GUITARIST'S GUIDE TO SCALES OVER CHORDS

The Foundation of Melodic Soloing

by Chad Johnson

ISBN 978-1-4234-8321-2

HAL•LEONARD®
CORPORATION
7777 W. BLUEMOUND RD. P.O. BOX 13819 MILWAUKEE, WI 53213

In Australia Contact:
Hal Leonard Australia Pty. Ltd.
4 Lentara Court
Cheltenham, Victoria, 3192 Australia
Email: ausadmin@halleonard.com.au

Visit Hal Leonard Online at
www.halleonard.com

CONTENTS

INTRODUCTION

Welcome to *The Guitarist's Guide to Scales over Chords*. This book is aimed at late beginner- to intermediate-level guitar soloists looking to improve their improvisational skills and expand their fretboard knowledge. Specifically, this book will help players who:

- Know some scales but don't know what to do with them.
- Don't understand how chord progressions work.
- Don't understand the connection between scales and chords.
- Have learned a bunch of licks but don't know where to apply them or how to use them in different keys.
- Are stuck in a box-position minor pentatonic rut.
- Don't know the notes on the entire fretboard.

If any or all of the above apply, you will undoubtedly improve by leaps and bounds with the concepts covered in this book.

Many players often have misconceptions about "improvising." It's actually quite rare that a solo is *completely* improvised. Sure, it may not be worked out in advance, but that doesn't mean it's comprised of completely new material that's never been played. When we improvise, we usually string together different known licks and phrases in unique ways. Think about it this way: music is a language. When we speak to one another, we don't make up words. We use the words we know to form sentences; the larger your vocabulary, the more freedom you'll have. The same applies to improvising guitar solos: the more licks you know, the more options you'll have.

However, beginners often have trouble with improvising because they aren't given much in the way of direction. It's kind of like traveling cross country without a map; you may get there eventually, but you'll surely waste lots of time and effort in the process, and you'll be limited in your scope should you need to travel somewhere else. Once you learn the *connection* between certain scales and the chords over which you're improvising, things become much clearer. You'll begin linking your inner ear to your fingers, allowing you to play what you hear in your head or mimic what you hear in your favorite solos. This concept is crucial in being able to turn those scales you learn into memorable melodies and phrases.

Besides the ones born entirely in your head, many licks are also created from slightly varying another learned lick; you can develop quite a vast repertoire this way. In order to create these variations, though, you need some context, and that's where *Scales over Chords* comes in.

So clear your mind, grab your guitar—maybe a refreshing beverage—and let's dive in.

ABOUT THE CD

When learning to make the connection between scales and chords, it's extremely helpful to hear one against the other. Therefore, for every full band example, the lead guitar is panned hard right in the stereo spectrum. By adjusting the balance on your stereo, you can remove the lead part when you're ready to try the licks by yourself. This is really a crucial ingredient in learning to effectively improvise over changes, so be sure to take advantage of this valuable tool.

It's also fun to jam with a friend when working on this stuff. You can take turns soloing over the chord progressions, which means you'll be getting some rhythm guitar practice too—always a good thing.

Recorded, mixed, and mastered by Chad Johnson at Tupperware Sounds Studio in North Carolina.

All instruments/programming performed by Chad Johnson.

ABOUT THE AUTHOR

Chad Johnson has written over 30 instructional books for Hal Leonard Corporation covering a wide range of topics, including *Pentatonic Scales for Guitar: The Essential Guide*, *The Hal Leonard Acoustic Guitar Method*, *All About Bass*, *25 Great Guitar Solos*, *The Best of Nirvana: Guitar Signature Licks*, *The Hal Leonard Fingerstyle Guitar Method*, and *The Best of Chet Atkins: Guitar Signature Licks*. He currently resides in North Carolina, where he keeps busy with session work, composing, gigging, recording, building amps and effects, and watching his two-year-old son's face light up when daddy plays guitar.

ACKNOWLEDGMENTS

Thanks to all the fine folks at Hal Leonard Corporation for their hard work in turning a simple manuscript into the beautiful book you now hold in your hands. It's always a pleasure working with everyone there.

I'd like to dedicate this book to my lovely wife, Allison, and our beautiful son, Lennon.
Y'all are always my most treasured source of inspiration.

CHAPTER 1: BASIC SCALE REVIEW

If you happened to purchase this book before learning any scales, then good for you! You'll be well-equipped to make the most out of everything you learn from the beginning. If you, like most, already know several scales and bought this book to help make sense of them, consider this chapter a refresher course. It's an essential one, though, so don't skip ahead! There are some concepts mentioned here that lay the groundwork for chapters to come.

MAJOR SCALE

The *major scale* is by far the most important scale you'll ever learn. In fact, we base our entire Western harmonic system off its intervallic structure. We're going to cover a bit more theory regarding this scale in Chapter 2, but for now, let's talk a bit about this structure.

Intervals

An *interval* is the name we use to describe the distance between two notes. In terms of scales, intervals are usually measured in *half steps* (one fret on the same string of the guitar) and *whole steps* (two frets on the same string). A major scale has seven different notes (the "eighth note" would simply be the first again in another octave), and each note is assigned a number: 1, 2, 3, etc. The *intervallic formula* for any major scale is always the same:

Whole step–**W**hole step–**H**alf step–**W**hole step–**W**hole step–**W**hole step–**H**alf step

So, from the first note (1) to the second note (2), the distance is one whole step, or two frets. The distance from 2 to 3 is also a whole step, or two frets. The distance from 3 to 4 is a half step, or one fret, and so on. This is demonstrated with the C major scale below:

C Major Scale

TRACK 01

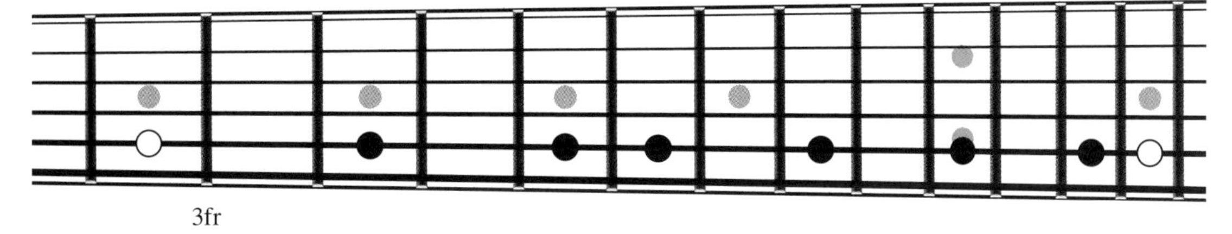

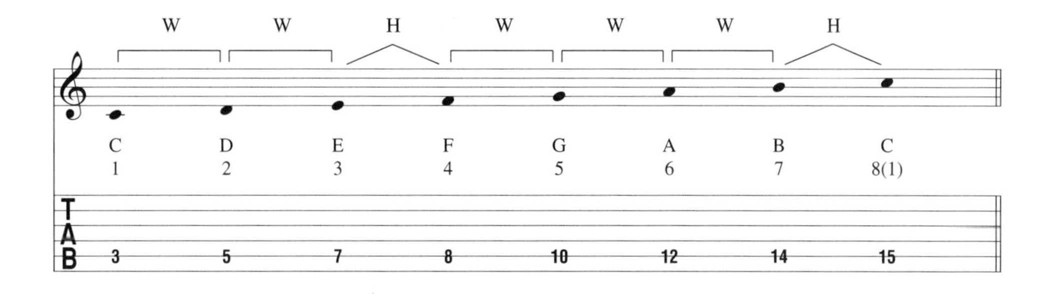

The Tonic

The 1st degree (1) of a scale is called the *tonic*; think of it as home base. This note feels resolved when you play it. You'll hear this term sometimes used interchangeably with "root." Also, you'll notice that sometimes the tonic appears at the top of a scale in a new octave, where it can be labeled as "8," and sometimes it does not. Don't be confused by this. A major scale has seven *different* notes. The "eighth" note, when it does appear, is just the same as the first; this relationship is referred to as an *octave*. It's sometimes helpful to see this, so you can see the interval from the 7th to the tonic.

Now, obviously, it's not very practical to play scales all along one string like this, but in the beginning, it's a great way to see the whole and half steps at work. In order to make this a playable scale shape, we move notes 3, 4, and 5 to the fourth string and notes 6, 7, and 8 to the third, like this:

C Major Scale

TRACK 02

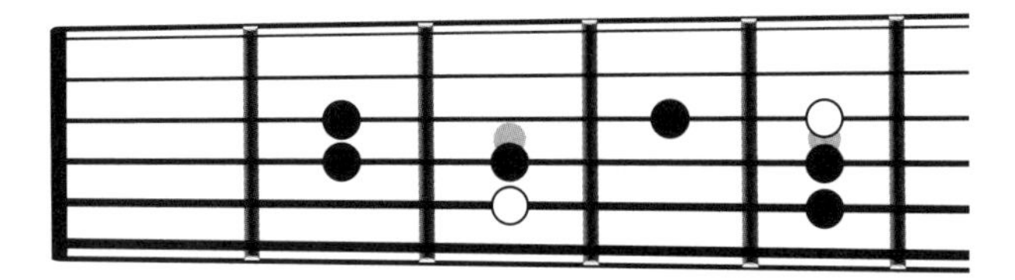

What's great about the guitar is that it's so easy to *transpose* (change keys). In order to make this a D major scale, for instance, all we need to do is move the shape up the neck so that the tonic note (indicated by the open circle) is D. This means moving everything up two frets.

D Major Scale

TRACK 02
(0:13)

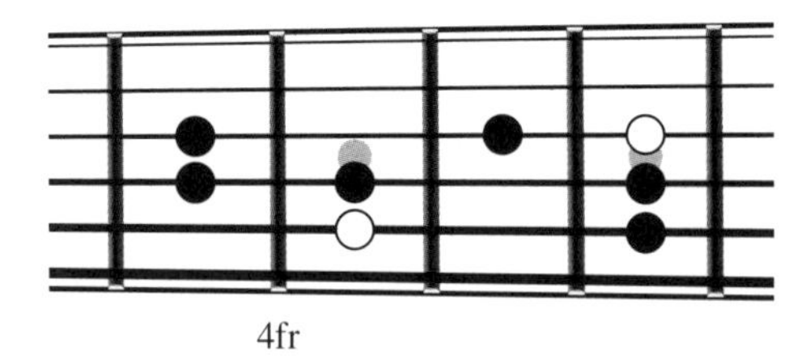

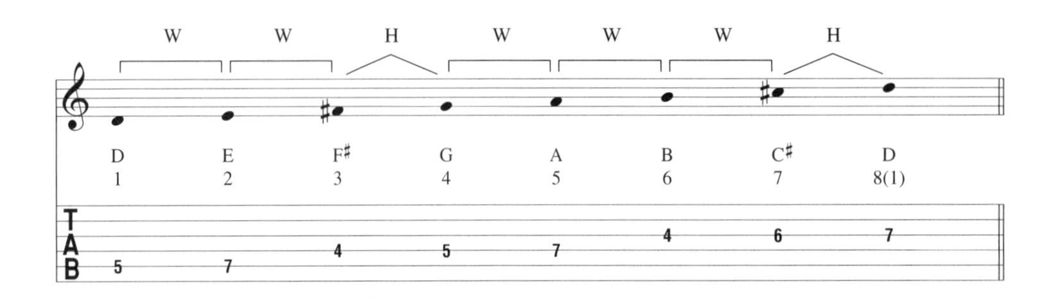

Notice that, in order to preserve our formula of W–W–H–W–W–W–H, we had to add two sharps: F♯ and C♯. This wasn't necessary in the key of C because the interval from E to F and from B to C is naturally a half step. This can most easily be confirmed on a piano keyboard, where the C major scale lays out on nothing but white keys.

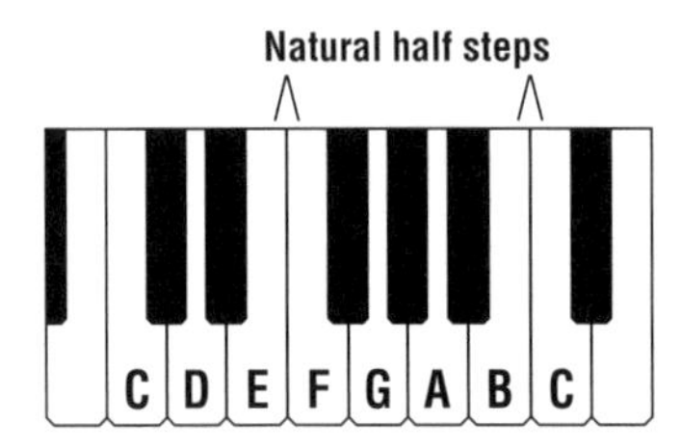

Consequently, C major is the only major scale that doesn't require any sharps or flats. More theory on sharps and flats will be covered in Chapter 2.

Two-Octave Major Scale Shapes

So now that we know how major scales are built, let's look at two different C major scale shapes that span two full octaves. The roots in all the diagrams are indicated with an open circle—in this case, all the C notes. The shapes may contain one or two more notes on top or bottom if they're within the fretboard position. (On the CD, all examples begin ascending with the root note; notes below the root, if any, will be included at the end of the descent through the shape.)

Our first C major scale shape begins with the fourth finger and lies mostly in fifth position.

Two-Octave C Major Scale—Shape 1

TRACK 03

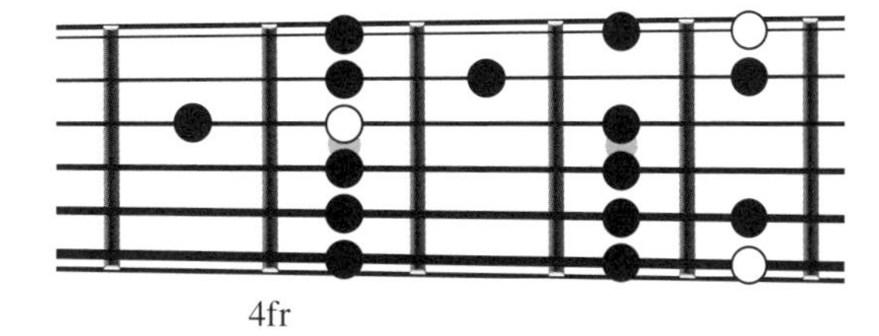

It's very helpful to visualize the accompanying chord shape for each scale as it greatly aids in fretboard knowledge and helps cement the connection between chords and scales. You can physically see on the guitar neck that the 3rd of a scale, for example, is also the 3rd of the chord. Realize that this scale shape resides within the architecture of this G-form C major barre chord (called "G-form" because it resembles the open-position G chord). The roots are open circles in each chord grid diagram.

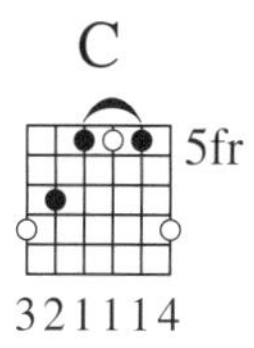

And here's our second shape, which begins with the second finger and lies in seventh position.

Two-Octave C Major Scale—Shape 2

TRACK 03
(0:25)

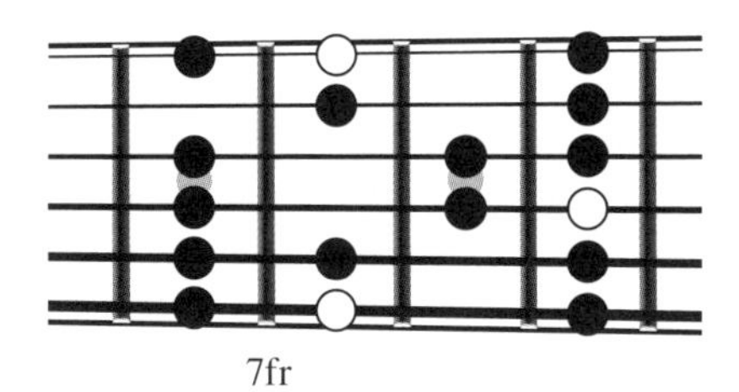

This scale pattern lies within this E-form C chord in eighth position:

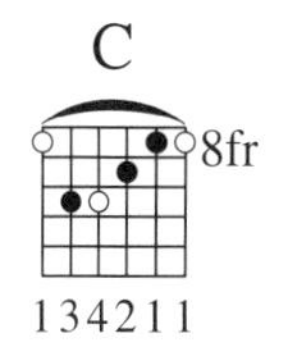

If these shapes are new to you at all, practice them with a metronome until you can play through them cleanly at a moderate tempo using alternate picking. Something around sixteenth notes at 90 beats per minute (bpm) is adequate for now.

MAJOR PENTATONIC SCALE

The *major pentatonic scale* is simply a five-note version ("penta" meaning "five") of the seven-note major scale. We just remove the fourth and seventh notes of the major scale, which leaves the notes 1–2–3–5–6. In a C major scale, this means we eliminate F (4th) and B (7th), leaving the notes C–D–E–G–A.

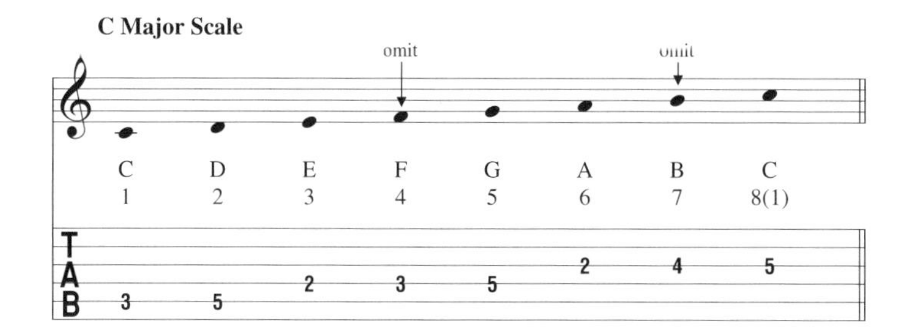

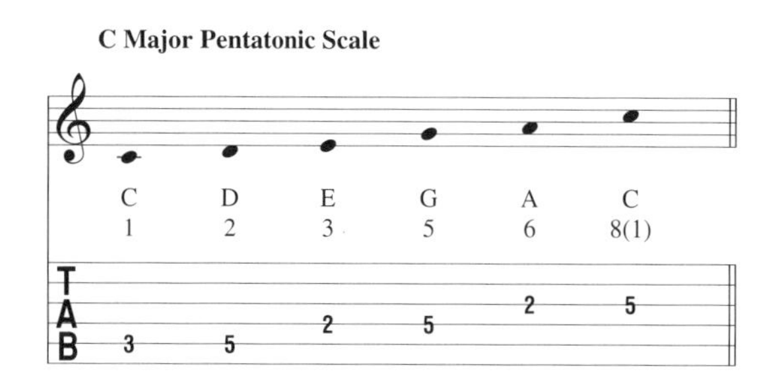

Two-Octave Major Pentatonic Scale Shapes

Now let's take a look at two major pentatonic scale shapes that span two octaves. Notice that these shapes are very similar to the major scale shapes you just learned; we've just eliminated two notes. Be sure you can play these cleanly at a moderate tempo before looking too far ahead in the book. The first shape begins with the fourth finger and lies in fifth position.

Two-Octave C Major Pentatonic Scale—Shape 1

TRACK 04

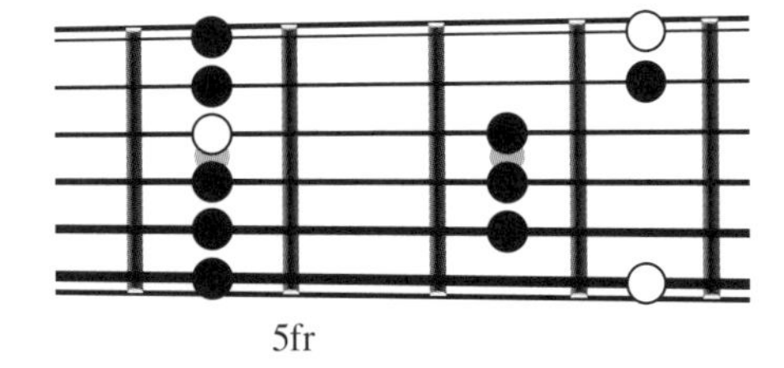

The second shape begins with the second finger and lies in seventh position.

Two-Octave C Major Pentatonic Scale—Shape 2

TRACK 04
(0:17)

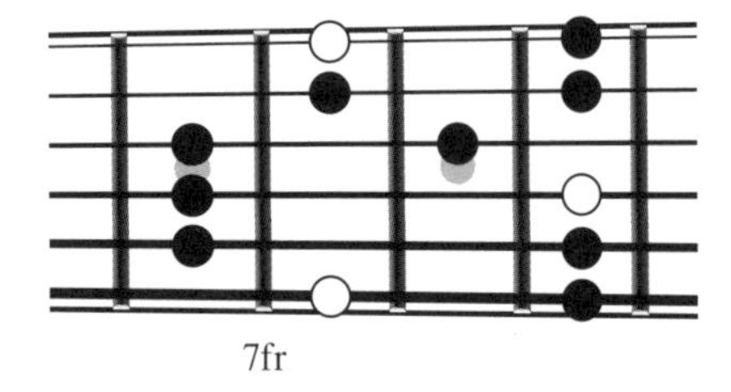

Again, be sure to realize that these two shapes are linked to the same two C chord forms as the similar major scale shapes.

MINOR SCALE

The *minor scale* is another seven-note scale but it has a different intervallic formula than a major scale. Where the major scale sounds happy or bright, the minor scale sounds sad or dark. There are two ways you can think about the construction of the minor scale. First, you can approach it from its intervallic formula:

Whole step–**H**alf step–**W**hole step–**W**hole step–**H**alf step–**W**hole step–**W**hole step

Alternatively, you can build it by altering the scale degrees of a major scale. This is another common way to look at scales. We look at the major scale as the standard, with its degrees numbered 1–7, and then we alter those degrees (raise or lower them by half steps) to create other scales.

To build a minor scale, we need to lower the 3rd, 6th, and 7th tones of a major scale. So its scale degrees would be numbered 1–2–♭3–4–5–♭6–♭7. This is demonstrated with the C minor scale below:

C Minor Scale

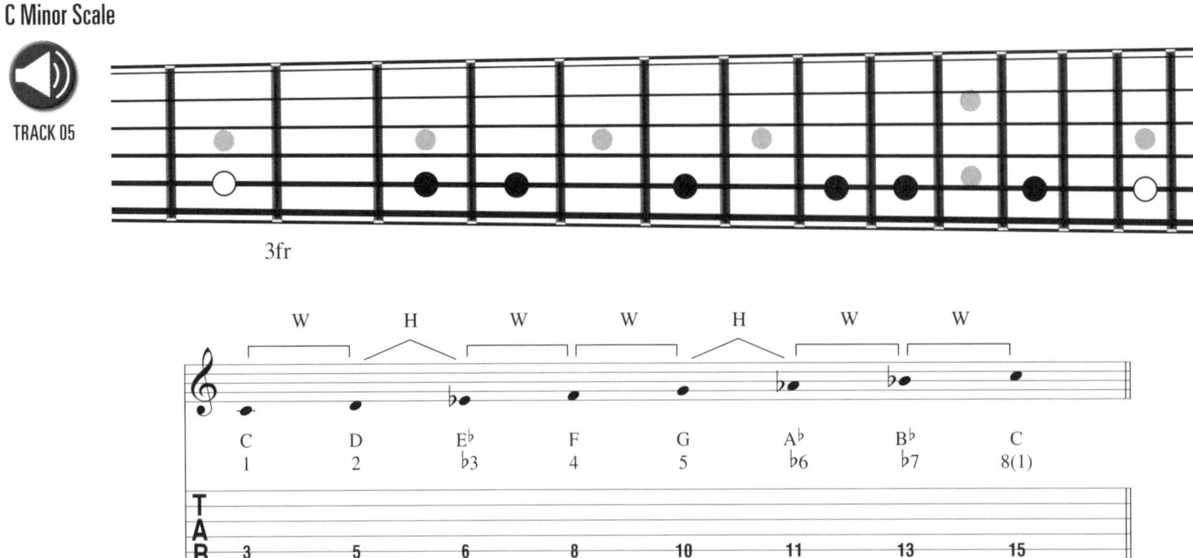

Notice that we must add three flats to spell this scale: E♭, A♭, and B♭. The C minor and C major scales are said to be *parallel* to each other because they share the same root: C. We'll talk more about this concept later.

Two-Octave C Minor Scale Shapes

Here are two different C minor scale shapes to learn. The first shape, in fifth position beginning with your fourth finger, is not as commonly used, but it's a good shape to compare against the C major scale shape in the same position.

Two-Octave C Minor Scale—Shape 1

TRACK 05
(0:13)

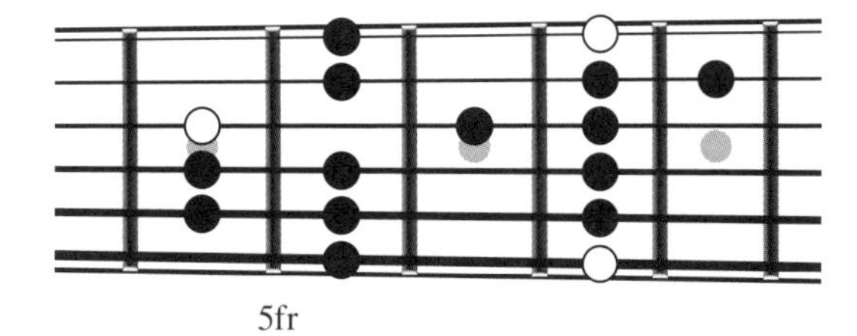

And here's the G-form Cm chord on which this scale is based. Again, it's not a chord form that's played often, but it's important to see the connection. (If you're from the planet Zortok, you may be able to barre your pinky and catch the high E string too. I can't do that.)

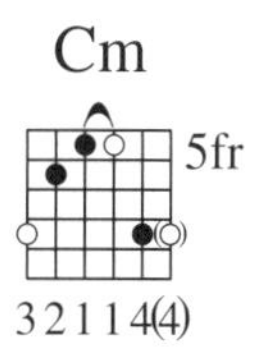

This second shape is by far the most commonly used minor scale shape. It begins with the first finger and is based around eighth position.

Two-Octave C Minor Scale—Shape 2

TRACK 05
(0:37)

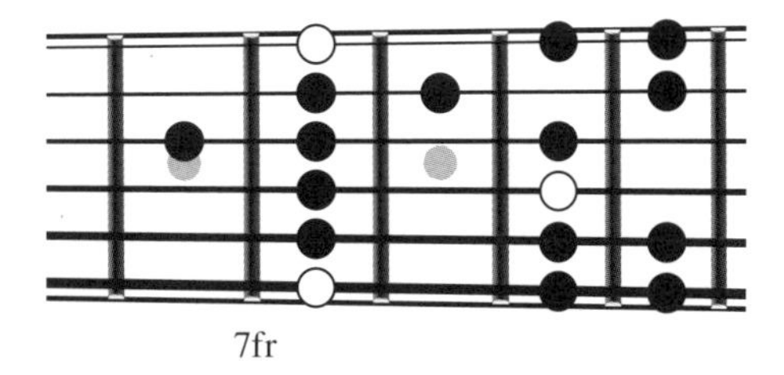

And here's the common E-form Cm chord to which this scale is attached.

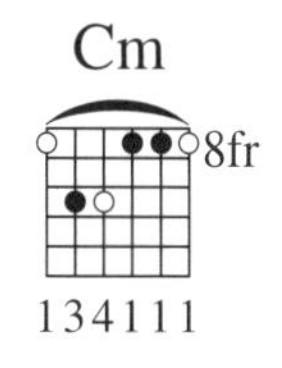

MINOR PENTATONIC SCALE

Just like the major scale has its companion major pentatonic, the minor scale has a five-note version called the *minor pentatonic scale*. We build it by eliminating two notes from the minor scale: the 2nd and ♭6th. So the minor pentatonic scale degrees are numbered 1–♭3–4–5–♭7. From a C minor scale, this means we eliminate D (2nd) and A♭ (♭6th), leaving the notes C–E♭–F–G–B♭.

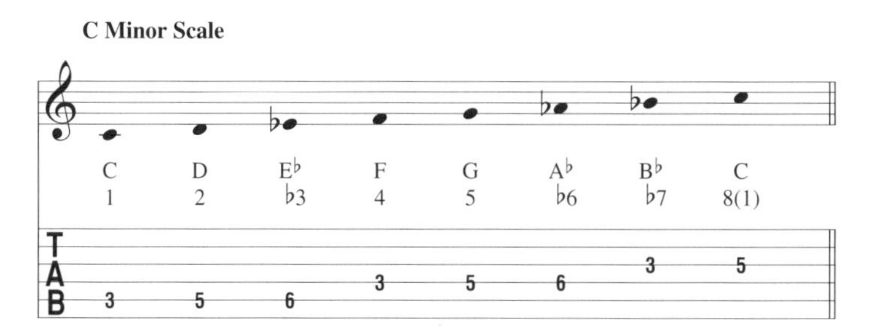

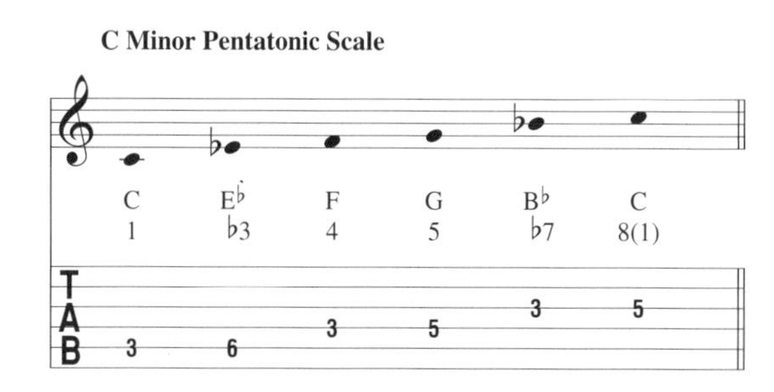

Two-Octave Minor Pentatonic Scale Shapes

Now here are our two minor pentatonic scale shapes. The first is in fifth position and begins with the fourth finger.

Two-Octave C Minor Pentatonic Scale—Shape 1

TRACK 06

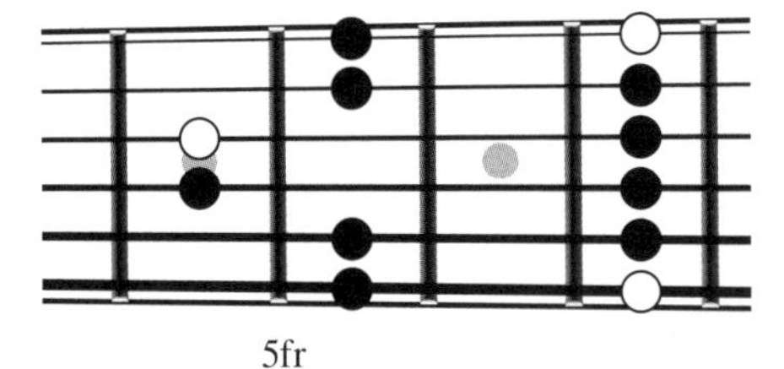

5fr

The second shape begins with the first finger and is found in eighth position. This is the extremely common shape and it's nicknamed the "box shape" because of the box-like figure it resembles on the fretboard.

Two-Octave C Minor Pentatonic Scale—Shape 2

TRACK 06
(0:17)

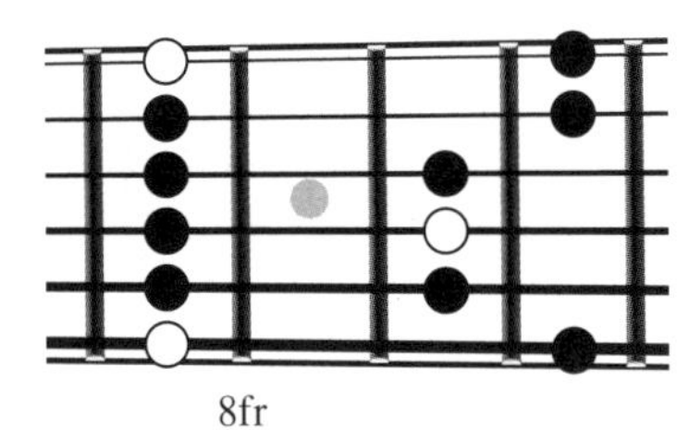

8fr

Again, these two minor pentatonic scale forms reside within the same chord forms as their respective minor scales.

TRANSPOSING THE SHAPES

Again, one of the guitar's greatest assets is its ease in transposition. All of the shapes we learned here are moveable and can easily be transposed to other keys by simply moving them up or down the neck. All you need to know are the names of the notes along the sixth string. And here they are:

Notes on the Sixth String

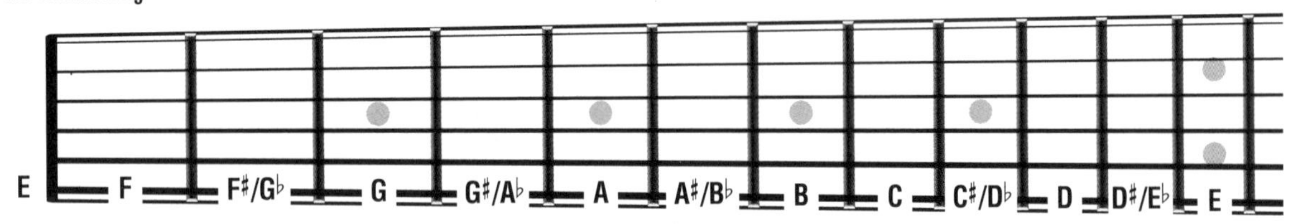

After the twelfth fret, the order starts all over again. So fret 13 is F, fret 14 is F♯/G♭, and so on. So, let's say you want to play Shape 2 of the minor pentatonic scale in the key of A minor. All you need to do is slide the shape down so the root note on the sixth string lies on the note A, and you have an A minor pentatonic scale. Since A is on the fifth fret of the sixth string, the A minor pentatonic shape would look like this:

TRACK 06
(0:35)

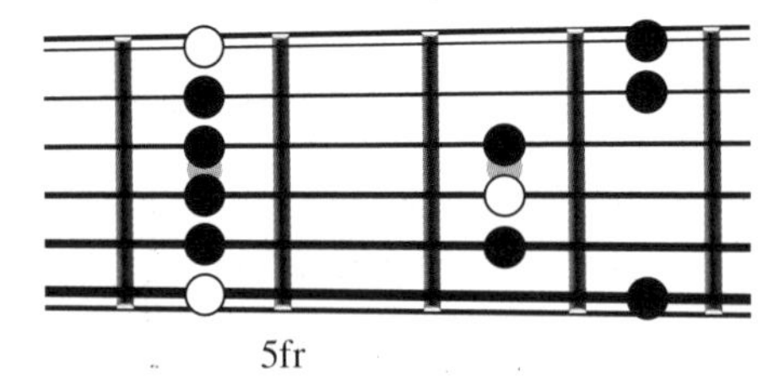

5fr

Or let's say you want to play an E♭ major scale using Shape 1. Find E♭ on string 6 and slide the shape until the root note is there. Since E♭ is on fret 11, your E♭ major scale shape would look like this:

TRACK 06
(0:53)

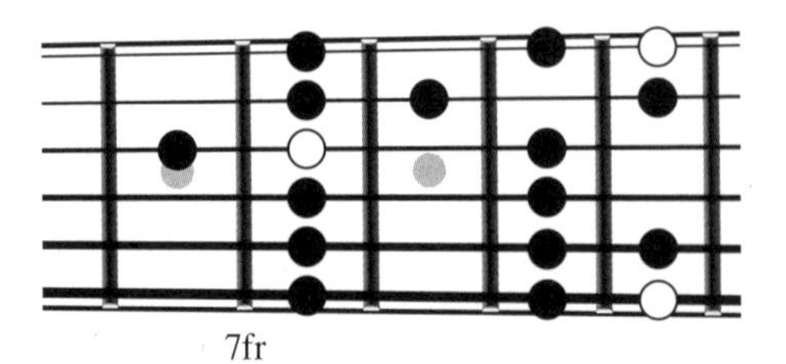

7fr

See if you can find the following scale shapes. Answers are on the bottom of the page (no peeking!).

- B Minor Scale—Shape 1.
- D Major Scale—Shape 2.
- B♭ Major Pentaonic Scale —Shape 2.
- G Minor Pentatonic Scale—Shape 2.

OK, so now we've learned how to construct and play four of the most common scales in all of music: the major scale, the major pentatonic scale, the minor scale, and the minor pentatonic scale. Believe it or not, this is where a good many players stop learning and begin noodling. They learn a few licks from these scales and never bother to learn why they sound the way they do—or, more importantly, why these licks seem to work sometimes and not others.

Noodling Run Amuck

I recall one instance when I was watching a band rehearse. They played through the same song, which began with a guitar solo, five or six times before moving on. The guitar player had worked out a little solo for the intro and played it verbatim each time. Everything sounded fine except for a few notes from a certain lick. Each time the song began, he would get into the groove and start bobbing his head as he played his solo. And *every time* he hit those few sour notes, he would roll his eyes and make a face. But he wouldn't change anything! He would play it the same way the next time, getting excited at first and then expressing the same disgust over and over.

This situation is not uncommon. It's what happens to many players who, for whatever reason, decide not to progress by learning more than just a few shapes on the fretboard. You're about to take the first step in breaking past this barrier that holds so many players back. Read on!

WHAT YOU LEARNED:

- Intervallic construction of the major and minor scales.
- Construction of the major and minor pentatonic scales.
- Two fingering patterns for major and major pentatonic scales, based on open chord forms.
- Two fingering patterns for minor and minor pentatonic scales, based on open chord forms.
- How to transpose the fingering patterns to any other root.

Answer Key

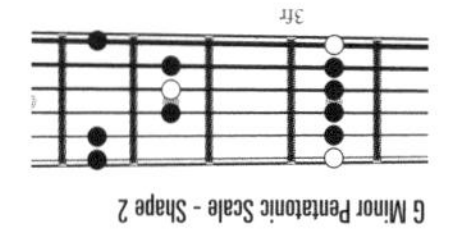

G Minor Pentatonic Scale - Shape 2

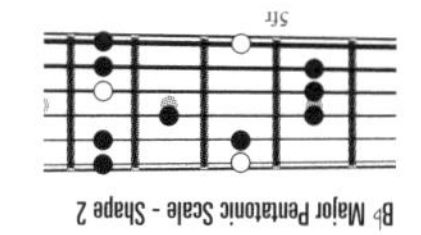

B♭ Major Pentatonic Scale - Shape 2

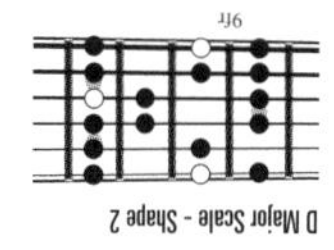

D Major Scale - Shape 2

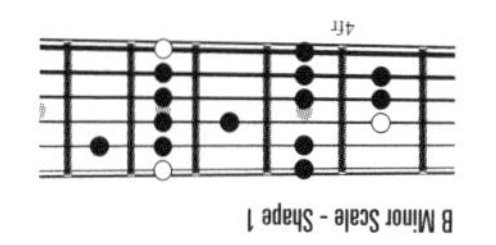

B Minor Scale - Shape 1

CHAPTER 2: DIATONIC HARMONY PRIMER

Before we get to the fun stuff, we need to learn some fundamentals that will pay off in a big way down the line. The knowledge you gain in this chapter will open the doors to a lifetime of learning and improvement on the guitar. These are the important first steps.

So, what exactly is *diatonic harmony* and what do we mean by it? The word "diatonic" stems from the Greek *diatonikos*, meaning "progressing through tones." Today, it basically means "in key" or "belonging to one key." We would say that the notes of a C major scale (C–D–E–F–G–A–B), for instance, are all *diatonic* to the key of C major. The notes E♭ and B♭, for instance, are then not diatonic (or non-diatonic) to the key of C major. Make sense?

MORE ON INTERVALS

An interval has two components: a *quantity* and a *quality*. The quantity is expressed numerically; we may say, for example, that C and E are a 3rd apart. This is because there are three note names involved in the distance between them, and we confirm this by counting forward through the musical alphabet: **C** (1), D (2), and **E** (3). By the same token, C and G would be a 5th apart: **C** (1)–D (2)–E (3)–F (4)–**G** (5). The notes D and E would then be a 2nd apart: **D** (1)–**E** (2). What about from G to B? Remember that the musical alphabet only goes from A to G, so we start over at A after G. Therefore, from G to B would be a 3rd: **G** (1)–A (2)–**B** (3).

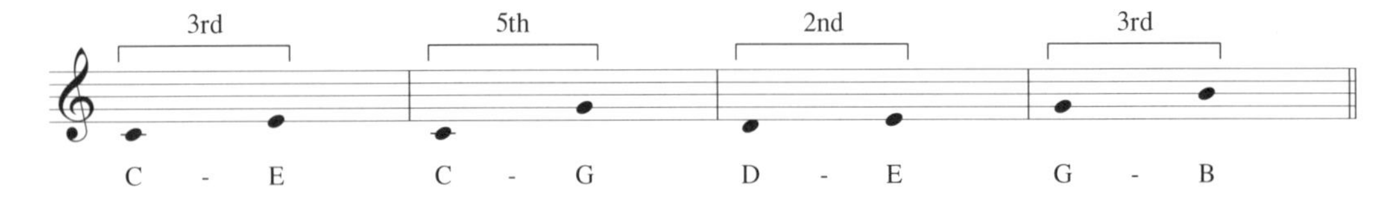

The quality is where we get a bit more specific. There are seven different notes in a diatonic major scale (or minor scale) before we reach the octave and start over. But there are a total of 12 notes in an octave when you include the non-diatonic tones as well. (If you counted every key on a piano—black and white—between one note and the same note an octave higher, you'd get 12.) This is where the quality comes in. There are five types of qualities used to describe intervals: major, minor, augmented, diminished, and perfect. The chart below shows the intervals for all 12 notes of the octave measured against a C root note.

Notes	# of half steps	Interval Name
C to C	0	Unison
C to D♭	1	Minor 2nd
C to D	2	Major 2nd
C to E♭	3	Minor 3rd
C to E	4	Major 3rd
C to F	5	Perfect 4th
C to F♯ C to G♭	6 6	Augmented 4th Diminished 5th
C to G	7	Perfect 5th
C to A♭	8	Minor 6th
C to A	9	Major 6th
C to B♭	10	Minor 7th
C to B	11	Major 7th
C to C	12	Octave

From this chart, we can deduce quite a bit regarding qualities. Here are some of the axioms on display:

1. **A minor interval is one half step *smaller* than a major interval.**

   C to E (4 half steps) = major 3rd

   C to E♭ (3 half steps) = minor 3rd

2. **An augmented interval is one half step *larger* than a perfect interval.**

   C to F (5 half steps) = perfect 4th

   C to F♯ (6 half steps) = augmented 4th

3. **A diminished interval is one half step *smaller* than a perfect interval.**

   C to G (7 half steps) = perfect 5th

   C to G♭ (6 half steps) = diminished 5th

4. **The terms "major" and "minor" do not apply to 4ths and 5ths.**

   We use "perfect," "augmented," or "diminished" to describe them.

5. **The term "perfect" does not apply to 2nds, 3rds, 6ths, or 7ths.**

   We use "major" and "minor" to describe them, although "diminished" and "augmented" are occasionally used as well. An augmented interval can also be one half step *larger* than a major interval, and a diminished interval can sometimes be one half step smaller than a minor interval.

The Enharmonic Interval Enigma

You'll notice that both F♯ and G♭ are listed, even though they are the same note. The term for a single note having two different names is *enharmonic*—i.e., F♯ and G♭ are enharmonic to each other. Don't get confused by enharmonic intervals. Always remember the rule of the interval's *quantity*. For an interval to be called a 2nd, there must be **two** note names involved. For an interval to be a 6th, there must be **six** note names involved, etc.

For example, what's the interval from C to E♭? First off, we know it's some kind of 3rd because there are three note names involved: C (1), D (2), and E♭ (3). We know that it's a *minor* 3rd because it's three half steps in distance (this is confirmed in the chart above).

However, what about the interval from C to D♯? E♭ and D♯ are enharmonic; they're the same note. But the interval from C to D♯ is technically *not* a minor 3rd because there are only two note names involved: C (1) and D♯ (2). We know that from C to D is a major 2nd, and since C to D♯ is one half step larger than a major 2nd, we say it's an *augmented* 2nd.

It *sounds* just like a minor 3rd, and if you heard it, you'd probably call it a minor 3rd, as that label is much more common. But there are instances where it will make sense to write it as C to D♯, instead of C to E♭, and in those instances, it's technically considered an augmented 2nd.

OK. At this point, I'd recommend taking a break. Go do some stretches, shake it out, and then come back and reread the first part of this chapter before moving on.

HARMONIZING THE MAJOR SCALE

A *chord* is created when three or more notes are sounded together. When we build chords from each note of a major scale, we say we're *harmonizing* the scale. It's a process that involves a technique called "stacking 3rds." You now know that a 3rd refers to an interval in which three note names are involved.

The most common chord (in rock and pop music, at least) is a *triad*, so named because it contains three different notes. We can build a triad by stacking two 3rd intervals from a major scale. We'll work in the key of C major again for starters.

Let's say we want to build a triad from the root of this scale, C. Our first note of the chord is going to be that root note, which is C.

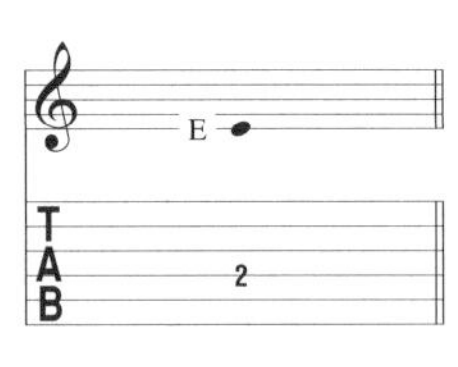

For the next note, we're going to stack a 3rd on top of that. Just count up the musical alphabet through the notes of the C major scale: C (1)–D (2)–**E (3)**. A 3rd above C is E.

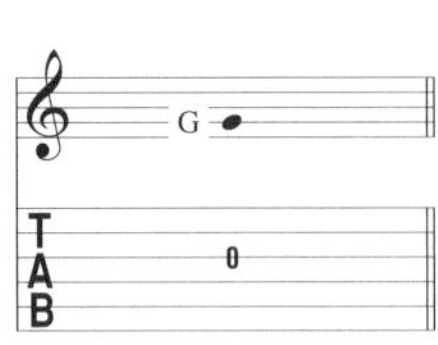

And now we need to stack another 3rd on top of that to get the last note.
A 3rd above E is G.

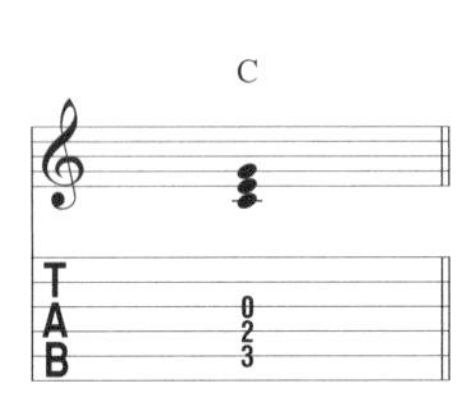

So, the triad built off the 1st degree of our C major scale is spelled C–E–G.
This is a C *major triad.*

Another way to look at this triad is in terms of intervals measured from the root note: C to E is a major 3rd (four half steps), and C to G is a perfect 5th (seven half steps). Knowing this, we can say that the formula for a major triad is root, major 3rd, and perfect 5th. This will hold true for any major triad.

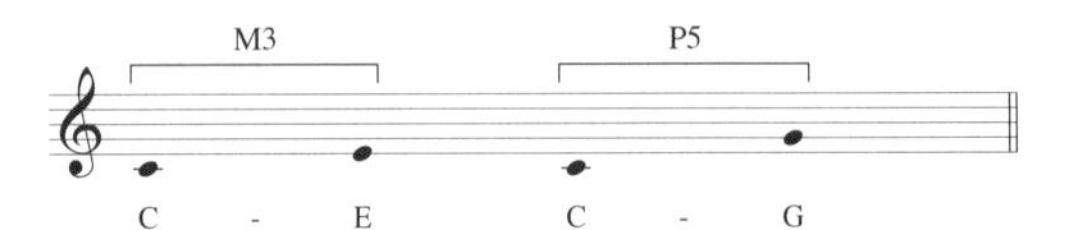

Now let's build a *minor triad* off the 2nd degree of our C major scale, D. If we continue the process of stacking 3rds, now from the note D, we get D–F–A. This is a D minor triad.

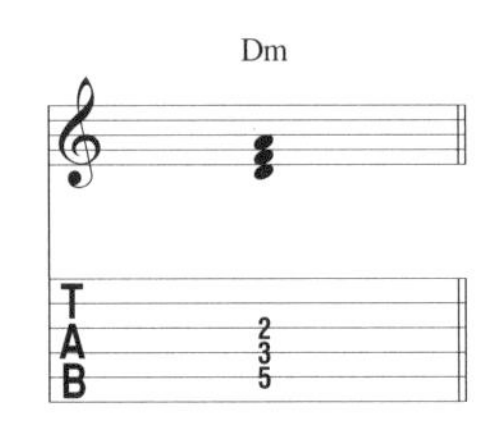

When we measure the intervals from the root of a minor triad, we discover that the formula is different than the major triad. D to F is a minor 3rd (three half steps), and D to A is a perfect 5th (seven half steps). So the formula for a minor triad is root, minor 3rd, and perfect 5th. Compared to a major triad, the only difference is that the 3rd has been lowered by a half step.

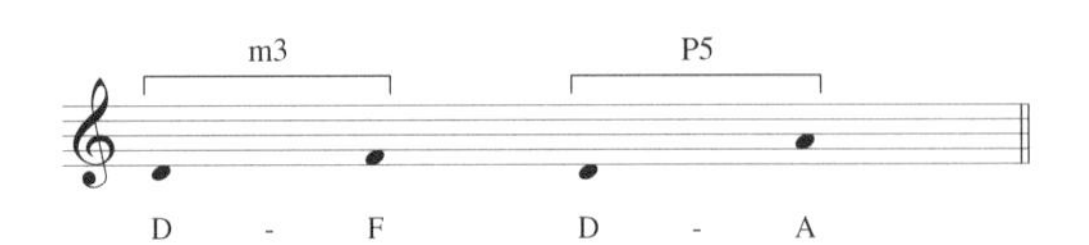

Continuing this process, we end up with several more major and minor triads from the C major scale: Em, F, G, and Am.

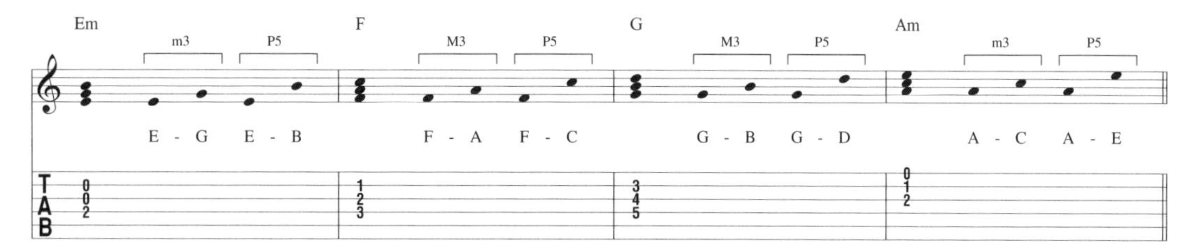

Remember: we're just using notes from the C major scale here (C–D–E–F–G–A–B). When we reach the last note, B, we get a different type of triad: *diminished*. The formula for a diminished triad is root, minor 3rd, and diminished 5th. It's close to a minor triad, but the 5th has been lowered by a half step. This makes quite a bit of difference in the sound, as you can hear. The chord symbol for diminished is °.

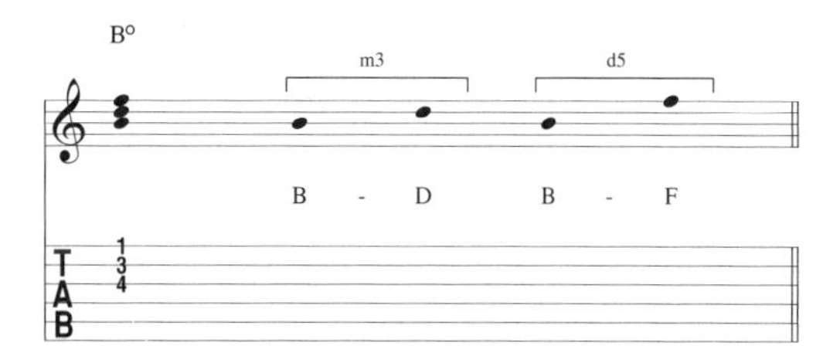

We use Roman numerals to indicate these chords within a key—uppercase for major chords, lowercase for minor, and lowercase with the " ◦ " symbol for diminished. Here are all the triads in the key of C and their corresponding Roman numerals:

TRACK 07

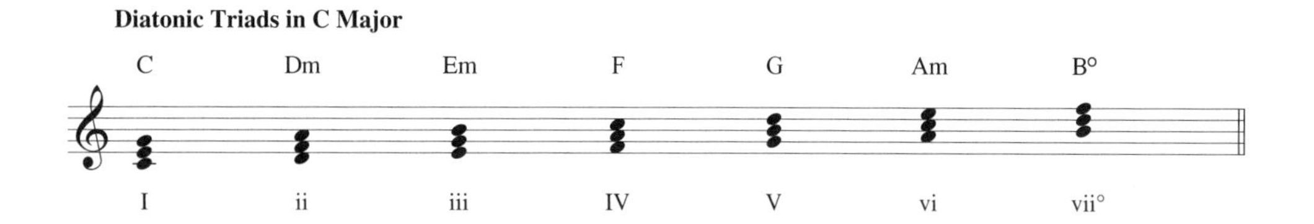

Like the W–W–H–W–W–W–H formula for the major scale we learned in Chapter 1, this is another formula that's always applicable in any key: The diatonic triads for any major key will always follow this pattern: major (I), minor (ii), minor (iii), major (IV), major (V), minor (vi), and diminished (vii°).

So, by harmonizing the major scale, we end up with three types of triads: major, minor, and diminished. Let's compare them all with a C root note, so we can see how notes are altered to create each type. First we have the C major triad:

TRACK 07
(0:17)

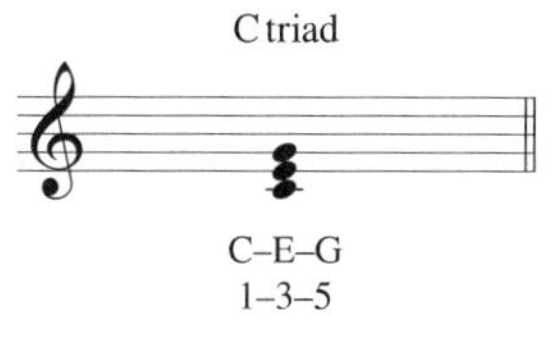

To make this a C minor triad, we just lower the 3rd, E, one half step to E♭:

TRACK 07
(0:22)

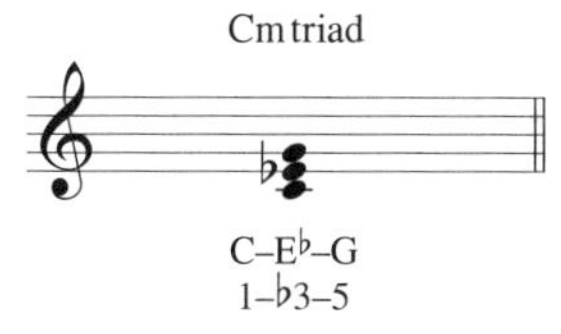

For a C° triad, we have a lowered 3rd (E♭) and a lowered 5th (G♭):

TRACK 07
(0:26)

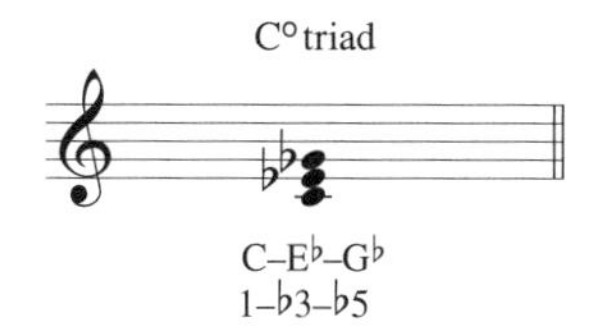

There's also one more type of triad to know. We haven't seen it yet because it doesn't occur within the harmonized major scale. It's called an *augmented* triad and is spelled 1–3–♯5. It's like a major triad with a raised 5th. The chord symbol is a + sign. Here's C+:

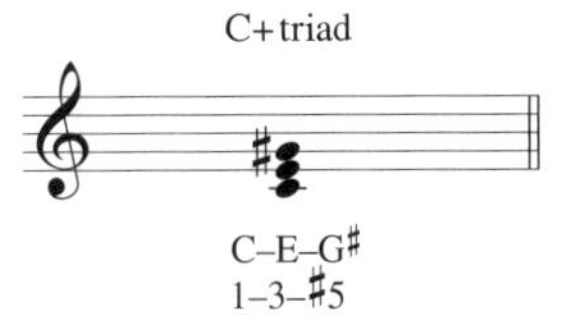

Since it doesn't occur within the harmonized major scale, the augmented triad is a non-diatonic chord. We'll talk more about this in Chapter 6.

The degrees of the major scale (and their harmonized triads) have labels that you'll hear—some more often than others:

1. **Tonic:** Home base (same as the key).
2. **Supertonic:** 2nd degree (directly "above" the tonic).
3. **Mediant:** 3rd scale degree ("middle" note of the tonic triad).
4. **Subdominant:** 4th scale degree (directly "below" the dominant).
5. **Dominant:** 5th scale degree (the most "dominant" harmonic note after the tonic).
6. **Submediant:** 6th scale degree (the "middle" note of the subdominant triad).
7. **Leading tone:** 7th scale degree (the note that "leads" to the tonic—also referred to as "subtonic").

But These Aren't the Chord Shapes I Learned!

Some of these triads probably don't look much like the familiar open-chord shapes we all learned on guitar. That's because these shapes only contain the three different notes that make up the triad. Those chords that we always play (open and/or barred) usually contain notes that are doubled in octaves to make fuller-sounding five- and six-string voicings that are well-suited for accompanying singers or making a big racket. However, the more you get into funk, blues, or Motown rhythm styles where the big, full chords don't sound quite as appropriate, the more you'll actually see smaller voicings like these being used.

KEY SIGNATURES

We use *key signatures* to avoid having to constantly write a bunch of sharps or flats (collectively known as *accidentals*) when playing in keys other than C major. It's a set of sharps or flats that appears on the staff at the beginning of a piece, telling the performer to always play those notes sharp or flat throughout. As there are 12 notes, there are 12 different key signatures.

By using our W–W–H–W–W–W–H major scale formula and starting on a root note other than C, we soon discover that we need to employ sharps or flats in order to build other major scales. If we build a G major scale, for example, we can start by writing out the seven note names starting from G:

G–A–B–C–D–E–F

In order for these notes to form a G major scale, they need to match the pattern of whole and half steps indicated in our formula. A piano keyboard is particularly helpful in this regard, because the sharp/flat keys are black.

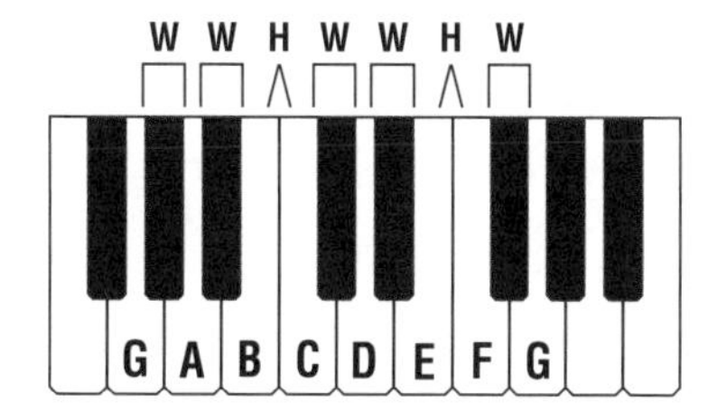

We can see that it's all fine until the end. From E to F is a half step, and from F to G is a whole step. This conflicts with our formula. So, we raise the F note to F♯, thereby creating the proper intervals needed.

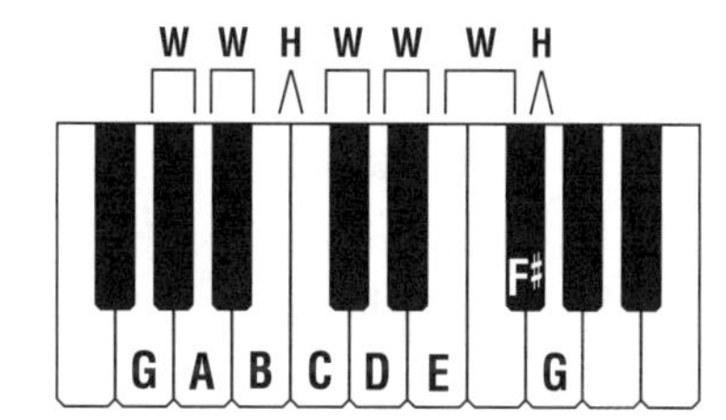

As a result, we say that the key signature for G major is one sharp: F♯. (Looking at a piano keyboard also reveals why C major has a blank key signature. There are naturally occurring half steps between E and F and between B and C.)

Let's try another one. If we build a major scale from the root of F, we encounter another problem.

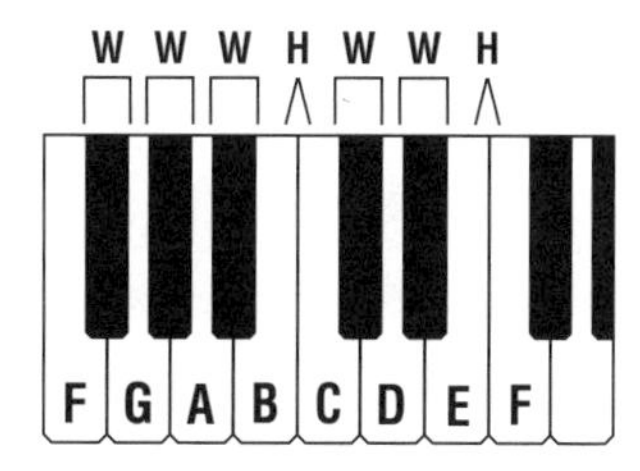

Instead of W–W–H in the beginning, we have W–W–W. We fix this by lowering B to B♭, thereby adhering to our major scale formula.

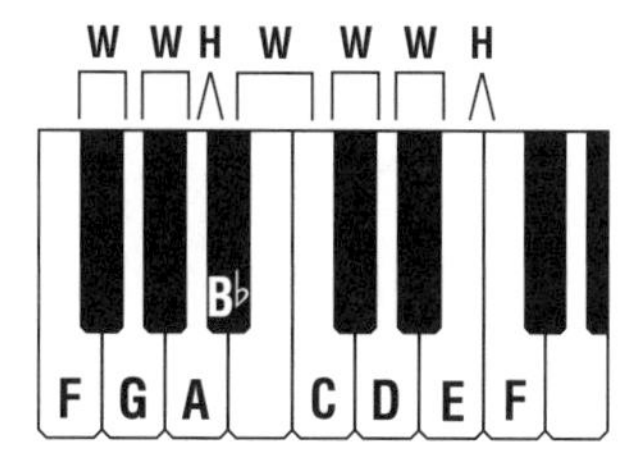

So, the key signature for F major is one flat: B♭. As this demonstrates, we have sharp keys and flat keys (and C major, which is neither). We can repeat this process for each of the 12 different notes; the resulting key signatures will be:

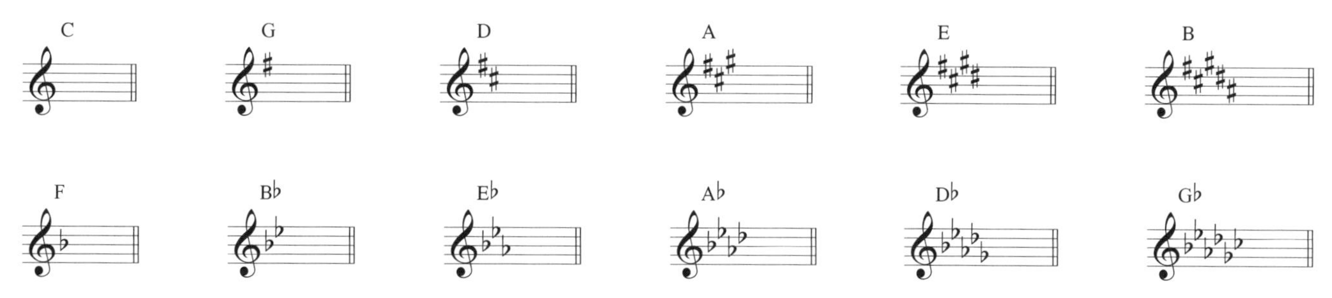

CIRCLE OF FIFTHS

To help demonstrate their relationship to each other and make the process of memorizing them easier, these 12 key signatures are grouped into a diagram called the *Circle of Fifths.* The keys are rearranged so that, when progressing clockwise, each key is a 5th higher than the previous one.

Notice that, when moving to the right (the "sharps" side), each new key contains the same sharps as the previous and adds one more; moving to the left (the "flats" side) works the same way. Keep this in mind when learning each new key signature. The parentheses indicate each major key's *relative minor* key. Relative major and minor keys use the same key signature, but they start and end the scale on different notes. The chords used in a song will usually let you know whether the song is in a major key or its relative minor key. For instance, if the key signature is one sharp (F♯), the song could be in G major or E minor. If the song begins and ends on Em, it's a sure bet that the song is in E minor. (More on this in Chapter 4: The Modes.)

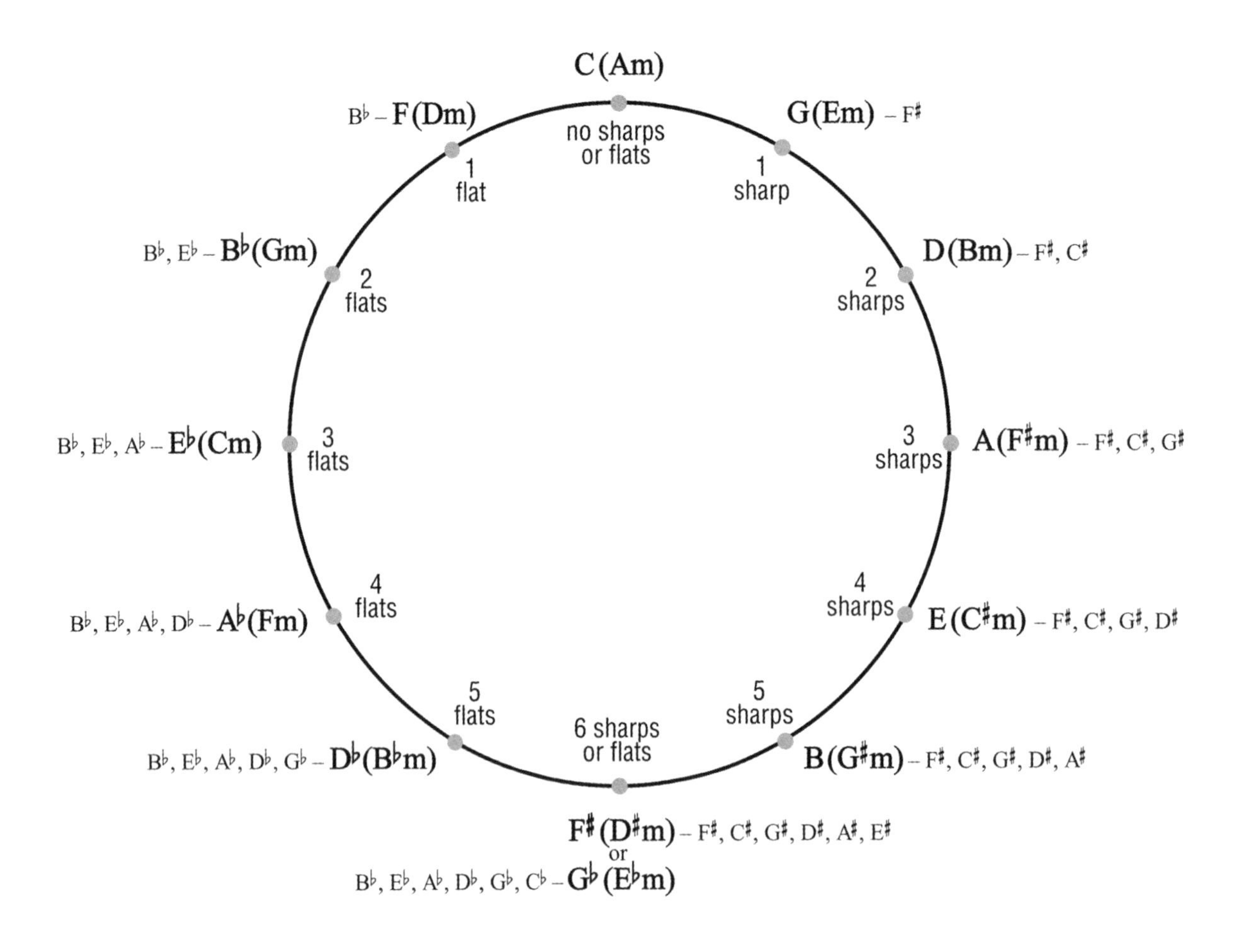

HARMONIZING THE MINOR SCALE

Just as we harmonized the major scale, we can do the same with the minor scale. We simply stack a diatonic 3rd and 5th over each degree of the scale. Let's do this with an A minor scale, which, as demonstrated by our Circle of Fifths diagram, uses the same notes as the C major scale; it just treats A as the root instead of C. Here's what we'll get:

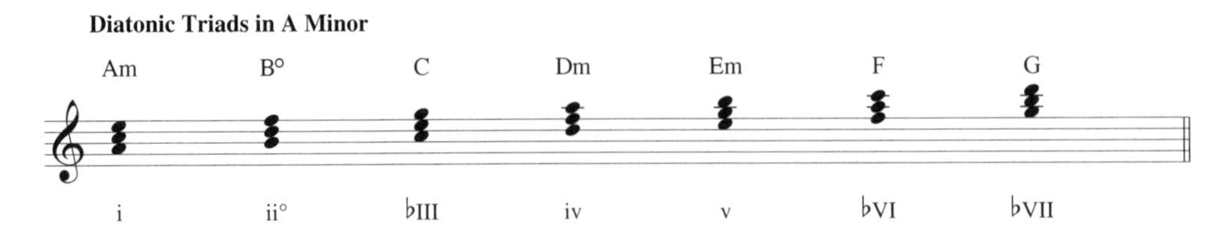

Notice that this is the same set of chords that we arrived at when we harmonized the C major scale, but we're starting from Am, and the Roman numeral analysis is reflecting that. Compare the Roman numerals to the 1–2–♭3–4–5–♭6–♭7 minor scale formula we discussed in Chapter 1 and you should see the relationship. We're still using uppercase for major chords and lowercase for minor chords, but the numerals have changed because the tonic is now A instead of C.

Just as with the major scale, there's a diatonic chord formula for every minor key: minor (i), diminished (ii°), major (♭III), minor (iv), minor (v), major (♭VI), major (♭VII).

The V Chord

In minor keys, an exception dealing with the V chord occurs so commonly that it's really more of a rule than an exception. Notice that the diatonic v chord in the key of A minor is normally Em (v). The problem with this is that it doesn't result in a very strong resolution to the i chord (which is the V chord's main function) because it lacks a *leading tone*—a note that's one half step below the tonic.

When we play the V chord in C major, which is G, the 3rd of the chord (B) is the leading tone of the key; it's one half step below C. This note pulls the ear toward the tonic, resulting in a strong resolution. However, in A minor, the 3rd of the v chord (Em) is G, which is one whole step below the tonic A. This one detail makes quite a difference.

So, in minor keys, we often change the v (Em) chord to a major chord (E) by raising the 3rd (G) by one half step (G♯), creating the leading tone necessary for a strong resolution. Listen to the following example to hear the difference this makes.

The former is heard in some folk music that draws heavily from modal sounds (modes are covered in Chapter 4), but the latter is what we usually hear most in rock, pop, jazz, classical, etc. When we raise this note (7th degree of a minor scale) by a half step, a new scale is created: the *harmonic minor scale*.

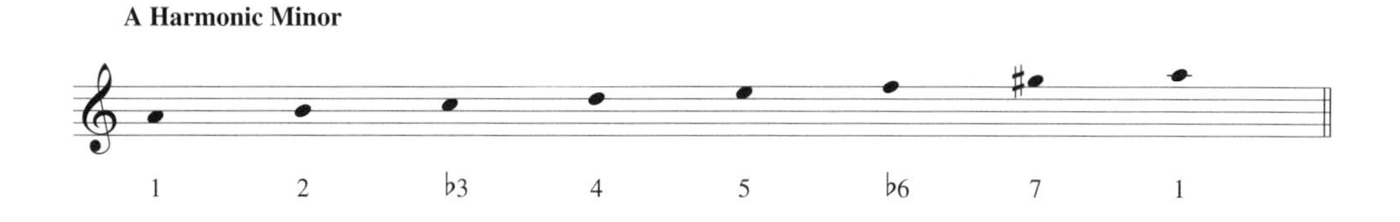

Here's a two-octave shape for A harmonic minor based around fifth position:

A Harmonic Minor

TRACK 09
(0:20)

4fr

We'll touch more on the harmonic minor scale and its applications later. For now, just remember that in minor keys, the minor v chord is often changed to a major chord to provide a stronger resolution to the tonic.

OK, that's plenty of theory for now. If your head hasn't exploded yet, go grab a beverage and relax. You may want to re-read this chapter when you feel up to it to make sure you're grasping all the concepts. It's time to play some licks!

WHAT YOU LEARNED:

- **Interval qualities** (major, minor, perfect, augmented, and diminished) and **quantities** (2nd, 3rd, etc.).
- The term **enharmonic**: the same note spelled two different ways (for instance, F♯ and G♭).
- The harmonization of the major and minor scales.
- Three types of **triads** (major: 1–3–5, minor: 1–♭3–5, diminished: 1–♭3–♭5).
- **Key signatures** and the **Circle of Fifths**.

CHAPTER 3: MAJOR AND MINOR SCALE APPLICATIONS

Now that we're familiar with several scale shapes and how basic diatonic harmony works, let's start looking at some licks using our newfound skills. We're going to start off fairly basic, concentrating on intelligent note choices above all else. Since you're now familiar with how to transpose these ideas, we'll work in several different keys throughout.

For these examples, we'll be using what's known as a *key-center* approach. This means that we'll use one scale to solo over all the chords in a progression. Note that this approach is best suited for *diatonic progressions*—i.e., those progressions in which all the chords belong to one key.

Determining the Key

How do we know what key the song is in if we don't have the sheet music to tell us the key signature? The first thing to try is to use your ear. Hum along with the song and see if you can tell what note sounds like the tonic, or the most resolved. This is often the last note of a melody (think of "Twinkle, Twinkle, Little Star" for instance) or often the final chord of a song. If you think you've located the tonic with this method, play the major scale along with the song and see if it sounds right. Does it sound way wrong? Maybe the song is in a minor key. Try playing the minor scale from that note.

If neither of those methods work but you know the chords to the song, you can determine the key by process of elimination. If a song has four chords in it—say, F, B♭, Dm, and C—you can plug those chords into different keys to see if they fit the harmonized major scale formula: I–ii–iii–IV–V–vi–vii°. Write out the formula and plug in the chords in three rows below it, treating each chord as the tonic, or I chord. (Remember, F and Dm are relative to each other, so the chords contained in their keys would be the same.) It will look like this:

	I	ii	iii	IV	V	vi	vii°
Key of F	F			B♭	C	Dm	
Key of B♭	B♭	~~C~~	Dm		F		
Key of C	C	Dm		F			~~B♭~~

After you cross out chords that don't fit the formula, you'll usually be left with only one choice. If we treat B♭ as the tonic, for example, we see that C is in the ii chord spot; the key of B♭ should have a Cm chord, though, so that's not right. The key of C works except for the B♭ chord, so that's wrong as well. In this instance, the key is most likely F major. The fewer chords there are in a song, the harder it can be to determine the key. But with this formula, combined with the ear approach above, you should be able to figure it out.

NOTE CHOICE

So, what exactly do we mean by "note choice?" This term refers to which notes you choose to play at a certain time, and it plays a crucial role in great, memorable solos. To demonstrate the concept in action, let's first take a look at some examples that *don't* consider note choice at all. These are the types of things that you'll often hear "noodlers" play—players that think mostly about shapes on the fretboard and don't really *listen* to what they're playing; they're just kind of playing "connect the dots."

This first one is in C major and uses the C major scale, Shape 1. Notice how the same sequence of notes is used on different strings throughout. This is a device that can sound good at times and, as demonstrated here, not so great other times. Most of the phrases land on an awkward note with respect to the underlying harmony, resulting in a line that seems to work against itself.

Example 1

TRACK 10

C5 F5 C5 A5 F5 C5

Now let's tweak this line a little to make it a bit stronger. We'll keep the rhythm and the basic contour the same, but we're going to adjust the note choice so that we're not accenting and/or landing on such awkward notes.

Example 1—Tweaked

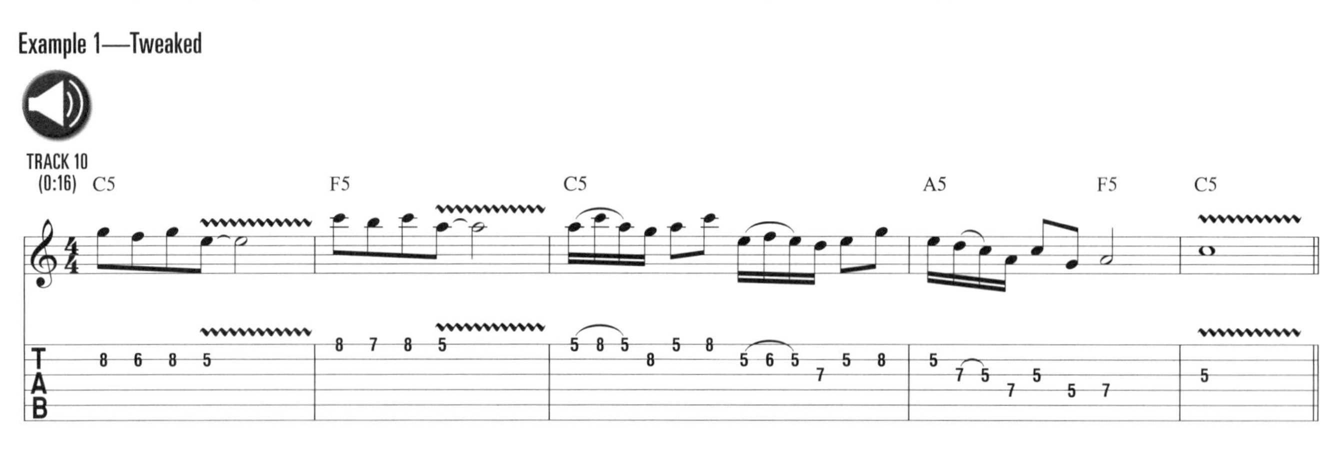

Here's one over a I–V–IV–ii–I progression in D major that uses Shape 2 of the D major scale. This is another case of fingering patterns dictating the line with no regard for how the notes sound against the chords. The final note really nails this concept home and shows just how badly things can go wrong if you're not listening to what you're playing!

Example 2

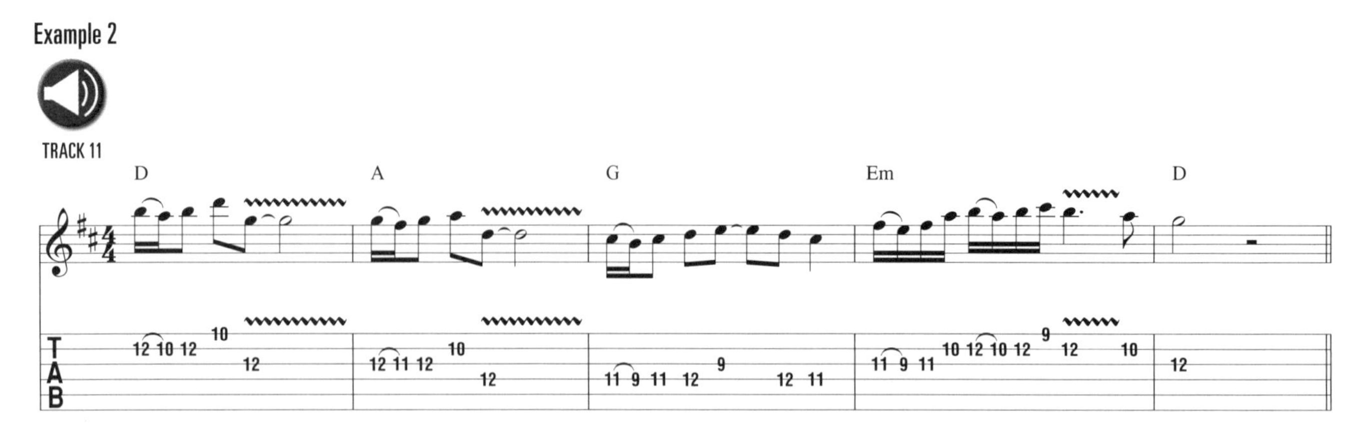

And here's that one adjusted to align a bit more with the underlying harmony.

Example 2—Tweaked

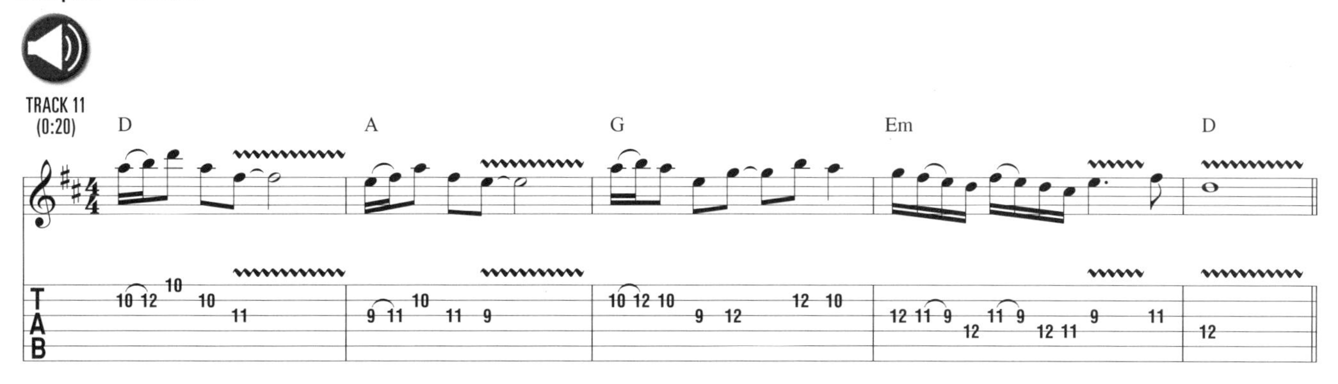

Now, obviously, this isn't the only way we could have adjusted these awkward lines, but I think most people would agree that the tweaked versions sound much more pleasant than the original ones.

> **Learn the Rules Before You Break Them!**
>
> I don't mean to insinuate that *everything* about the original examples was bad and vice versa. In fact, eventually, you'll want to accent more colorful notes (i.e., notes other than just chord tones) in your solos. However, by learning the basics first, you'll be armed with the knowledge of how to *resolve* those colorful notes, and resolution plays a huge role in their effectiveness. So for now, let's just concentrate on building that solid foundation; we'll get to the fancier stuff soon enough.

MAJOR SCALE EXAMPLES

Now that we have a good idea of what *not* to do, let's take a look at several major scale examples that implement good note-choice technique. This means that the notes we come to rest on at the end of a phrase will usually be a chord tone of the underlying harmony. We'll be working in different keys and using all the scale forms we've learned thus far, including the major pentatonic.

Example 3 uses a I–IV progression in G major, a very typical progression in major keys. We're working out of the G major scale Shape 1 here in twelfth position. Notice that all the sustained notes are chord tones of the underlying harmony. Also be aware that the lines over the G chords are derived from the G major pentatonic scale, including the 4th-based descending sequence at the beginning of measure 2.

Example 3

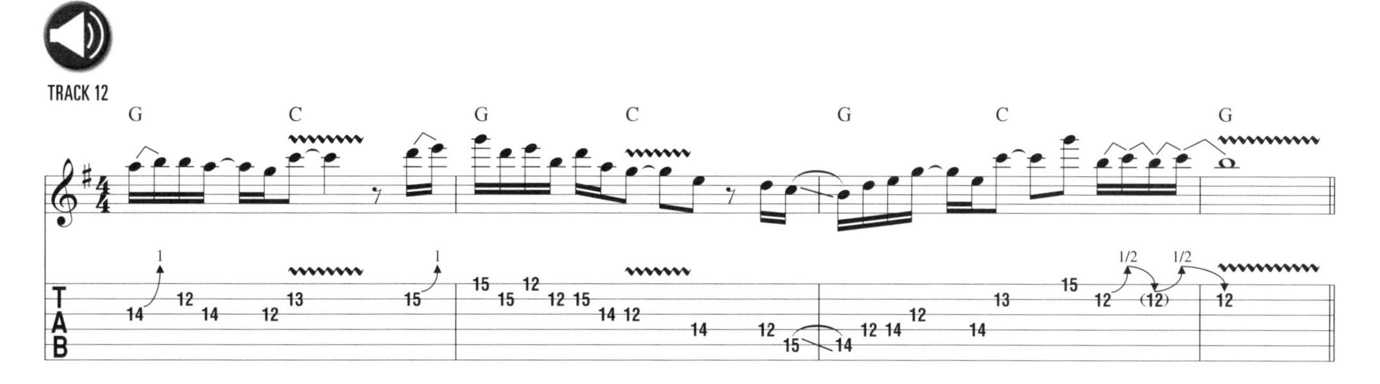

Phrasing Tip: Grace Has a Place!

Implementing *grace notes* can really infuse your lines with personality. A grace note is a very short note played just before the main note. They take up very little metric time and are meant as an ornament. They're written on the staff as a smaller note with a line through the flag and a slur connecting them to the main note. On the guitar, we normally perform grace notes with hammer-ons, pull-offs, or slides, as demonstrated below with several C major scale phrases.

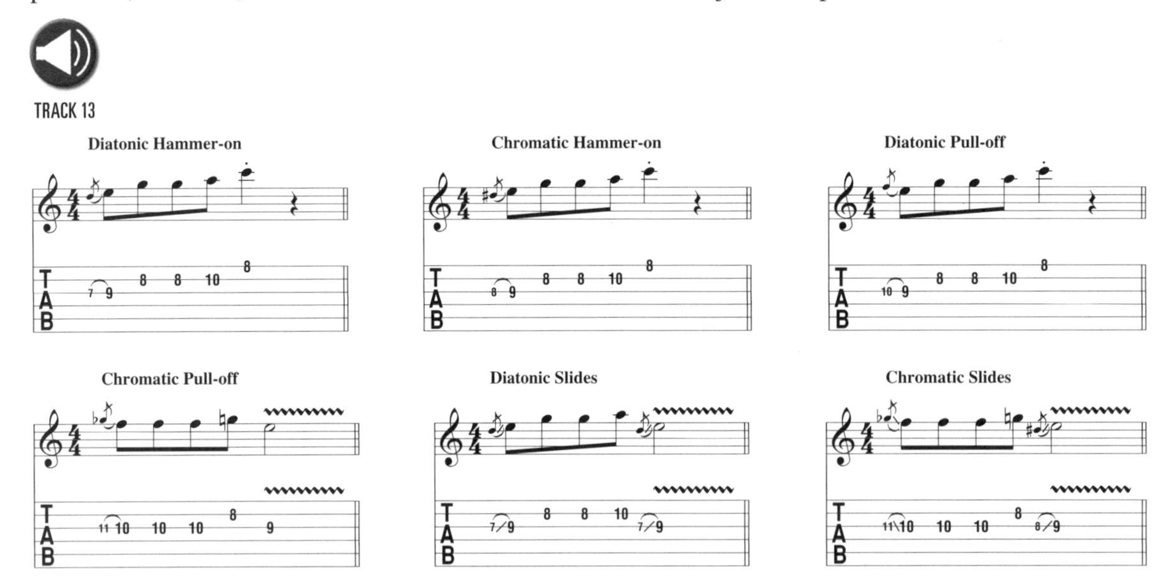

Grace notes can be diatonic, but they're just as often *chromatic* (notes outside the key), especially in blues or jazz styles. Watch out for the grace notes appearing in the remaining examples.

Check out the grace notes in example 4, which is played over a I–vi–IV–I in D major using Shape 2 of the D major scale. Both diatonic (measure 2) and chromatic (measures 3 and 4) grace notes are used, and don't miss the *double-stop lick* (two strings played at once) in measure 3—a staple of the blues/R&B style.

Example 4

Example 5 makes use of the E♭ major scale, Shape 1, over a I–iii–ii–V in E♭. The colorful major 7th of the scale, D, is carefully targeted to highlight the iii chord, Gm, where it functions as its 5th (G–B♭–**D**).

Example 5

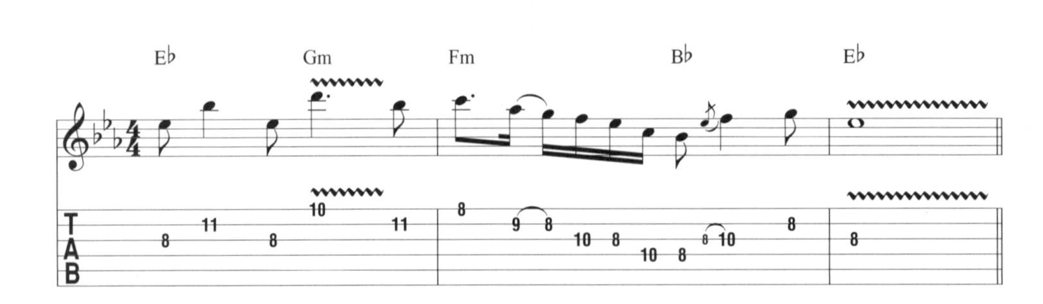

In example 6, the phrase accents the rhythm of the chord changes in this I–IV–vi–V progression in A♭. We're working out of the A♭ major scale, Shape 2, and targeting a lot of 3rds here.

Example 6

TRACK 16

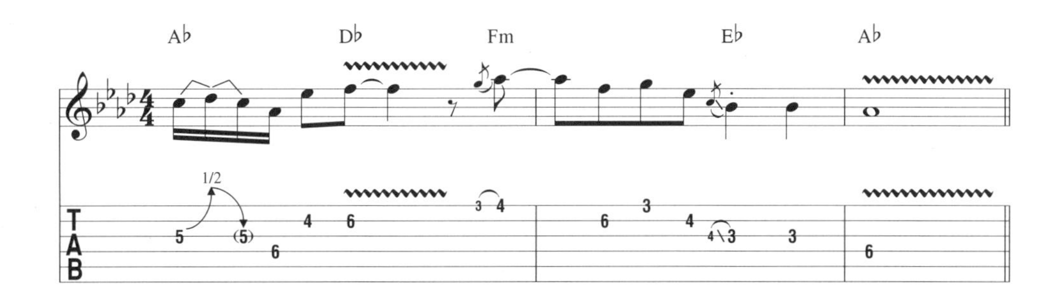

Phrasing Tip: Playing "Across the Bar"

In order to prevent your licks from sounding too rhythmically predictable, it's a good idea to vary where you begin and end your phrases. If you make it a habit of always starting a lick on beat 1 (or always ending there), for example, it's going to get old quickly. Playing "across the bar line" is a great way to mix it up. This means that, instead of beginning a phrase on beat 1, you begin on beat 4 or beat 4½ of the previous measure. This can really make your phrases stand out and keep things interesting.

For example, here's a typical C major pentatonic phrase. Notice that it begins and ends on beat 1.

TRACK 17

Now, there's nothing wrong with this phrase, but it's just a little square in terms of rhythm. Listen to what happens when we alter it so that we're phrasing over the bar line. In this example, we haven't changed any notes; we've just moved both the first and last notes back by an eighth note. Check out how it comes to life.

TRACK 17
(0:07)

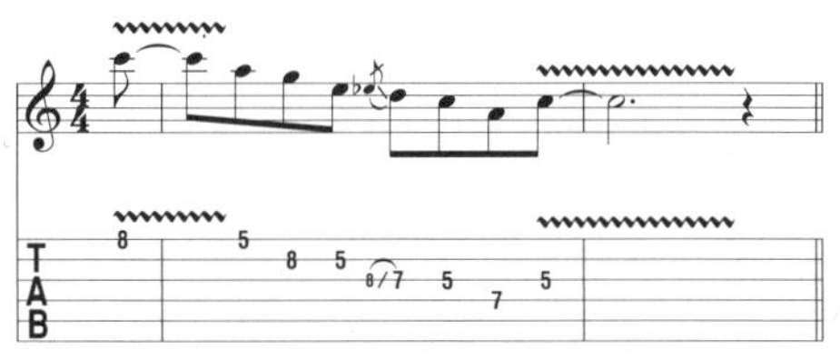

And here's how it sounds with the first and last notes moved back a full beat. Notice that we omitted one C note toward the end in order to accomplish this.

TRACK 17
(0:15)

Generally speaking, the faster the tempo, the earlier you can get away with starting and ending your phrases—i.e., beat 4 or even beat 3 or 2 of the previous measure. For slower tempos, it may sound better to move back by an eighth or just a sixteenth note. However, there are no rules, so feel free to experiment. Also note that you can move the phrase beginnings and endings independently of each other.

MINOR SCALE EXAMPLES

Now let's check out some minor scale examples in several keys and scale forms. We'll be using both the minor scale and minor pentatonic.

For example 7, we're in *12/8 time*, which is usually counted as four beats of triplets per measure: **1**–2–3, **4**–5–6, **7**–8–9, **10**–11–12. Over a i–♭VI–♭III–♭VII progression in C minor, we're employing two common bends in the Shape 1 form. Be sure to notice the anticipated B♭ note at the end of the phrase. While this isn't technically "phrasing across the bar" (since it's not happening across a bar line), the principle of anticipating a resolution is the same.

Example 7

TRACK 18

Cm A♭ E♭ B♭

Example 8 is set over a driving i–♭VII progression in D minor. We're phrasing across the bar throughout here, working out of the D minor scale, Shape 2.

Example 8

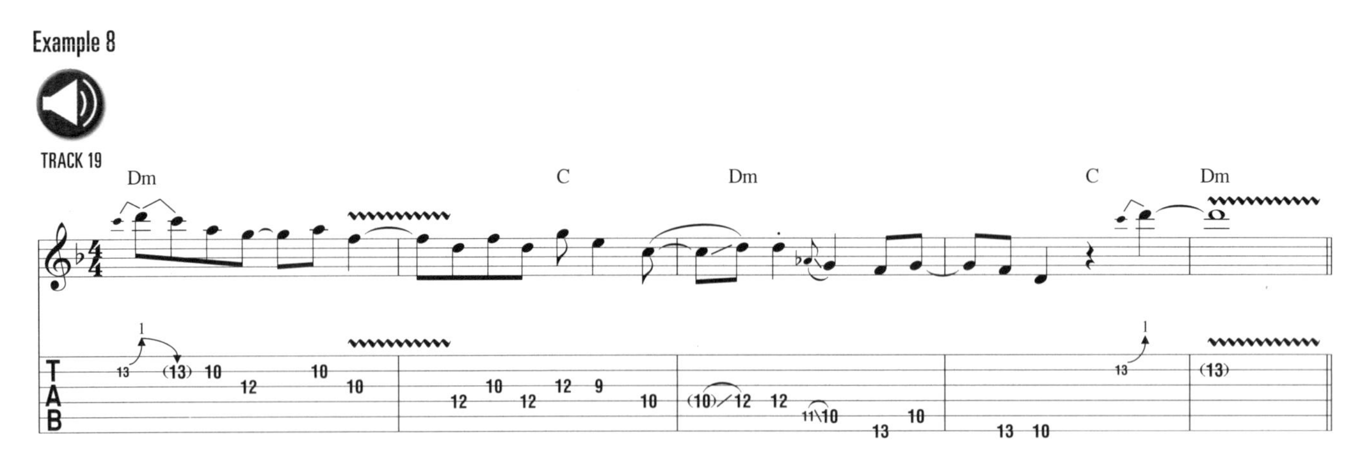

In example 9, we're playing over a funky i–iv *vamp* (repetitive progression of one or two chords) in G minor. This time, though, we get a little fancy. Over the Gm chords, we play out of the G minor pentatonic scale, Shape 2. Over the Cm chords, though, we move up to eighth position and play out of the C minor pentatonic scale, Shape 2. Notice how each phrase is still resolved to a chord tone (all roots in this case), even though we're moving between two different positions. This is just a glimpse into what we'll be covering later in the book, where we'll be moving through many different scale forms.

Example 9

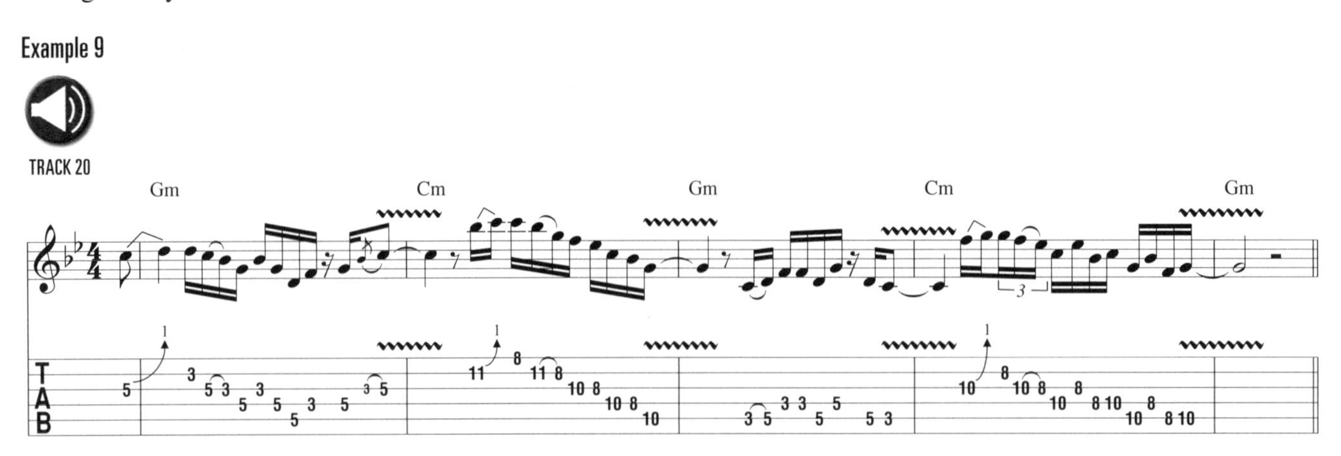

But wait! I thought we were using the key-center approach for this chapter? This means we only use one scale to solo over the whole progression, right? That's right. However, switching from G minor *pentatonic* to C minor *pentatonic* is technically still using a G minor key-center approach because all of the notes from C minor pentatonic (C–E♭–F–G–B♭) are found within the G minor scale: **G**–A–**B♭**–**C**–D–**E♭**–**F**. (If we had switched to a C *natural minor* scale over the Cm chord, instead of C minor pentatonic, we would no longer be using the G minor key-center approach.)

So, we really could have said that the previous example just uses the G minor scale and we would have been technically correct, but we're not thinking of it like that—especially on guitar, where the pentatonic scale creates such a recognizable visual pattern.

WHAT YOU LEARNED:

- The **key-center approach**: using one scale to solo over the whole progression.
- Fundamentals of good note choice: resolving to chord tones and not accenting awkward or dissonant tones.
- Phrasing Tips: **grace notes**, playing **across the bar**.

CHAPTER 4: THE MODES

Ah, the modes—one of the most misunderstood concepts in all of guitardom. (I suppose they may be equally misunderstood by other instrumentalists too, but guitar players are notoriously puzzled by them.) For a long time, guitarists have looked to modes to expand their options after growing tired of the major and minor scales. And this is a logical progression; it's no coincidence that we're covering modes immediately after the major and minor scales in this book. However, without an understanding of how to apply them, "knowing your modes" isn't going to do much good at all.

There are seven modes, and I believe they can be viewed in two ways:

1. **The Relative Method:** Seven different ways to play one major scale.

   or

2. **The Parallel Method:** Seven different scales in their own right.

These two ways of understanding modes aren't mutually exclusive at all; there are many bits of information that overlap from one method into the other. But, with regards to practical application, the differences are more pronounced. By the way, while "relative" and "parallel" aren't new musical terms, they're not usually applied to the modes in this way. The reason I attach these terms to them is that, in my opinion, it makes the concept of modes easier to understand.

MODES: THE RELATIVE METHOD

We heard the term "relative minor" earlier in the book. In a major key, you find the relative minor by counting up to the 6th degree of the scale. In C major, this would be A: C (1)–D (2)–E (3)–F (4)–G (5)–**A (6)**. So, we'd say that A minor is the relative minor of C major. Consequently, C is the *relative major* of A minor. Alternatively, you may have heard the "down three frets" trick. That will get the same result. C is on fret 8 of the sixth string; take away 3 from 8 and you get fret 5, which is A.

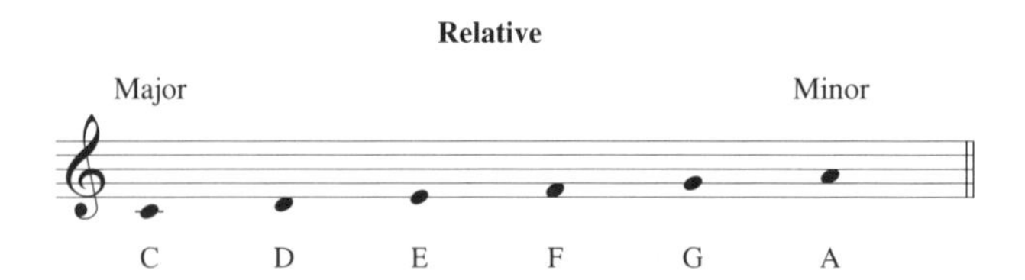

Relative majors and minors share the same key signature and, therefore, the same set of seven notes; they just have two different roots. In other words, the key of C contains the notes C–D–E–F–G–A–B, but C major treats C as the root, while A minor treats A as the root. You can remember this by thinking that they're "relatives" of each other—i.e., from the same "family" of notes.

So how does this relate to modes? Well, the seven modes are just an extension of this concept. If we can treat C or A as the root of this family of notes, what about the other notes? Yep, we can do the same for them, and that's where you get the modes. This is why I call this the "relative method." Since there are seven notes in a major scale, there are seven modes:

1. **Ionian**
2. **Dorian**
3. **Phrygian**
4. **Lydian**
5. **Mixolydian**
6. **Aeolian**
7. **Locrian**

So, if we were working in the key of C major, for example, we would name these based on each note of the C major scale (C–D–E–F–G–A–B). So the first mode of C major is C Ionian, the second mode is D Dorian, the third mode is E Phrygian, and so on. We can harmonize these modes if we'd like by playing them over the appropriate chord for each degree of the scale, as demonstrated below.

Modes in the Key of C Major

TRACK 21

C Ionian

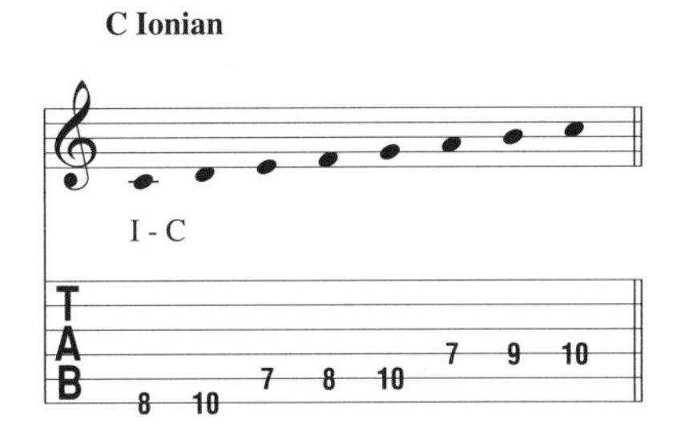

D Dorian

ii - Dm

TAB: 10 7 8 10 7 9 10 7

E Phrygian

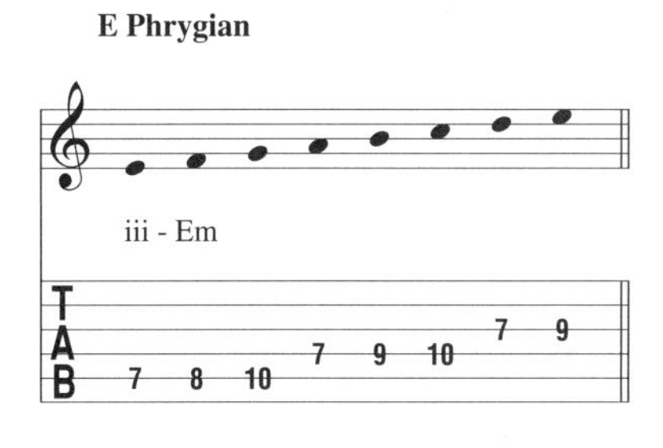

F Lydian

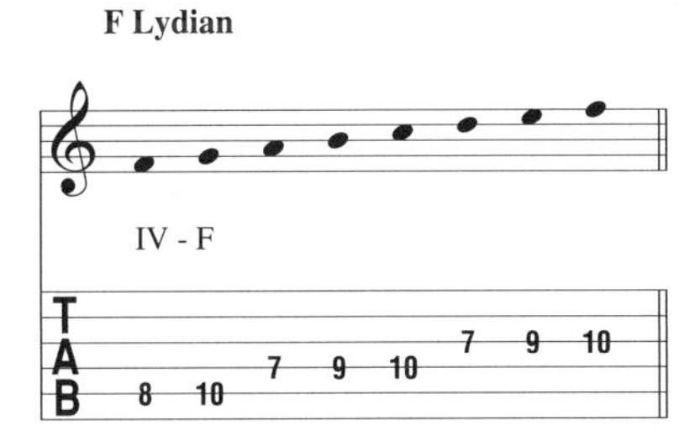

G Mixolydian

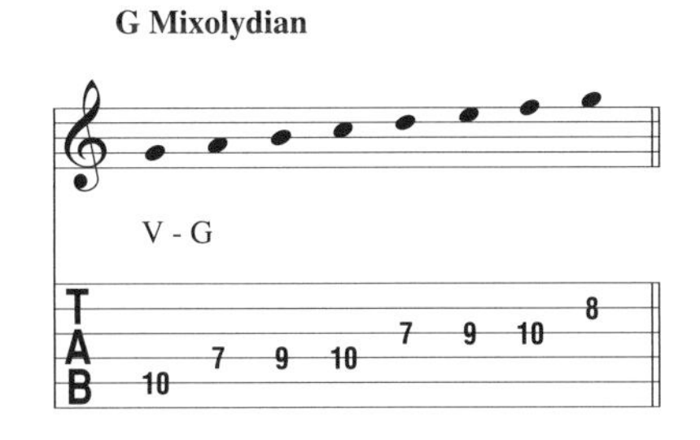

A Aeolian

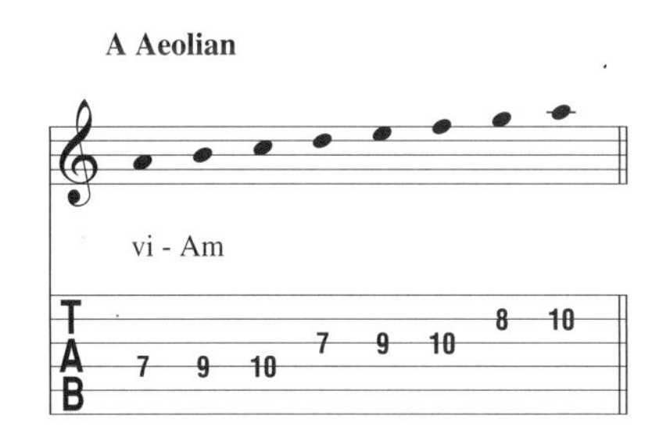

B Locrian

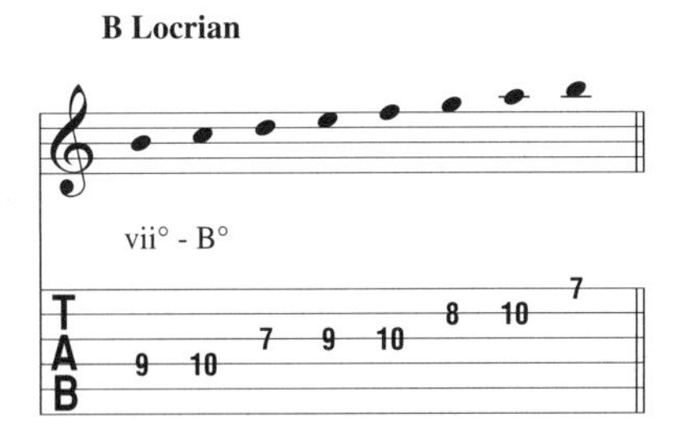

> **Déjà vu?**
>
> If you're on top of things, you may have noticed that two of these modes look very familiar: Ionian and Aeolian. There's good reason for this: the Ionian mode is simply another name for the major scale (i.e., C major scale = C Ionian mode), and the Aeolian mode is another name for the minor scale (i.e., A minor scale = A Aeolian).

This relationship holds true to any key. If you're in D major, for instance, you will find its modes by spelling out the notes of the D major scale (D–E–F♯–G–A–B–C♯) and playing the scale from each one of those notes treated as the root. Here's what you'd get:

D Ionian: D–E–F♯–G–A–B–C♯

E Dorian: E–F♯–G–A–B–C♯–D

F♯ Phrygian: F♯–G–A–B–C♯–D–E

G Lydian: G–A–B–C♯–D–E–F♯

A Mixolydian: A–B–C♯–D–E–F♯–G

B Aeolian: B–C♯–D–E–F♯–G–A

C♯ Locrian: C♯–D–E–F♯–G–A–B

If you were to play these all as two-octave shapes with each root falling on the sixth string, you would cover an entire octave span (12 frets) on the neck:

Modes of D Major

D Ionian (D–E–F♯–G–A–B–C♯)

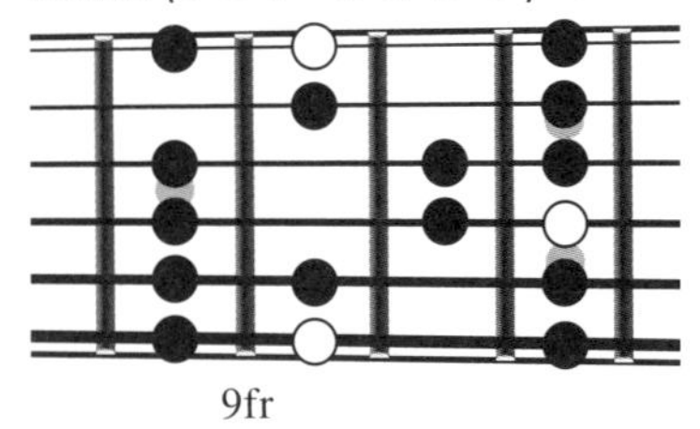

9fr

E Dorian (E–F♯–G–A–B–C♯–D)

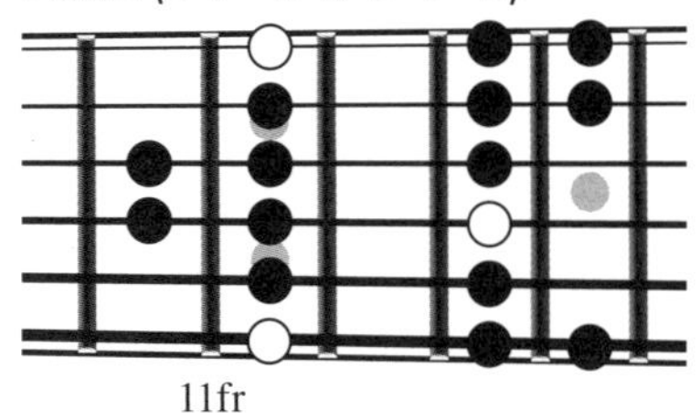

11fr

F♯ Phrygian (F♯–G–A–B–C♯–D–E)

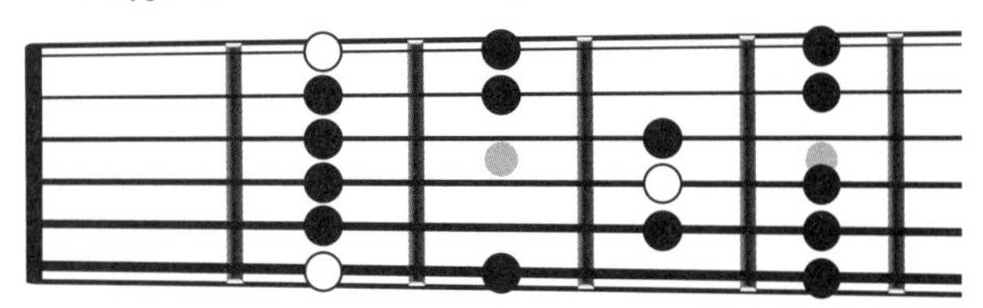

G Lydian (G–A–B–C♯–D–E–F♯)

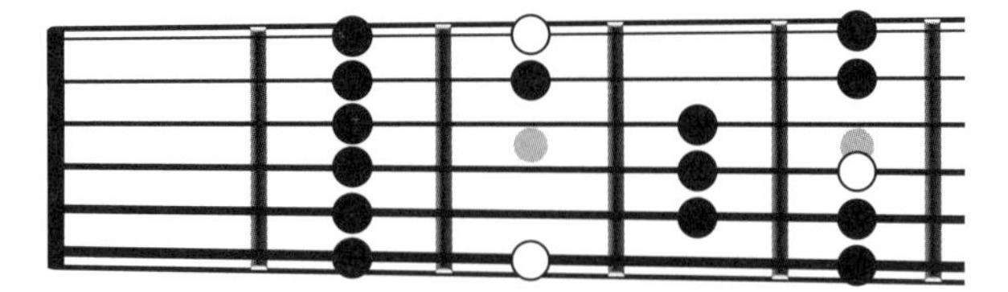

A Mixolydian (A–B–C♯–D–E–F♯–G)

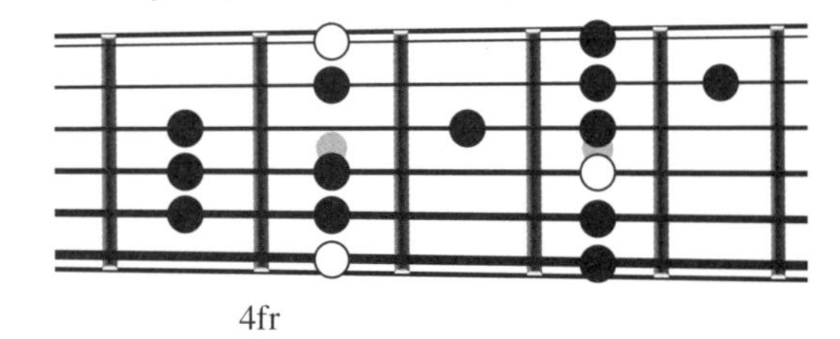

4fr

B Aeolian (B–C♯–D–E–F♯–G–A)

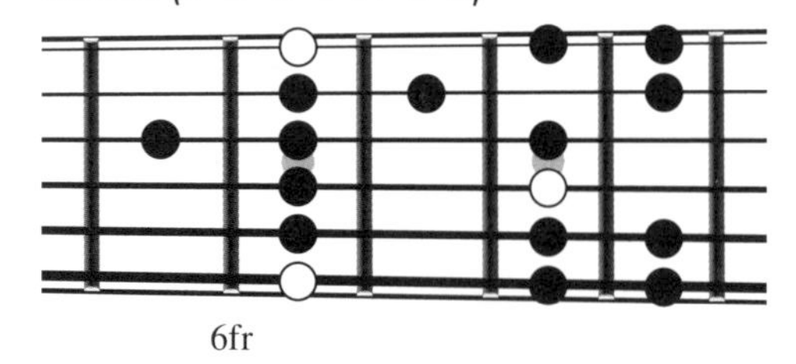

6fr

C♯ Locrian (C♯–D–E–F♯–G–A–B)

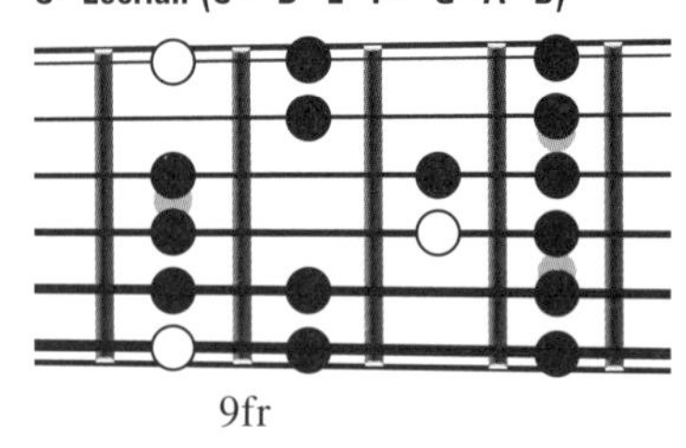

9fr

Another way to view this is simply the D major scale in seven patterns. Here are the same seven patterns with all the D notes indicated:

D Major Scale in Seven Patterns

Pattern 1

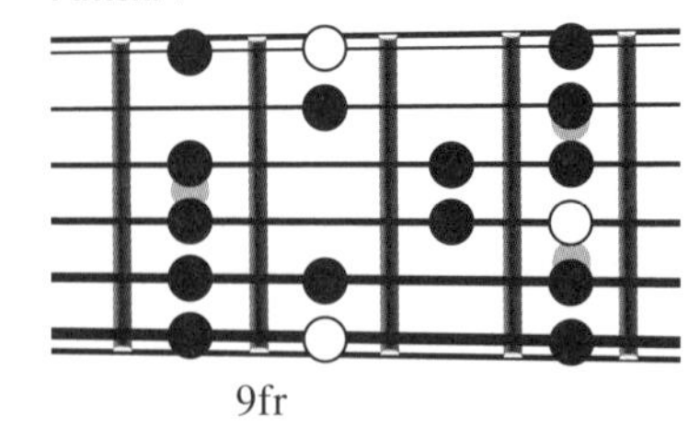

9fr

Pattern 2

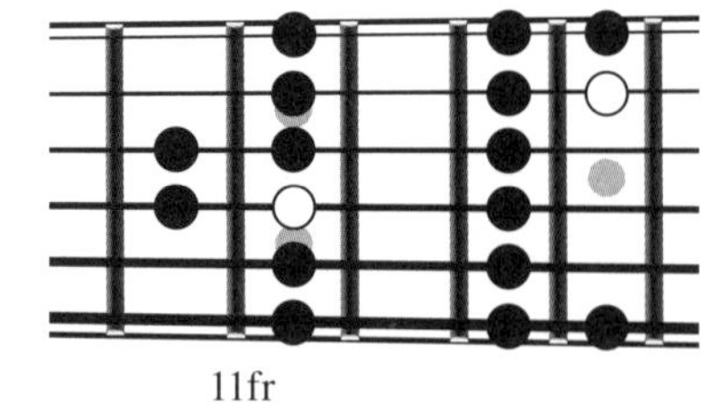

11fr

Pattern 3

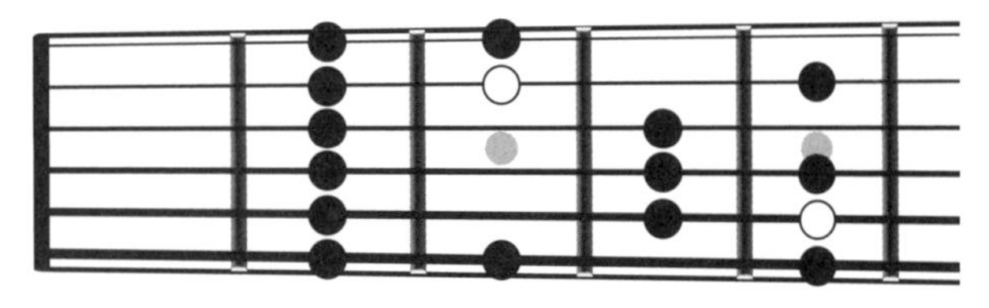

Pattern 4

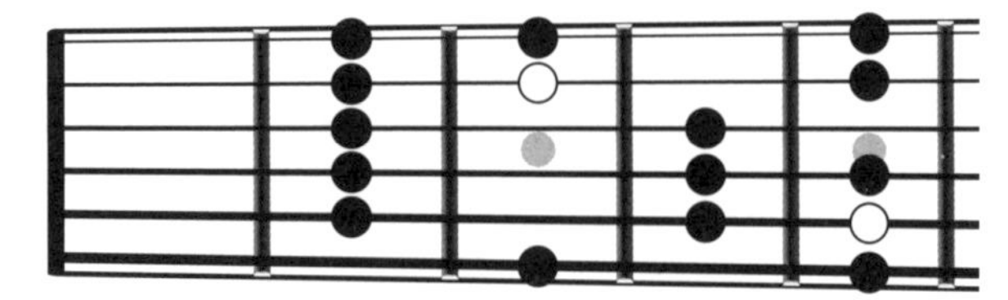

Pattern 5

4fr

Pattern 6

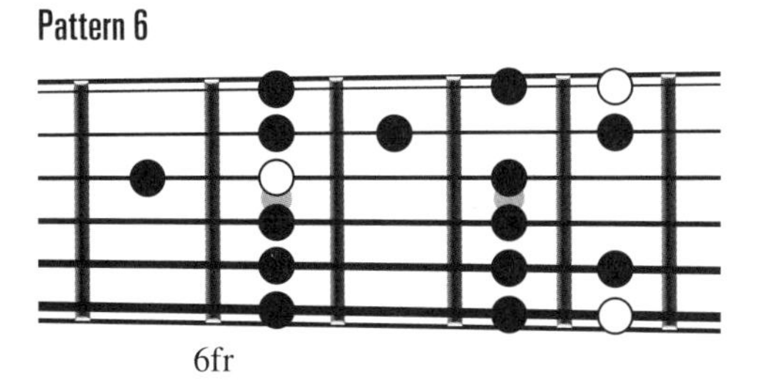

Pattern 7

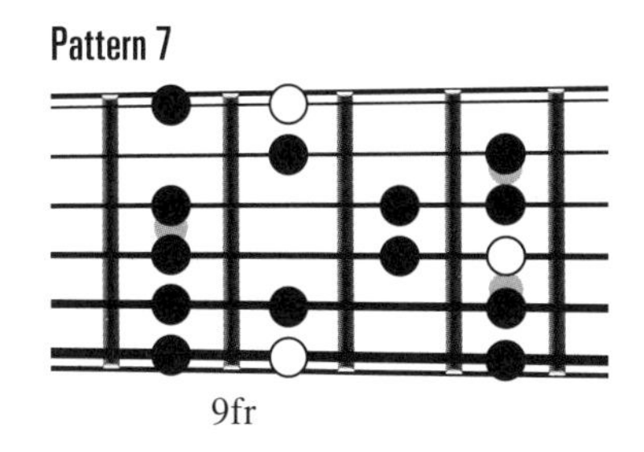

That's pretty much all there is to the relative method of thinking about modes. It's a good introduction to modes, but it doesn't teach you much in the way of practical application. Therefore, we need to examine the other side of modes.

A Half-Developed Modal Picture

Many players get this far with their modal knowledge and stop. They think, "OK, I get it! I know all the modes now," but all they really know are fingerings for the major scale all over the neck. Although this is certainly helpful, it's not going to provide any different sounds. If the player is sharp, he or she may deduce that they can play the appropriate mode over its matching chord in a diatonic progression, which is certainly true.

For example, if you have a I–V–vi–IV progression in E major (E–B–C♯m–A), you could solo over the progression using the matching mode for each chord: E Ionian over E, B Mixolydian over B, C♯ Aeolian over C♯m, and A Lydian over A.

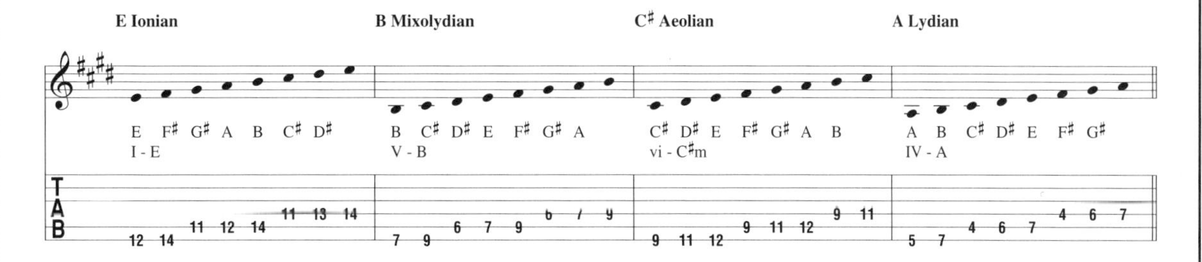

The problem with this is that it's unnecessarily complicating things. In the end, it's just going to sound like an E major scale; it doesn't matter what scale form you're using. If you're playing over a diatonic major or minor progression such as this and you only want to use diatonic notes, then there's really no need to involve the modes. The key-center approach works perfectly well; you'll use your ear and knowledge of harmony to make the correct note choices.

However, if you're soloing over a non-diatonic progression (one in which not all the chords belong to one key) and you need to treat one or more of the chords with a different specific scale, then you're most likely going to need to call upon a mode or two. This is where the other half of the modal picture comes in.

MODES: THE PARALLEL METHOD

In the parallel method of looking at modes, we're going to look at each mode as a scale in its own right. We learned earlier that the major scale's intervallic formula is 1–2–3–4–5–6–7; all other scales can be represented by altering one or more of these numbers (i.e., adding sharps or flats). Now we're going to do the same thing with the modes.

But Modes Aren't Scales! Or Are They?

You'll hear some people go on endless tirades about how modes are *not* scales. In my opinion, this is really just a silly matter of semantics. We've already seen evidence of the contrary with two modes: Ionian and Aeolian, also known as the major and minor scales, respectively. So let's get this out of the way right now: Yes, modes are scales! Just as the minor scale (Aeolian mode) has a unique formula (1–2–♭3–4–5–♭6–♭7) that's different from the major scale, each mode has its own unique formula, too. And that's the essence of the parallel method.

Instead of examining all of the diatonic modes of C major, for instance, now we're going to examine all the modes using C as the root note. In the relative method we were looking at the same notes but with different roots, whereas now we're looking at the *same root but with different notes*. For each mode, we'll spell the notes and look at a suggested two-octave shape.

Seven Modes with C as the Root

Ionian mode: 1–2–3–4–5–6–7
C Ionian: C–D–E–F–G–A–B

Construction: As we've already learned, the Ionian mode is simply the major scale. Its formula is the standard by which we judge all other scales, so there are no altered numbers. Its matching diatonic harmony is the I chord; it's played here over a C chord.

Sound and application: The Ionian mode sounds happy and sunny and is the most widely used mode of all, prevalent in almost all forms of film scores, pop, jazz, classical music, and more.

TRACK 22

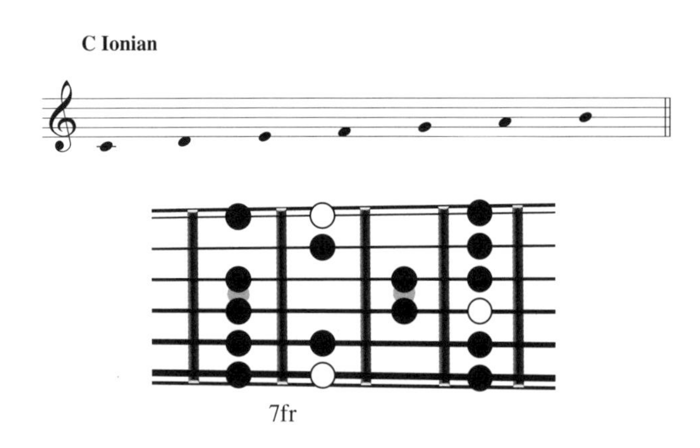

Dorian mode: 1–2–♭3–4–5–6–♭7
C Dorian: C–D–E♭–F–G–A–B♭

Construction: The Dorian mode can be thought of as a minor scale (Aeolian mode) with a natural 6th degree (instead of the ♭6th). Its matching diatonic harmony is the ii chord; it's played here over a Cm chord.

Sound and application: Though it's still a minor mode (due to the ♭3rd degree), the Dorian mode sounds brighter than Aeolian. It's widely used in rock, blues, jazz, pop, and lots of Celtic music, as well.

TRACK 22
(0:17)

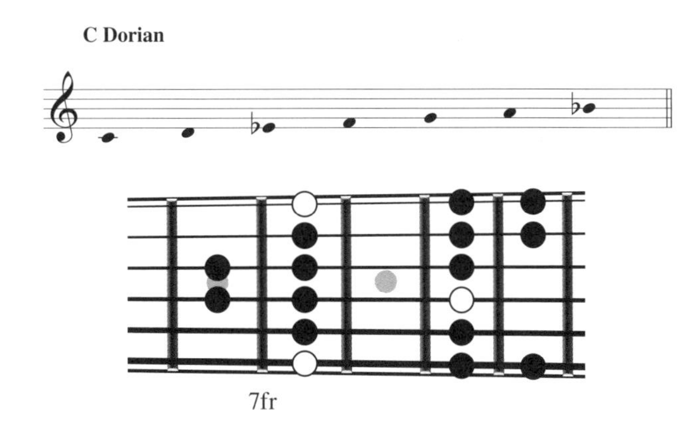

Phrygian mode: 1–♭2–♭3–4–5–♭6–♭7
C Phrygian: C–D♭–E♭–F–G–A♭–B♭

Construction: The Phrygian mode can be described as a minor scale (Aeolian mode) with a ♭2nd. Its matching diatonic harmony is the iii chord; it's played here over a Cm chord.

Sound and application: The ♭2nd degree of Phrygian gives it a slightly exotic sound that's prevalent in some Spanish music and also some metal.

TRACK 22
(0:32)

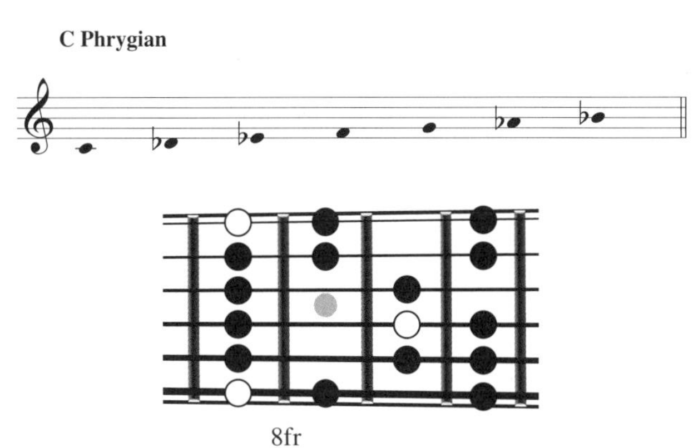

Lydian mode: 1–2–3–♯4–5–6–7
C Lydian: C–D–E–F♯–G–A–B

Construction: The Lydian mode is like a major scale (Ionian mode) with a ♯4th degree. Its matching diatonic harmony is the IV chord; it's played here over a C chord.

Sound and application: This is a bright, dreamy-sounding scale that has a mysterious quality to it. You hear it often in jazz and a lot of film scores as well.

TRACK 22
(0:47)

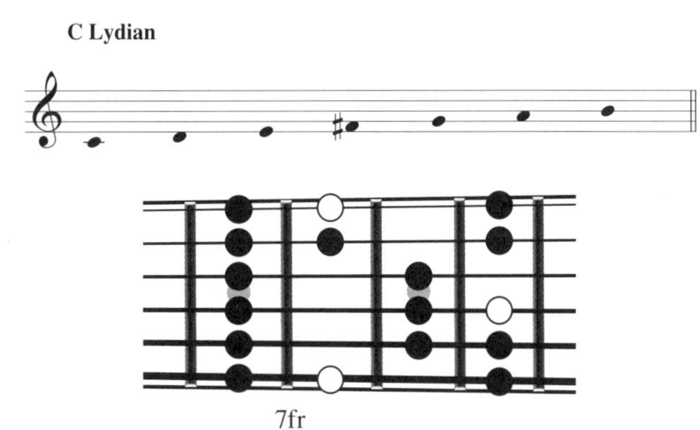

Mixolydian mode: 1–2–3–4–5–6–♭7
C Mixolydian: C–D–E–F–G–A–B♭

Construction: Mixolydian can be thought of as a major scale (Ionian mode) with a ♭7th degree. Its matching diatonic harmony is the V chord; it's played here over a C chord.

Sound and application: The Mixolydian mode sounds kind of like a bluesy, funky major scale. It's very common in blues, jazz, rock and all kinds of pop.

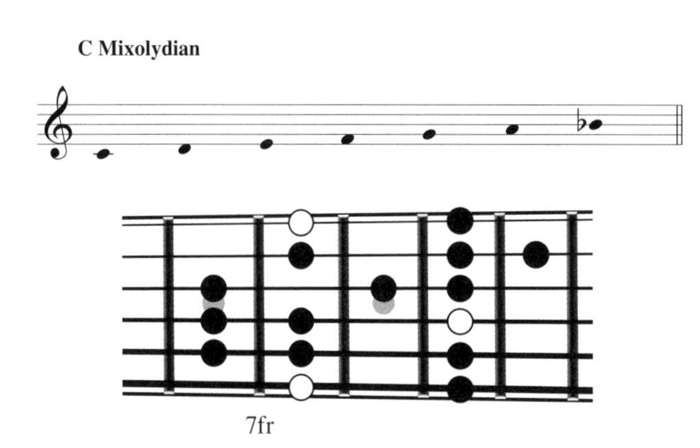

Aeolian mode: 1–2–♭3–4–5–♭6–♭7
C Aeolian: C–D–E♭–F–G–A♭–B♭

Construction: The Aeolian mode is the same thing as the natural minor scale. Compared to the major scale, it has lowered 3rd, 6th, and 7th degrees. Its matching diatonic harmony is the vi chord; it's played here over a Cm chord.

Sound and application: The Aeolian mode sounds dark, sad, and sometimes gothic. You hear it in lots of pop, rock, metal, some jazz, classical music, and film scores.

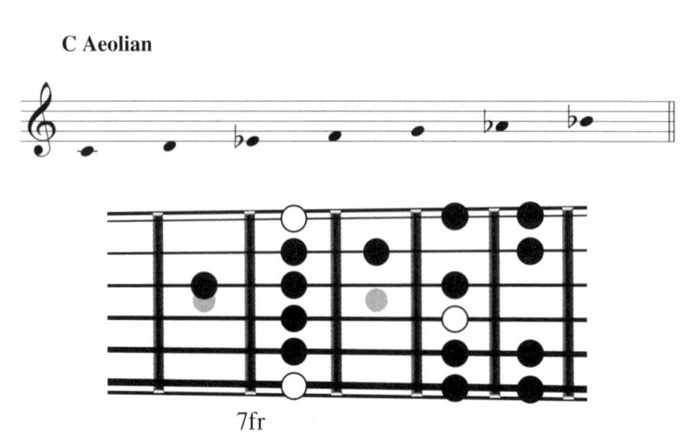

Locrian mode: 1–♭2–♭3–4–♭5–♭6–♭7
C Locrian: C–D♭–E♭–F–G♭–A♭–B♭

Construction: The Locrian mode is like an Aeolian mode with a ♭2nd and ♭5th. Its matching diatonic harmony is the vii° chord; it's played here over a C° chord.

Sound and application: The ♭5th degree of this mode makes it very unstable. In fact, its matching harmony is a diminished chord—not exactly the pillar of resolution. Outside of jazz, the Locrian mode sees some action in certain metal genres, but that's about it.

TRACK 22
(1:32)

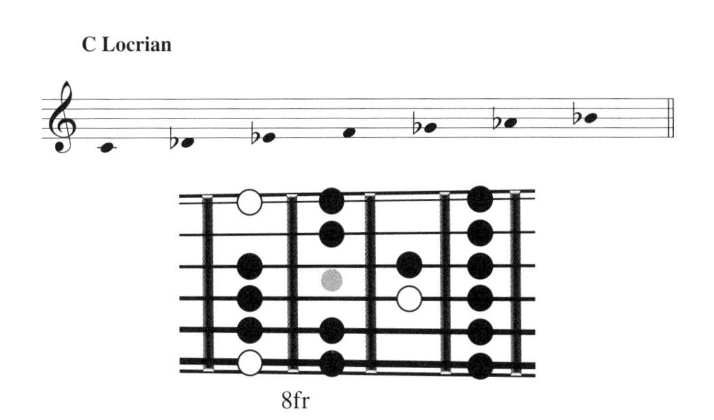

Major/Minor Distinction

These modes can be roughly broken down into one of two groups: major-sounding or minor-sounding. The determining factor is the 3rd degree.

Major modes:

- Ionian
- Lydian
- Mixolydian

Minor modes:

- Dorian
- Phrygian
- Aeolian
- Locrian*

*Locrian isn't technically a minor mode since it also contains a ♭5th, so it qualifies as a diminished scale. But for our purposes, the minor label will suffice.

At this point, all you really need to take from this is that you normally play a mode over the appropriate chord type. For example, over a C chord, you would play C Ionian, C Lydian, or C Mixolydian; over a Cm chord, you would play C Dorian, C Phrygian, or C Aeolian; over C°, you would play C Locrian. There are a few factors that would help in determining which mode would be most appropriate, and that's what we'll look at in the next chapter.

WHAT YOU LEARNED:

- Names and fingerings of the seven modes: Ionian, Dorian, Phrygian, Lydian, Mixolydian, Aeolian, and Locrian.
- Two modal relationships: **relative** and **parallel**.
- Modes are scales!
- Intervallic formulas for each mode.
- Modes are grouped as either **major modes** or **minor modes**.

Learn That Neck!

At this point, jump ahead to the appendix and take a look at the remaining three scale forms for the major and minor scales and the pentatonic versions of each. Just like the first two forms we learned, they're each based on an open-position chord form. The licks in the remainder of the book, though usually based on one form, will freely move through others, so familiarize yourself with all five forms and work on playing them all over the neck. We still have a lot of ground to cover, so I have to trust you to do a little of this legwork on your own!

CHAPTER 5: MODAL APPLICATIONS PART 1— ONE-CHORD VAMPS

OK, after all that talk about modes in the previous chapter, how about we get down to making some music with them? In this chapter, we're going to learn how to choose the right mode(s) to play over a chord that doesn't clearly fit into a diatonic set of harmonies.

If you're in the key of C and you have C, F, G, and Dm chords, that's no problem. All those chords are diatonic to the key of C. Therefore, the C major scale and/or C major pentatonic scale will sound great. However, what if you have a D chord instead of the Dm? Or an Fm instead of the F? What do you do then? Or what if you just have a one-chord vamp? What do you play over that? In each of these instances, you have some options, and we'll talk about those in this chapter.

ONE-CHORD VAMPS

Occasionally, you have a song or a solo section that consists of nothing but one chord. It could be E, A7, Dm7, Bmaj7, or whatever. But that's it. That's all you have to work with—just one chord. How do you determine what you should play over it? There are a few simple steps that will help point you in the right direction.

The Ear Is the Final Judge

It's important to realize that there are no hard-and-fast rules in music. You're not going to be arrested if you choose to play a C major scale over a Cm chord. (You may not be hired on another gig, but … that's neither here nor there.) All of these concepts we're discussing are really just conventions; they're what *most* people play *most* of the time because *most* people agree that they sound good.

Our C major scale over a Cm chord example seems blatantly wrong to most people, but not all situations are that cut-and-dried. (And, believe it or not, even that specific application can be made to work if done carefully and in the proper context!) There will be many times when more than one scale choice would "work," and it's in those instances where your ear, among other possible factors, will be the judge in what sounds best or most appropriate. So, while the following steps will be applicable for most situations, you should always feel free to experiment.

Determining the Appropriate Mode for a One-Chord Vamp

Let's look at some helpful methods in determining what to play over a one-chord section:

1. **Use the chord's 3rd to choose the major or minor modes**
   This is pretty self-explanatory. If the chord has a major 3rd (i.e., it's major or dominant), you'll start with the three major modes. If it has a minor 3rd (i.e., it's minor, half-diminished*, or diminished), start with the minor modes.

* *Half-diminished* is another name for a minor seventh flat five chord, which we'll examine more closely in Chapter 8.

2. **If present, compare the chord's 7th to that of the mode choices remaining**
   If the chord is a C7†, for example, which is spelled C–E–G–B♭, the 7th is B♭. Since the presence of the major 3rd already narrowed down your choice to the three major modes (C Ionian, C Lydian, C Mixolydian), you can now check those modes to see which has a B♭. Both C Ionian and C Lydian have a B♮, but C Mixolydian has a B♭, which makes it the logical choice.

† Seventh chords will be fully covered in Chapter 7.

So let's take a look at a few examples to see how this works. Example 1 is a repetitive groove over a Bm7 chord, which is spelled B–D–F♯–A. We know from the minor 3rd (D) that we need a B minor mode, and we know from the ♭7th (A) that the mode should contain A as well. Consequently, all three B minor modes (B Dorian, B Phrygian, and B Aeolian) contain A. Therefore, if we were given no other information, the choice would be left up to the soloist. Let's try out all three options.

Here's what it sounds like using B Dorian:

Example 1A

Now here's what B Aeolian (minor scale) sounds like:

Example 1B

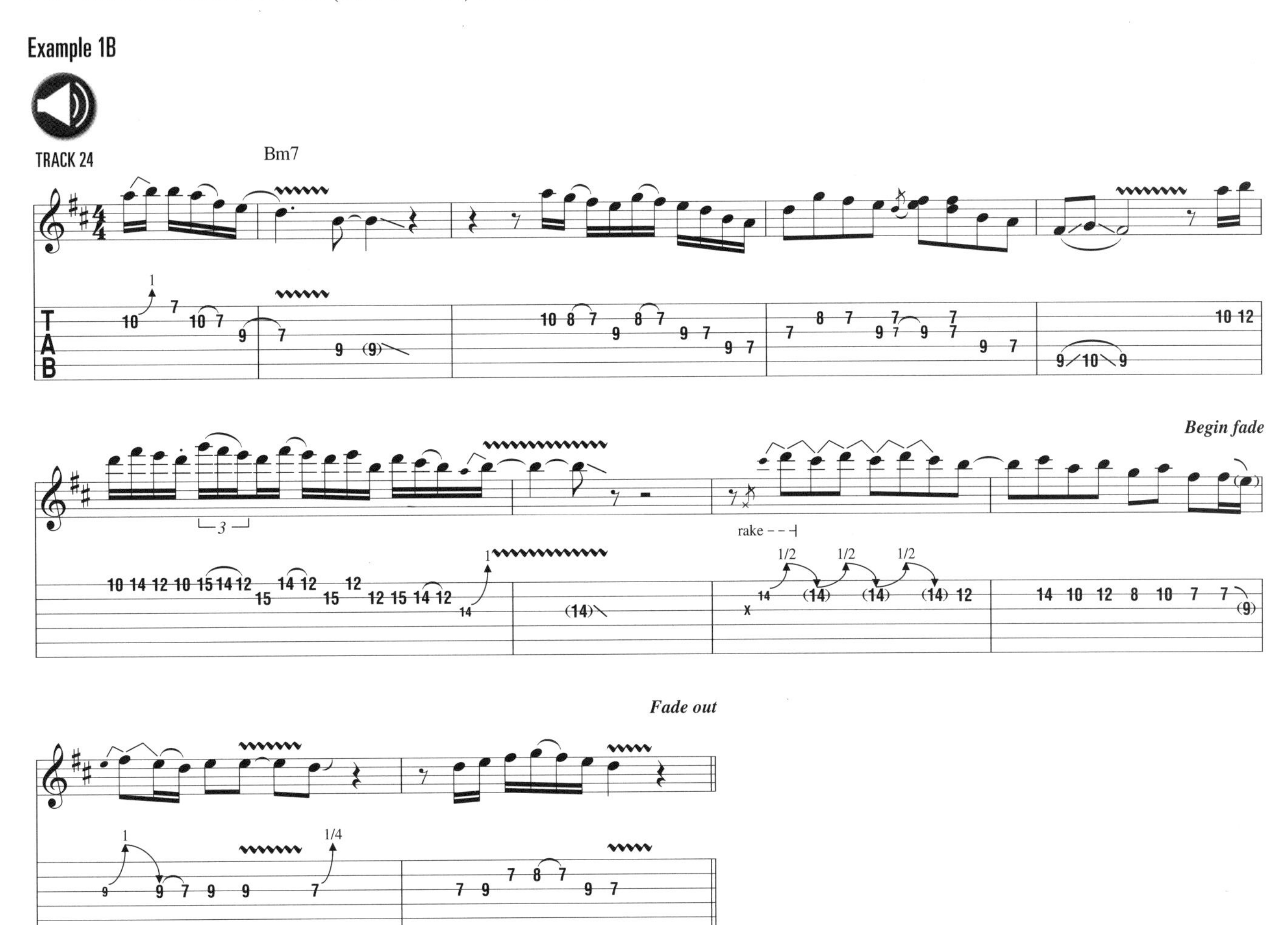

And finally, here's the B Phrygian approach:

Example 1C

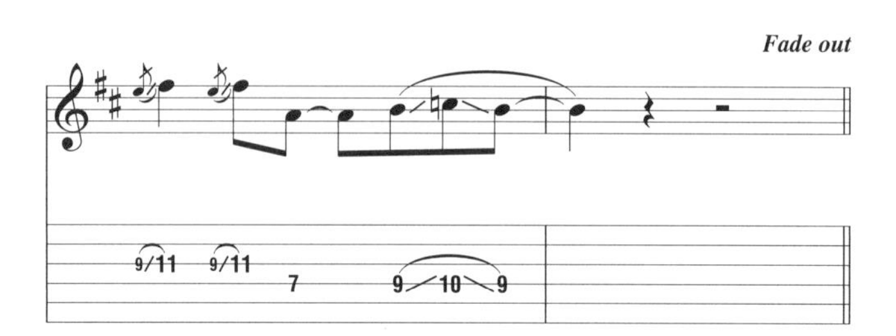

Could you hear the difference? Certain licks sounded similar because all three of these modes share several notes—specifically, they share the notes of the B minor pentatonic scale (B–D–E–F♯–A). But occasionally you'd hear the definitive notes—the different 2nds and/or 6ths—that set apart the sound of each. The more you familiarize yourself with the sound of each mode, the quicker you'll be able to determine which one will suit your needs in situations such as these.

Example 2 takes place over a G7 vamp. This is a fairly common occurrence if you're playing in a funk band, for instance. As mentioned earlier, with a dominant seventh chord, the only logical choice of mode is the Mixolydian.

Example 2

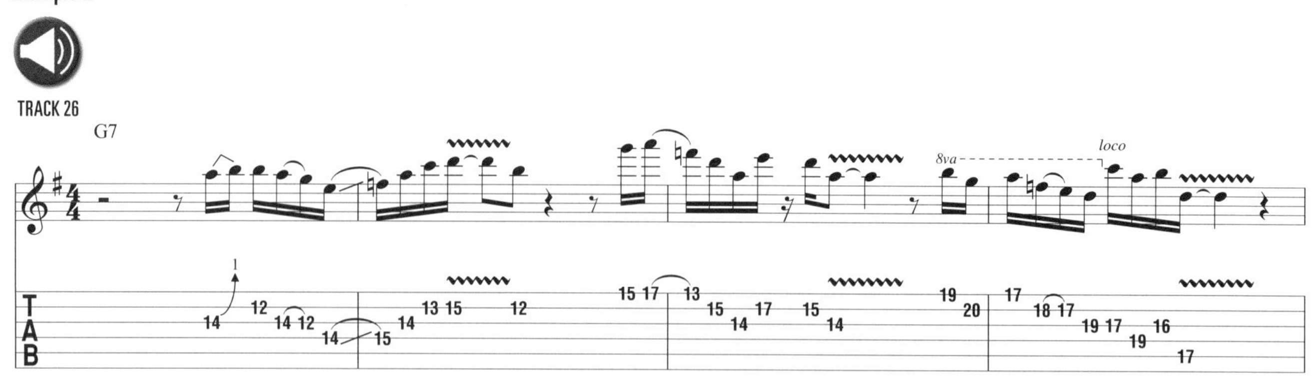

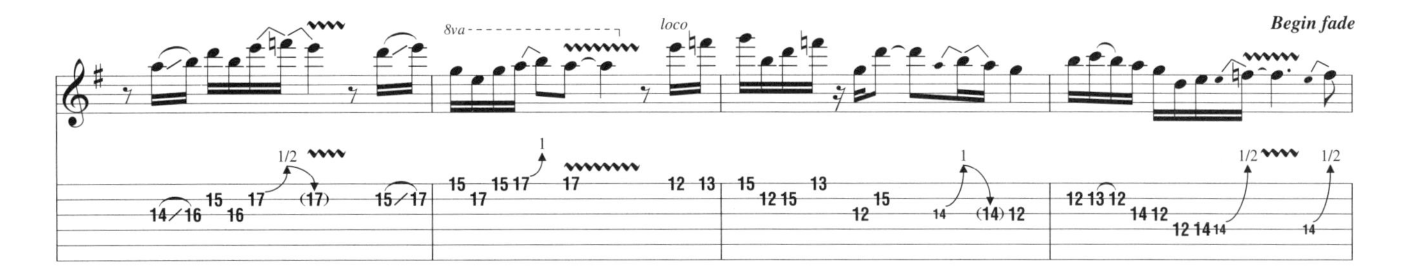

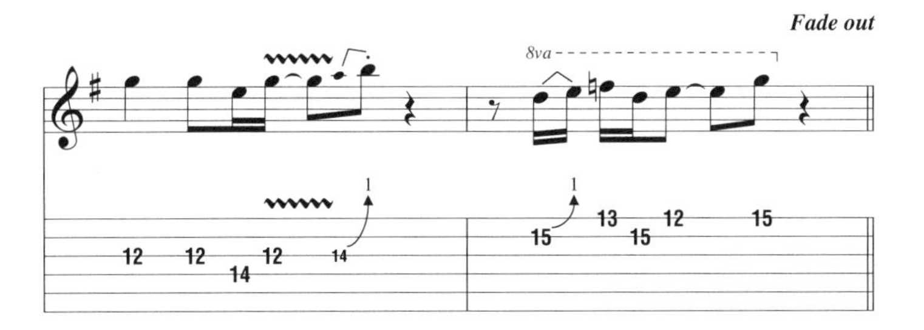

Grain of Salt Alert!

Remember that these guidelines are not rules. I bring this up now because we've just stated that the only scale you may play over a dominant chord is the Mixolydian mode. Now, anyone who's ever played a 12-bar blues knows this is not even close to correct. The minor pentatonic and its close cousin, the *blues scale*, have been played over dominant chords for decades with astounding results.

While this practice would theoretically clash—a dominant chord contains a major 3rd, while the minor pentatonic and blues scales contain a minor 3rd—history has shown us that our ears have no problem adapting to this sound when it's used in a certain way. (Interestingly, the opposite approach—using scales with a *major* 3rd over *minor* chords—usually sounds just flat-out wrong to us.) We'll cover this idea thoroughly in Chapter 9: The Blues. For now, just remember that these are conventions and not rules.

In example 2, we were left with only one choice that fit the criteria established by the 3rd and 7th of the chord. But what if the vamp takes place over just a C triad? Theoretically, any one of the three major modes would be an option. However, there are a few factors that may aid in the decision.

1. **Context:** Does the vamp chord fit within the context of the rest of the song? In other words, does the C chord vamp, for example, take place in a song that's in C major, F major, G major, or some other key to which a C chord is diatonic? If so, it will likely sound best to choose the appropriate diatonic mode for the C chord. However, the longer the vamp is, the more liberty you have with stretching out a bit into other scales.
2. **Melodic or Harmonic Contributions from Other Instruments:** Sometimes the presence of notes played by other instruments may make the decision for you. For example, if you've got a vamp on C, and the bassist is playing a line that includes a B♭, then that would strongly suggest C Mixolydian (C–D–E–F–G–A–B♭). Or maybe the keyboard player is incorporating a suspended 4th (F) to the C chord occasionally as an ornament. This would make C Lydian an unlikely choice, since it contains an F♯. This type of deduction requires a bit of listening on your part and/or communication with other band members if playing live.

Let's look at an example of soloing over a single, major triad. Example 3 takes place over a C chord vamp and utilizes several different C major-family modes.

Were you listening closely? If so, you may have caught on to the fact that, during measures 1–8, the bass line consisted of only roots (C) and 5ths (G), and the keyboard was playing only a C major triad with the occasional suspended 2nd (D). This meant that any of the three C major-family modes could be used. I chose to play in C Lydian here to conjure up a dreamy sound.

However, at measure 9, the groove changes to something a bit funkier, and the bass begins to include a B♭ in its line. The keyboard also begins to incorporate a suspended 4th (F) and a ♭7th (B♭) in its comping pattern. The combination of these two elements makes C Mixolydian (C–D–E–F–G–A–B♭) the logical choice.

WHAT YOU LEARNED:

- How to determine an appropriate mode for soloing over a one-chord vamp by comparing 3rds and 7ths (if applicable).
- How to consider context and contributions from other instruments when making scale choices for soloing over a one-chord vamp.

CHAPTER 6: MODAL APPLICATIONS PART 2—NON-DIATONIC CHORDS

Now it's time to tackle another common soloing obstacle: that one pesky chord (or several) that sounds different than the rest. You know what I'm talking about. The Beatles did this all the time. Think of "Here Comes the Sun," for example; the chord at measure 4 of the chorus is a good example. Or the chord that happens during the third chorus line of "All You Need Is Love" is another good example.

These are called *non-diatonic* chords because they don't normally occur in the key of the song. They contain notes that are outside the tonic major scale and, therefore, must be given special consideration when soloing. In instances like these, the key-center approach will probably work great most of the time, but you're likely to get in trouble over the non-diatonic chord unless you make an adjustment.

By far, the most common non-diatonic chords you'll encounter will fit into two categories: *secondary dominants* and *borrowed chords*. Let's look at each.

SECONDARY DOMINANTS

We've already seen that the V chord in any key is called the dominant chord. This is the chord that wants to resolve up a 4th (or down a 5th) to the tonic, or I chord. Well, a secondary dominant is a dominant seventh chord (or sometimes just a major chord) built on a key's scale degree other than the V. (In the case of a secondary dominant that's just a major chord, as opposed to a seventh chord, it would be one built on a degree other than I, IV, or V.)

For example, in the key of C, the ii chord is normally Dm. However, you sometimes see a D7 (or just a D) chord in songs in the key of C, especially in bridge sections. This D or D7 chord is an example of a secondary dominant. In this case, we would say that the D chord is a V/V, which is read "five of five." In other words, it's acting like a temporary dominant chord of the V chord, G. Usually this chord would be followed by G (V), which would likely be followed by C, the tonic. However, that's not always the case, as we'll discover later on.

In Roman numeral analysis, you'll see this chord notated as either "V/V," "V7/V" (more common in classical studies), or sometimes "II." The uppercase Roman numeral "II" indicates that a major chord should be played instead of the diatonic minor (ii) chord. Sometimes "II7" will be used to designate that D7 specifically should be played. This is the type of chord (II) referred to in the "Here Comes the Sun" example.

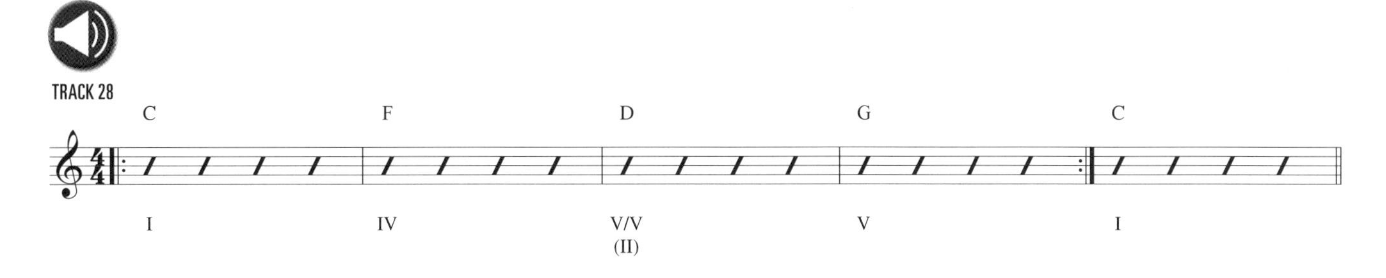

Another very common secondary dominant is a V/IV. In our key of C example, this would mean that our C chord would appear as a C7, instead of just a C triad. In Roman numeral analysis, you'd either see this as "V/IV" or "I7." This chord would normally be followed by the IV chord (F), as illustrated below.

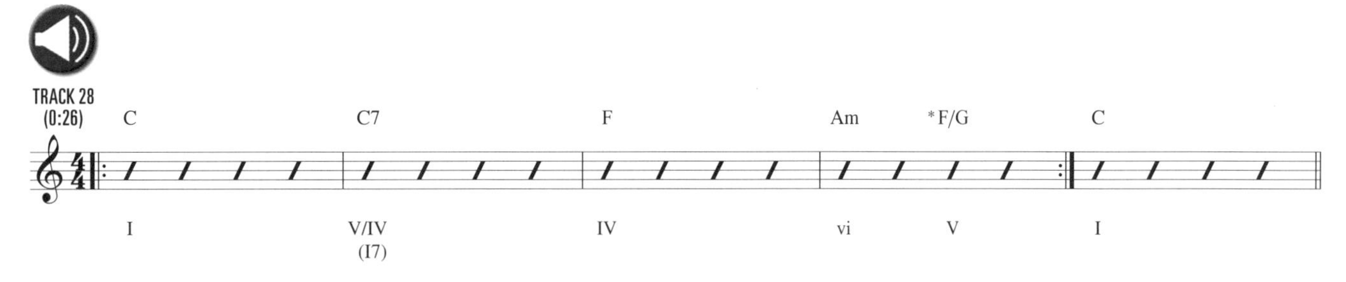

* The F/G chord is what's known as a *slash chord*. It's read "F over G" and it's simply an F major triad played over a G bass note. It still functions as a V chord (G) but it's a little dressier. Another (more complicated) name for it would be G9sus4.

Still another you often see is V/vi. This would mean, in the key of C, that our iii chord, Em, would be changed to E or E7, as demonstrated here. This is the type of secondary dominant (III) referred to in the "All You Need Is Love" example. It has a recognizable sound that really pulls the ear to the vi chord.

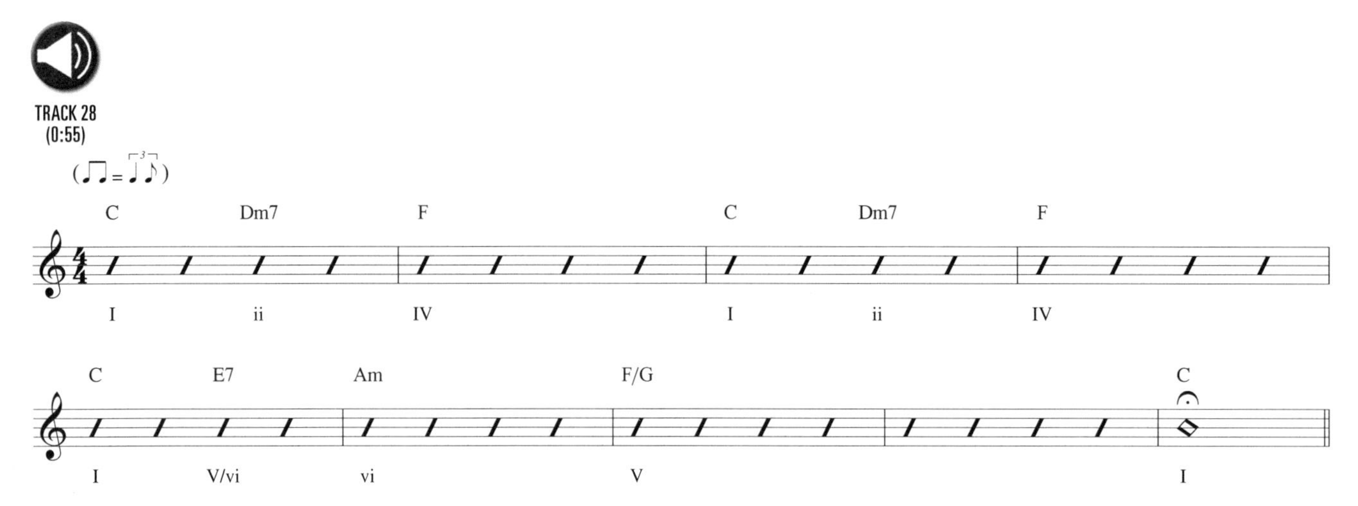

Scale Choices

OK, so now you've gotten a taste of how these secondary dominant chords sound, but how do you solo over them? This can actually be somewhat tricky, and it requires a bit of forethought. Again, there is more than just one scale that can be used in these instances, but, for now, we're going to look at the most "inside"-sounding approach.

When the secondary dominant is the V of a *major* chord (V/IV or V/V), use the Mixolydian mode built off the root of the secondary dominant.

Example 1 contains a progression in C that uses a D7 chord, which is a V/V. So, we use the C major scale for the bulk of it. But, when that D7 chord shows up, we play the D Mixolydian mode. After that, we switch back to the C major scale.

Example 1

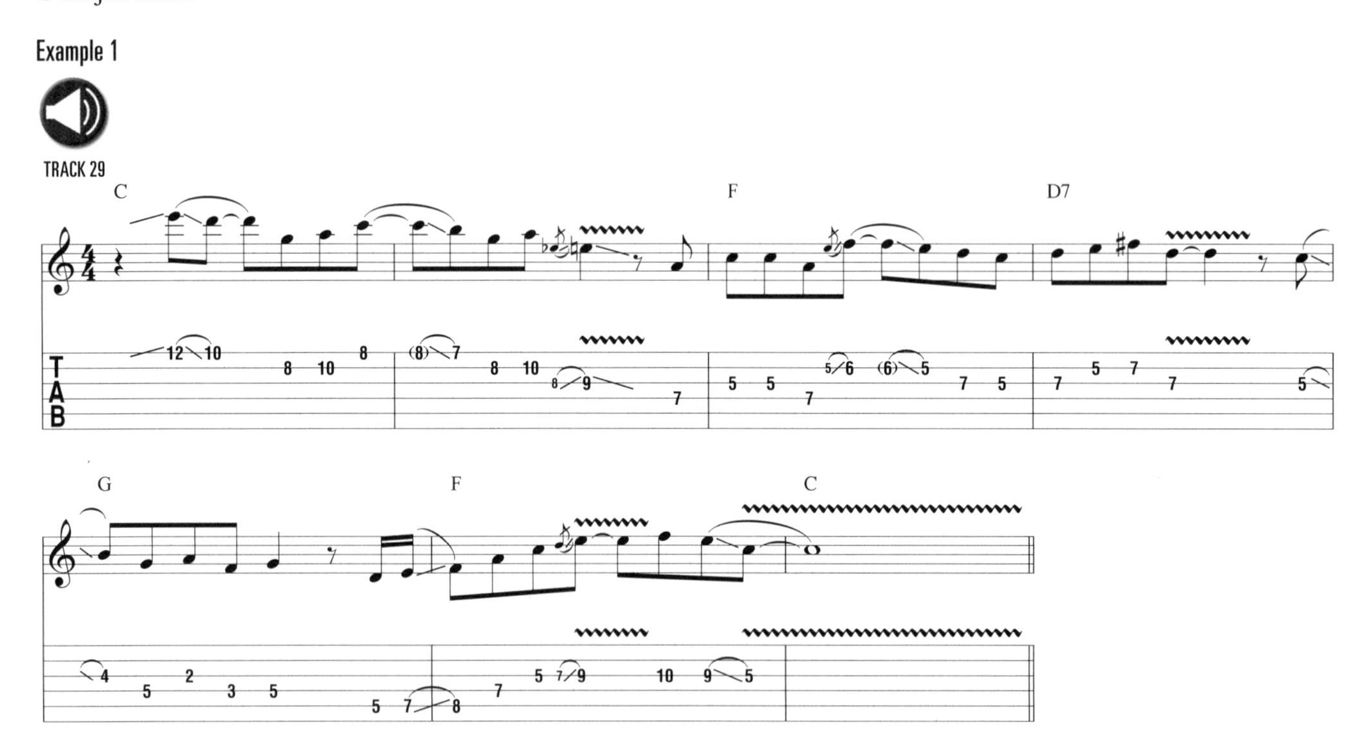

In example 2, we see the other possible major chord-resolving secondary dominant: V/IV. We've changed keys to A major here, so that means our V/IV secondary dominant will be an A7, and we'll play the A Mixolydian mode over that chord. The rest of the lines will come from the A major scale. Since we played it very "bare bones" over the secondary dominant in example 1, this time we'll play a slightly jazzy sixteenth-note line over the secondary dominant so you can hear how that sounds.

Example 2

TRACK 30

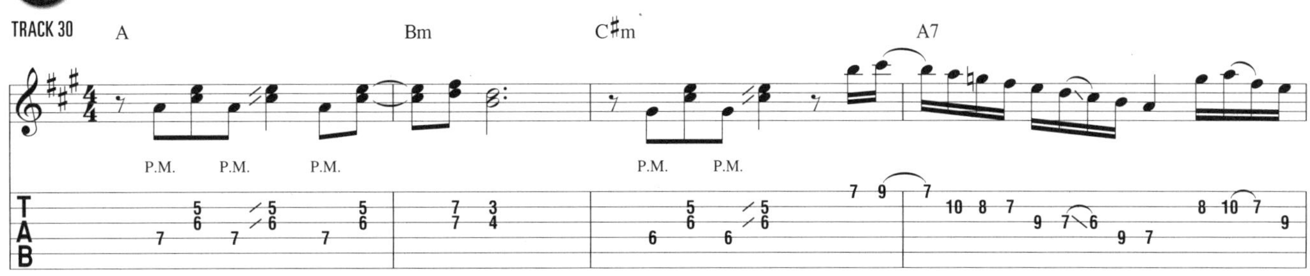

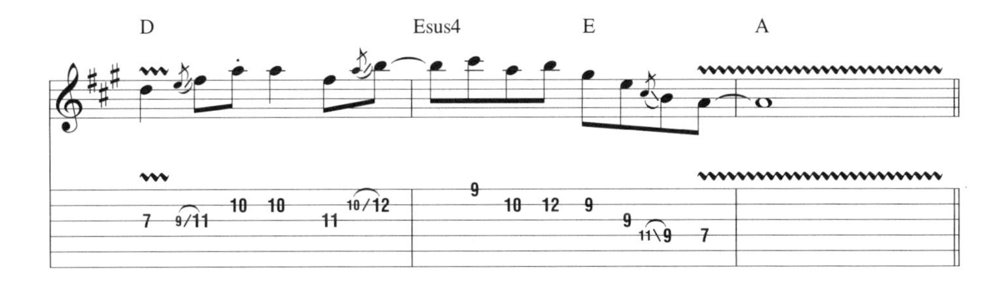

When the secondary dominant is the V of a minor chord, it's a little trickier. The best bet here is to use the harmonic minor scale based on the root of the chord to which the secondary dominant would normally resolve. In other words, if the chord is a V/vi, such as an E7 chord in the key of C, then you'd play an A harmonic minor scale since Am is the vi chord in C. (E7 is the V of Am.) There are a few other ways to say this:

1. Play a *harmonic minor scale* that's a 4th above the root of the secondary dominant. A is a 4th above E.
2. Play the *Phrygian dominant mode* based on the root of the secondary dominant. The Phrygian dominant scale is simply a mode of the harmonic minor scale—namely, the fifth mode. So, if you played the A harmonic minor scale from E to E instead of A to A, you'd have the E Phrygian dominant mode.

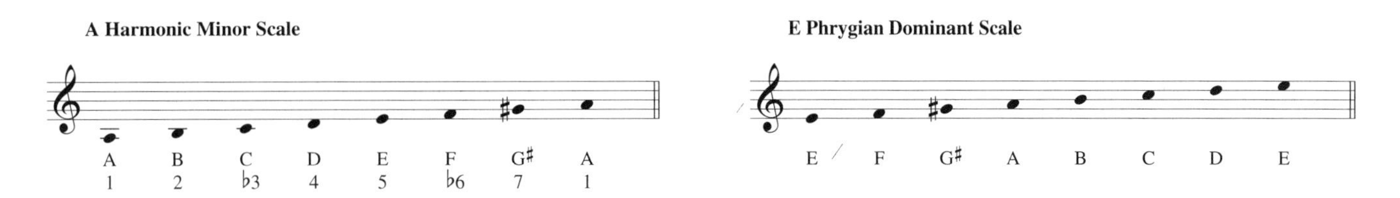

Here's a two-octave fingering pattern for E Phrygian dominant:

E Phrygian Dominant

TRACK 31

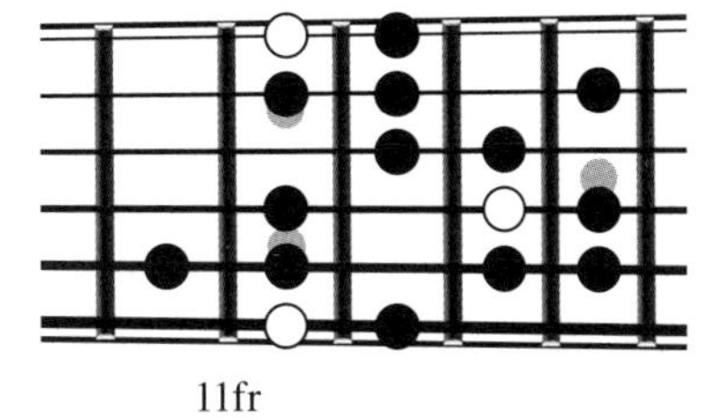

It's the same set of notes; the only difference lies in what you consider the root. As long as you use your ear and listen to what you're playing, the name you choose for the scale isn't all that important.

Example 3 demonstrates the sound of the E Phrygian dominant mode (A harmonic minor) against the E7 secondary dominant chord.

Example 3

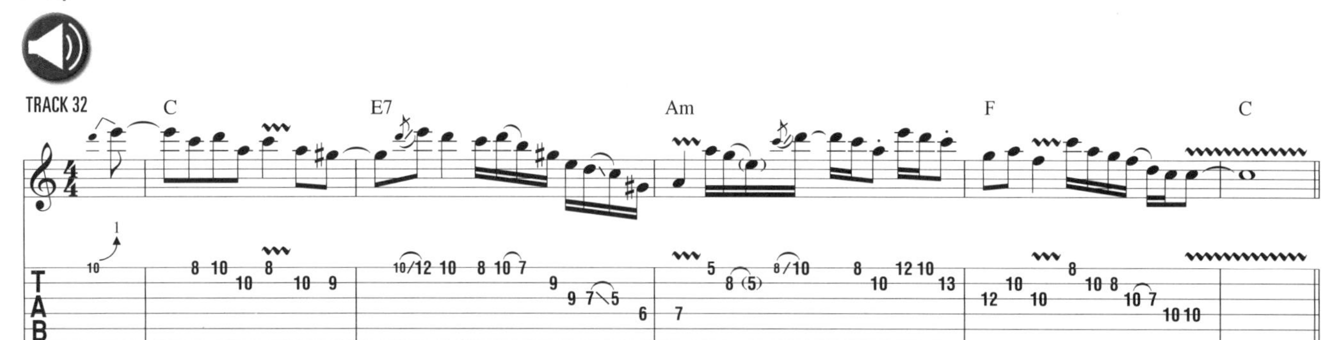

Let's take a look at this same secondary dominant, V/vi, but in the key G. This would be a B or B7 chord, usually resolving to Em. Example 4 demonstrates what the B Phrygian dominant mode sounds like over B7 with the G major scale covering all the other chords.

Example 4

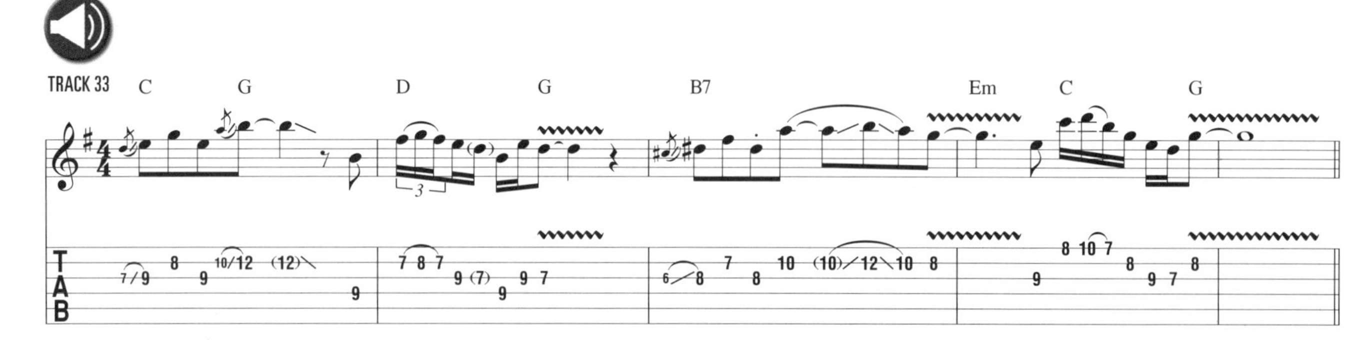

> **Two Ways to Skin a Cat**
>
> Remember that you'll occasionally see these secondary dominants with their alternative Roman numeral analyses, which will be just an uppercase numeral instead of the normal lowercase one. So, in the key of A, for example, you may see a B chord referred to as "V/V" (V of E, the V chord of A) or simply "II" (as opposed to the normal "ii" used for the diatonic Bm).

Let's take a look at another secondary dominant. Example 5 demonstrates another V/V, or II chord, in the key of D. We've already seen an example of this secondary dominant in example 1, but there's a catch: this II chord is followed by a IV chord, instead of the expected V chord. This makes the II chord (E) a *non-resolving secondary dominant*. This is just a fancy way of saying it doesn't resolve up a 4th as expected. This particular case—a II chord moving to IV—is particularly common in rock. We still use the same scale (E Mixolydian in this case), but we just need to take care in how we resolve the line.

Example 5

BORROWED CHORDS

The other common non-diatonic chord is the *borrowed chord*. This is a chord that we say is "borrowed" from the parallel mode. Let's say you're in C major, for instance, and you see an Fm chord. Well, Fm normally doesn't appear in C major, but it does appear in C minor (parallel minor). So we call the Fm a borrowed chord. It's more common to borrow from a parallel minor mode while in a major key than it is to borrow from the parallel major mode while in a minor key, so we'll look at examples of those first.

Major Key Borrowing from Parallel Minor:

The ♭VII Chord

Probably the most common borrowed chord of all is the ♭VII. You've heard this chord in about 10 million classic rock songs. In the key of C, this would be a B♭ chord.

TRACK 35

The v Chord

Somewhat similar to the ♭VII, but not nearly as common, is the v chord. In the key of C, this would be a Gm chord.

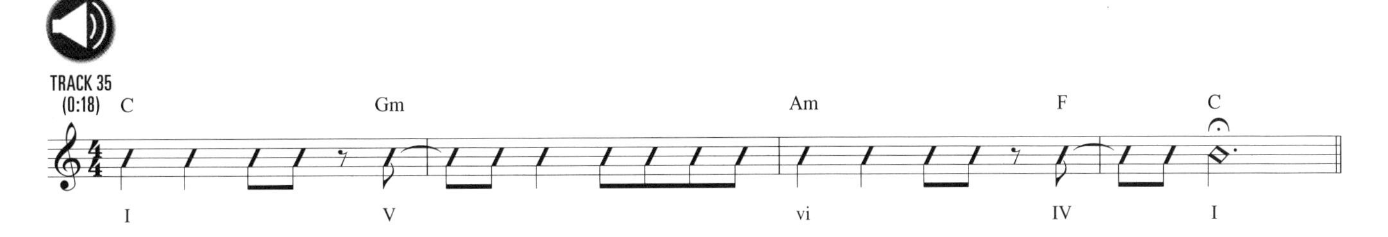

The iv Chord

This is one that's heard in lots of Beatles songs. It's a sad, wistful chord that almost always resolves to the I chord. In the key of C, this would be Fm.

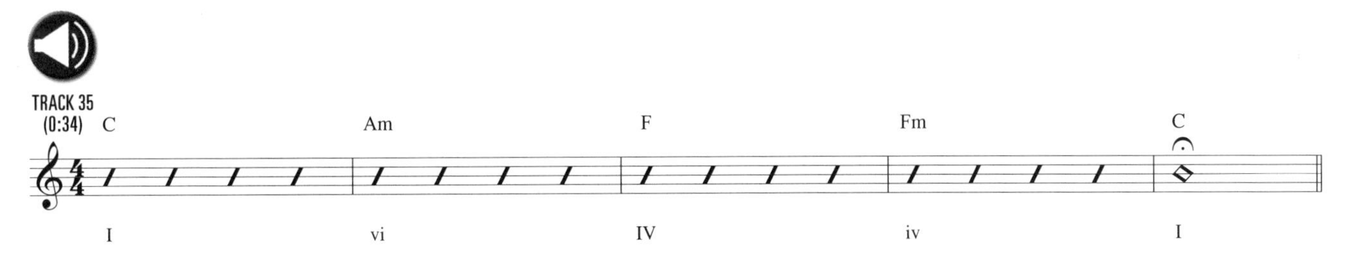

The ♭VI Chord

This one has a similar effect to the iv, but its effect is usually a bit more dramatic than wistful. In the key of C, this would be an A♭ chord.

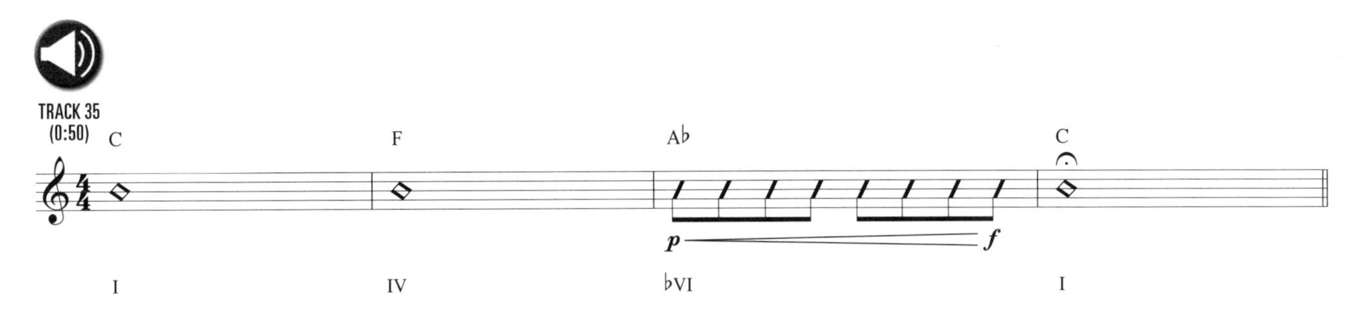

The ♭III Chord

Classic rock makes good use of this one as well. If sustained, it can sound dramatic, but it's more often used in passing to add grit to a chordal riff. In the key of C, this would be an E♭ chord.

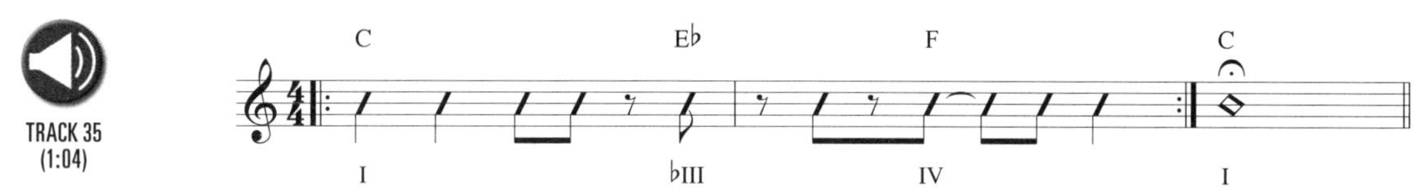

Scale Choices

Here's a list of the scales that are commonly played over these borrowed chords:

- **♭VII and v chords:** Tonic Mixolydian mode—In the key of C, this would be the C Mixolydian mode over B♭ and Gm chords.
- **iv, ♭VI, and ♭III chords:** Tonic Aeolian mode (minor scale)—In the key of C, this would be the C Aeolian mode over Fm, A♭, and E♭ chords.

Again, there are other options, but these are safe and common choices. Let's hear what they sound like. We'll stay in the key of C so that you can hear the different sounds all against a common tonic, but you should work on transposing these ideas to all the keys.

Example 6 features the C Mixolydian mode over the ♭VII chord, B♭. The C major scale and C major pentatonic handles the rest of the chords.

Example 6

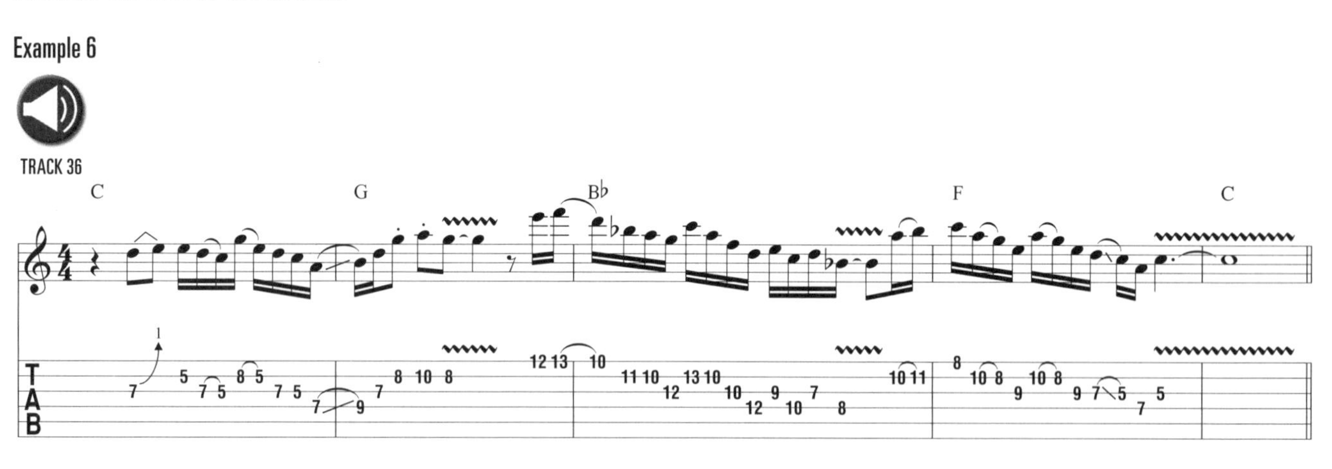

Example 7 makes use of the v chord, Gm, over which we solo with C Mixolydian. The rest is C major pentatonic. Notice how similar the Mixolydian lick is to example 6.

Example 7

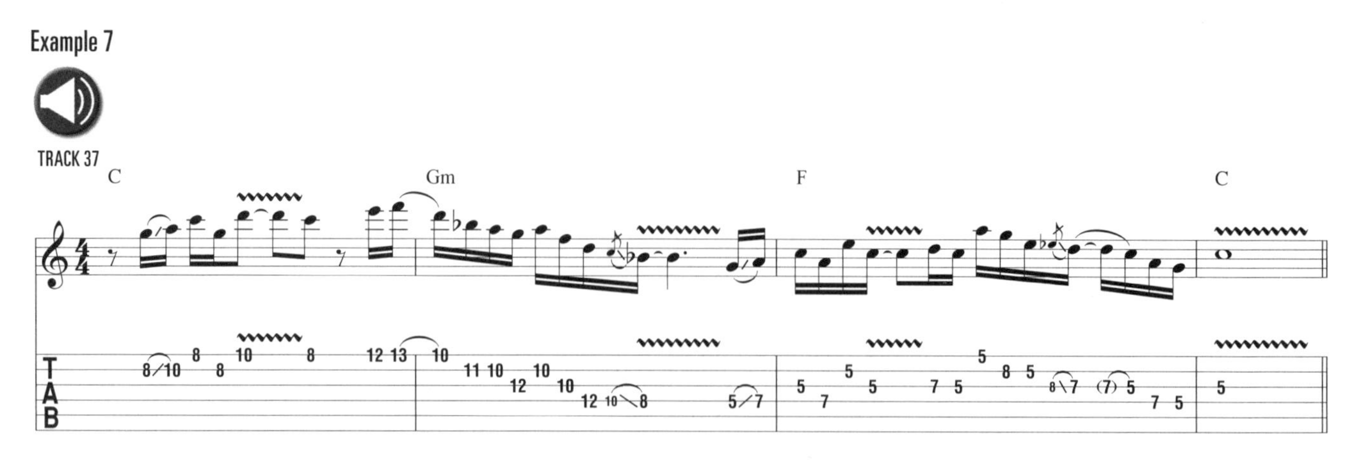

We get a dose of the iv chord in example 8. In the key of C, this is an Fm chord. We're playing a C major scale until then, where we switch to the C minor scale.

Example 8

TRACK 38

C Am F Fm C

rake

Check out the dramatic sound of the ♭VI chord, A♭, in example 9. We're playing the C major scale over all the chords except for that one, where we switch to the parallel C minor scale.

Example 9

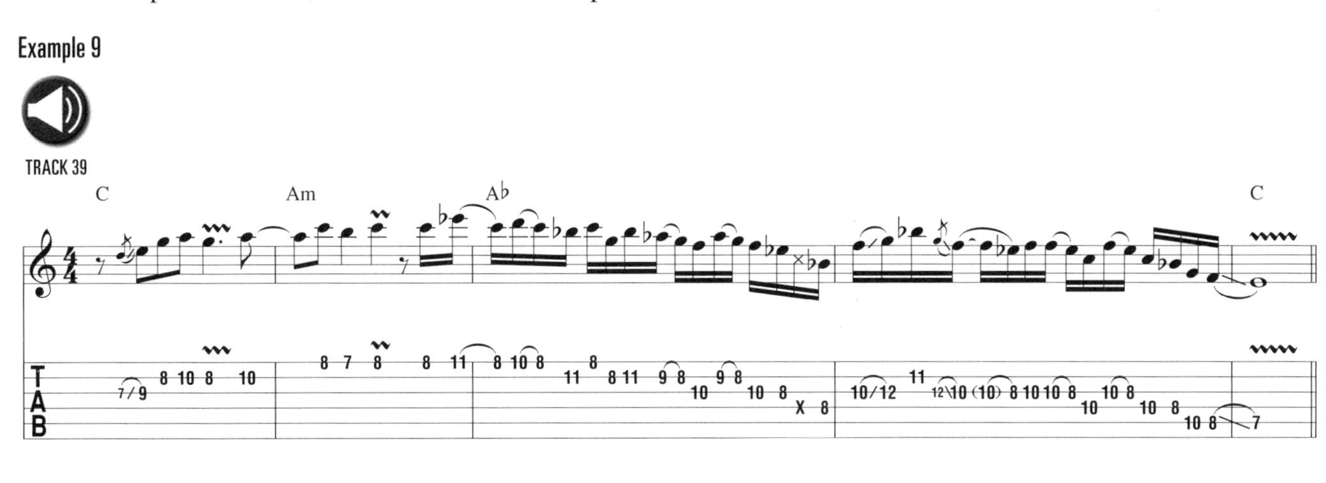

Example 10 demonstrates the classic rock-approved ♭III chord with a ballsy riff that makes typical use of the chord—as a connector between I and IV. In the key of C, the ♭III is an E♭ chord. We mine the C major pentatonic over everything else and use the parallel C minor pentatonic over the E♭ chord.

Example 10

Minor Key Borrowing from Parallel Major

The V Chord

As we mentioned earlier, it's very common to substitute a V chord for a v chord, and this is essentially borrowing harmony from the parallel major. In the key of C minor, this would be a G chord.

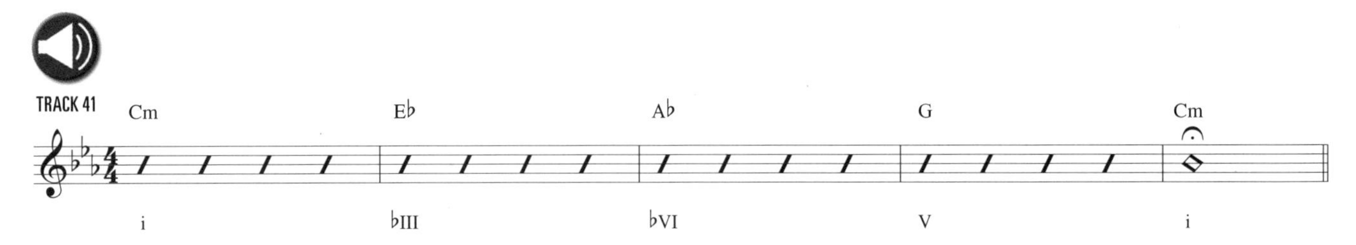

The IV Chord

This is another very common one that you'll hear in lots of classic rock and R&B. In the key of C minor, this would be an F chord.

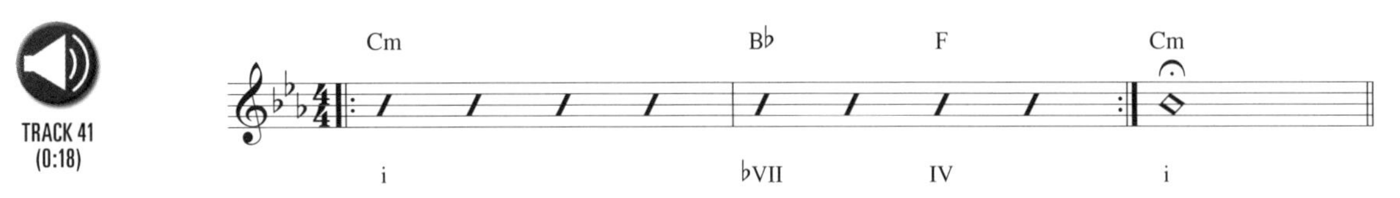

The ii Chord

This one has a bit of a jazzy sound to it. Think of Van Morrison's "Moondance" for an example of this. In the key of C minor, this would be a Dm chord.

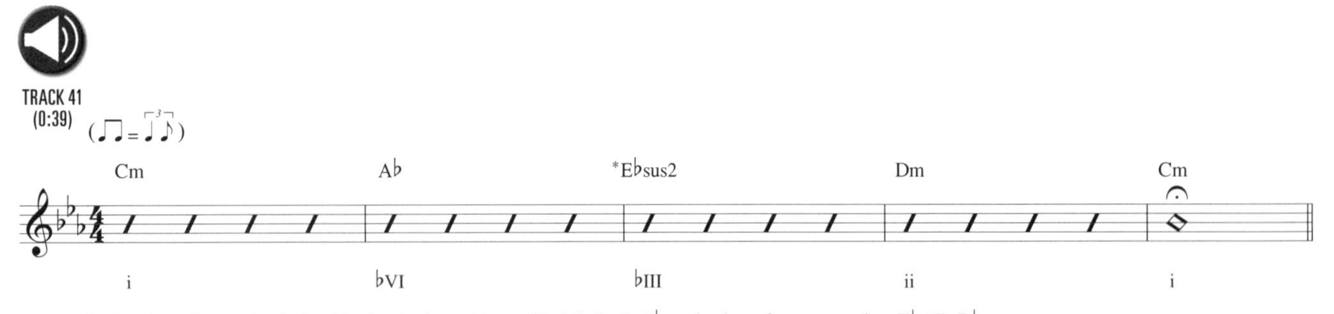

* A sus2 chord replaces the 3rd with the 2nd, so it's spelled 1–2–5. E♭sus2, therefore, contains E♭–F–B♭.

Scale Choices

Here's a list of the scales that are commonly played over these borrowed chords:

- **V chord:** Tonic harmonic minor scale—In the key of C minor, this would be the C harmonic minor scale over a G chord.
- **IV and ii chords:** Tonic Dorian mode—In the key of C minor, this would be the C Dorian mode over F and Dm chords.

Again, there are other scales to experiment with, but these are just the common choices. Let's hear what they sound like.

In example 11, we hear the sound of the V chord, G. After using the C minor scale in measures 1–3, we switch to C harmonic minor over the G chord to acknowledge the change of B♭ to B♮. This scale is Yngwie Malmsteen's best friend.

Example 11

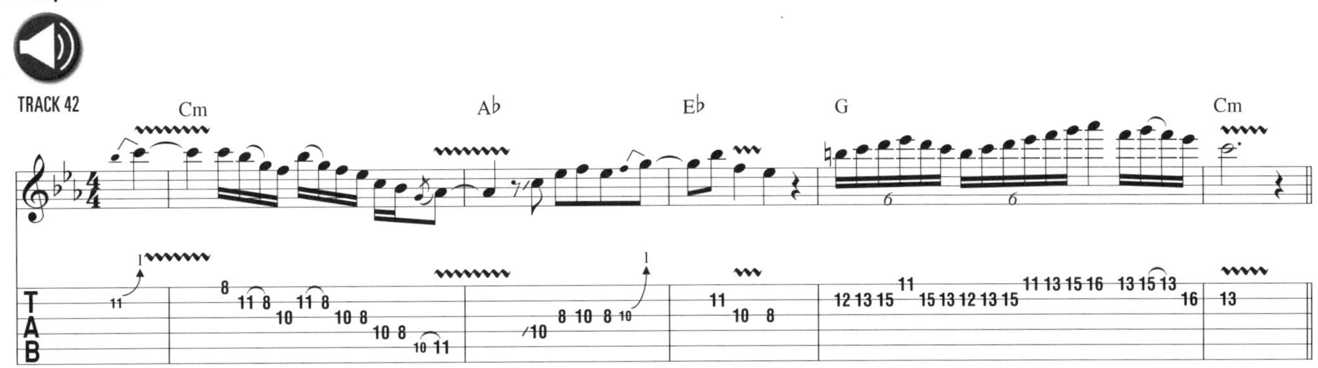

Example 12 lets us hear how the C Dorian mode sounds over a IV chord, F. We stick to C minor pentatonic the rest of the time.

Example 12

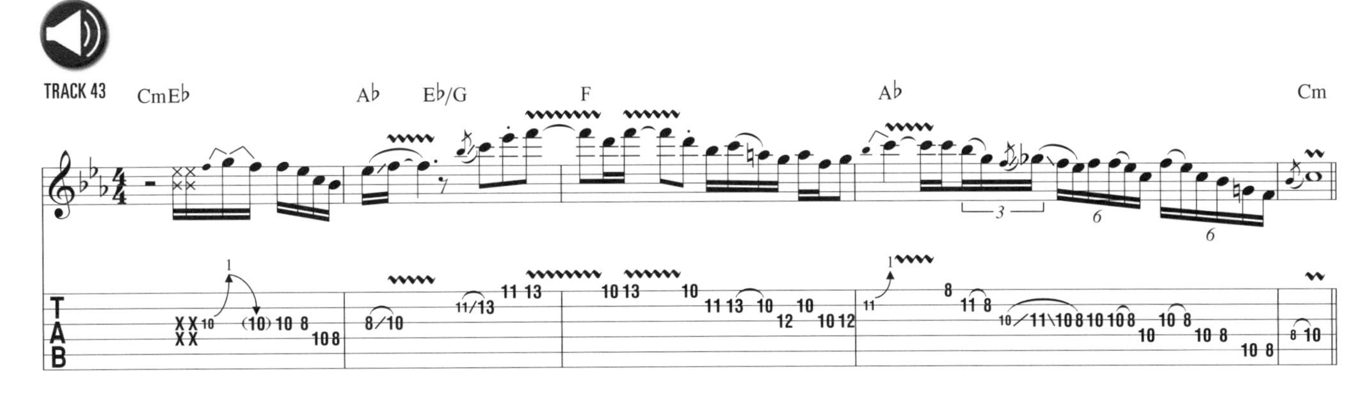

Finally, we hear the jazzy ii chord, Dm, in example 13 and solo over it with C Dorian again. It's straight C minor otherwise.

Example 13

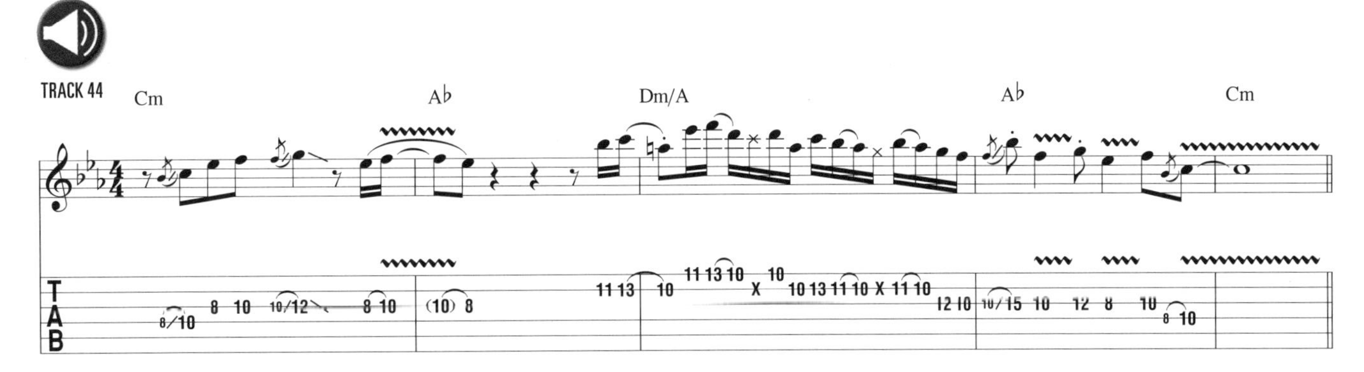

WHAT YOU LEARNED:

- Two common non-diatonic chords: **secondary dominants** and **borrowed chords**.
- Typical scale choices for common secondary dominants and borrowed chords.

CHAPTER 7: MODAL APPLICATIONS PART 3—MODAL PROGRESSIONS

Now that you're familiar with how modes are constructed and the concept of borrowed chords, it's time to introduce *modal progressions.* A modal progression is one that's built upon chords from a harmonized mode. Just as we've already harmonized two modes, Ionian and Aeolian (also known as the major and minor scales, respectively), it's possible to form triads from the remaining modes we know. When we play over a modal progression, we simply solo with the mode from which the chords are derived.

For example, if a song is in C Mixolydian, we'd use the C Mixolydian mode. If it's in C Dorian, we'd use the C Dorian mode. It's just like the key-center approach we used earlier, only we're using modes other than just Ionian (major scale) and Aeolian (minor scale).

MIXOLYDIAN MODE

The Mixolydian mode is commonly used for progressions. When we harmonize each note of a Mixolydian mode, using the same stacking 3rds method, we get yet another set of seven triads. Here they are in the key of C:

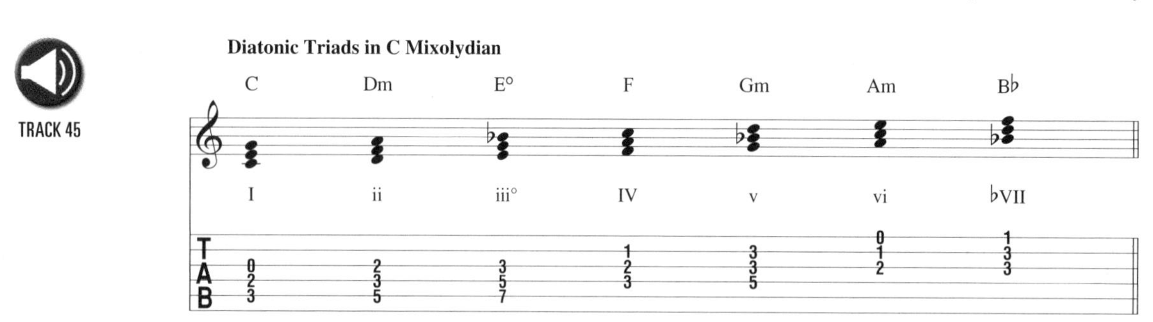

When a song is in a Mixolydian mode (or sometimes you hear "Mixolydian key"), it uses these chords as the foundation—not the set of triads from the major scale. Generally speaking, if you have a song that clearly identifies a C chord as the tonic yet you repeatedly see a B♭ chord (♭VII) and no G chord, it's a safe bet that the song is using the Mixolydian mode. Let's look at a few examples, again in the key of C.

Example 1 makes use of a time-tested classic rock progression: I–♭VII–IV. These three chords may have been in as many songs as the I–IV–V progression—in the seventies at least!

Example 1

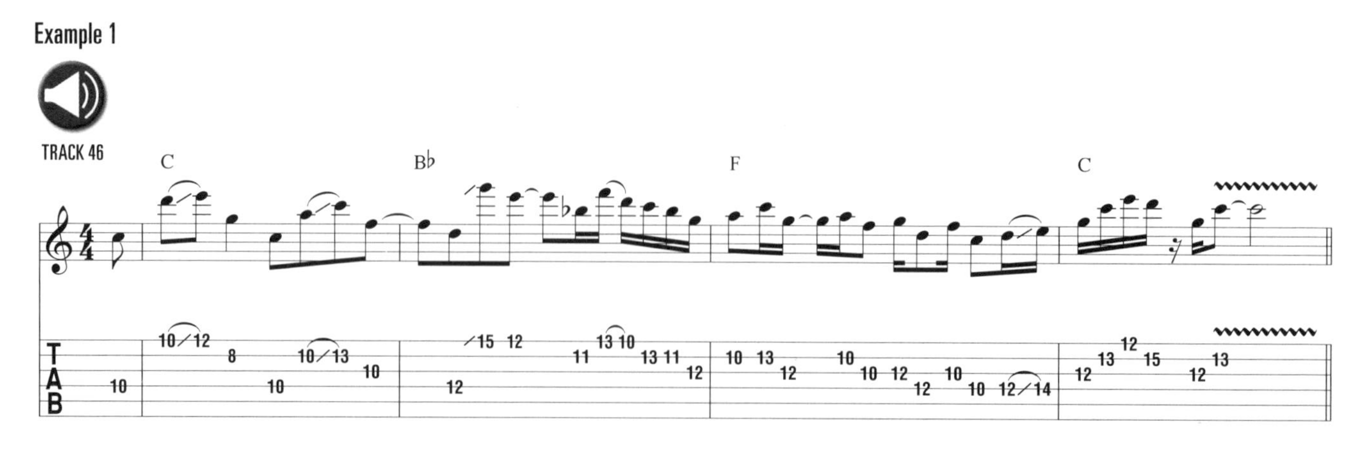

Example 2 is a more laid-back example that uses some other chords from the C Mixolydian mode. The lines here are a little jazzier but still use only the C Mixolydian mode.

Example 2

TRACK 47

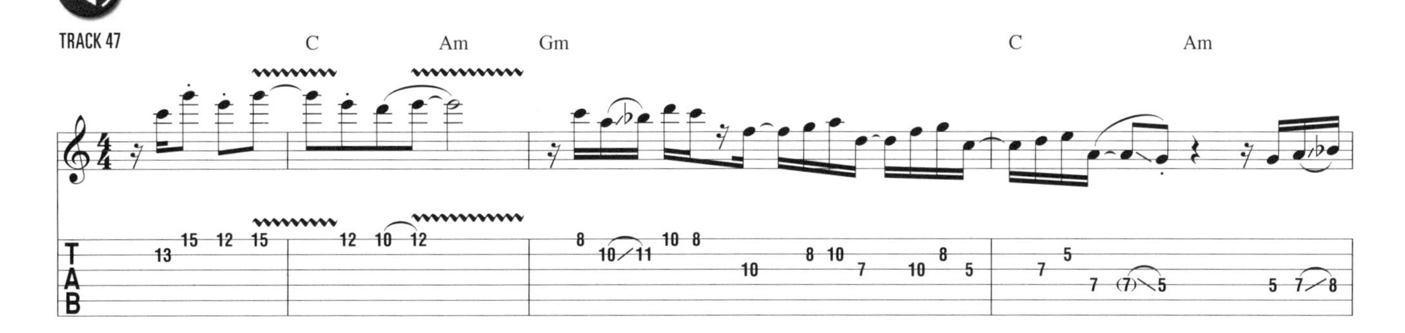

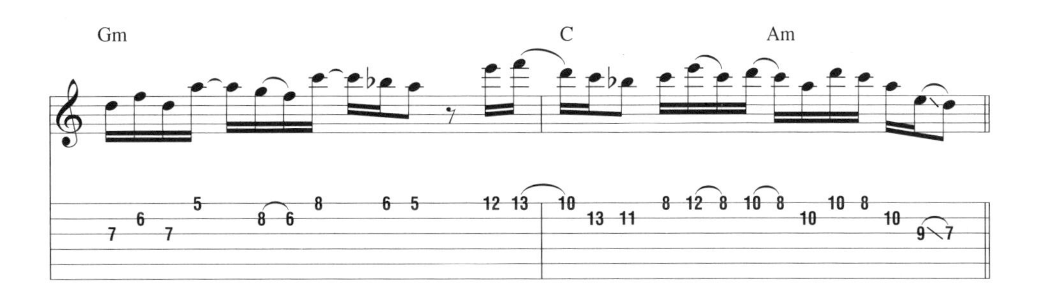

What About the Key Signature?

Notice that the key signature is still blank, indicating C major, as opposed to one flat. This topic (that of modal key signatures) is one in which there really is not a set standard in the music community. Some people will write a song that's in C Mixolydian with one flat in the key signature so they don't have to keep rewriting that flat over and over. Others will leave the key signature as a major key (blank in the case of our C Mixolydian song) because they feel it clearly defines C as the tonal center, even though we're consistently using B♭ instead of B♮. I tend to agree with the latter method, but you will come across both presentations.

DORIAN MODE

The other mode commonly used to build progressions is the Dorian mode. A tell-tale sign of a Dorian progression is often a minor tonic (i) with a major IV chord. The characteristic trait of the Dorian mode is the natural 6th degree (as opposed to the ♭6th of Aeolian) and that's exactly what the IV chord highlights; its major 3rd is the natural 6th of the scale. This is a very common sound in rock, blues-rock, jazz, and pop. When we harmonize the C Dorian mode, we get the following set of triads:

TRACK 48

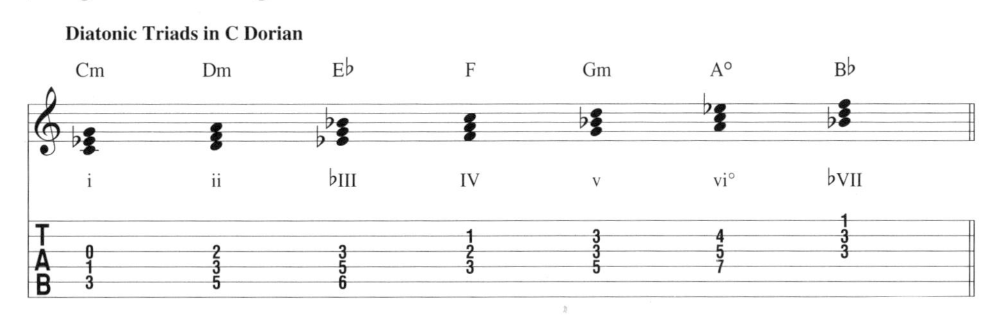

In example 3, we rock out with the C Dorian mode over a Tom Petty-style progression. The IV chord is on prominent display here.

Example 3

TRACK 49

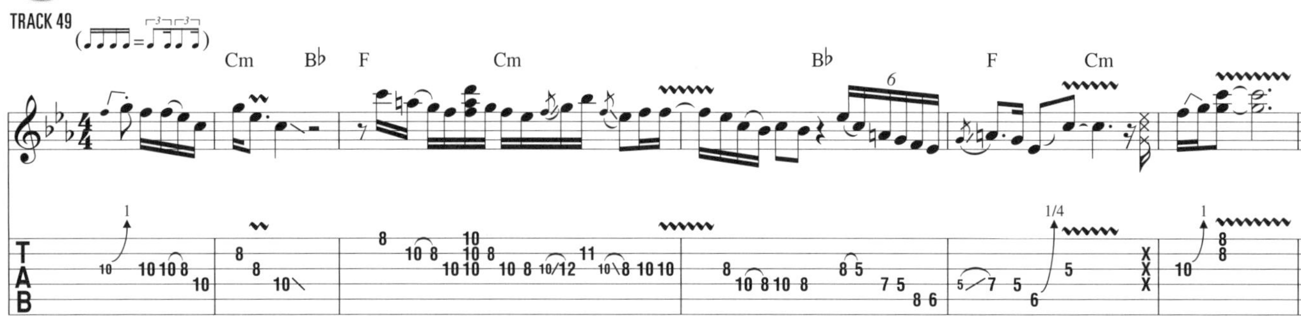

Example 4 is a much more moody-sounding progression in C Dorian. The phrases here are a bit more angular than your typical rock lines.

Example 4

TRACK 50

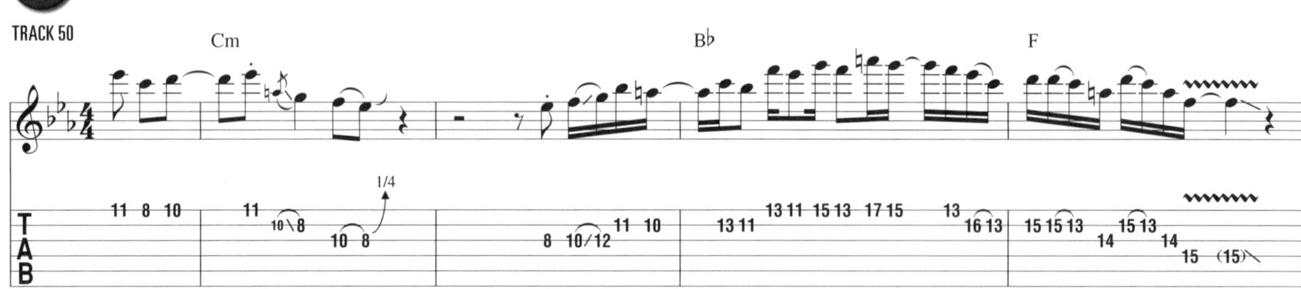

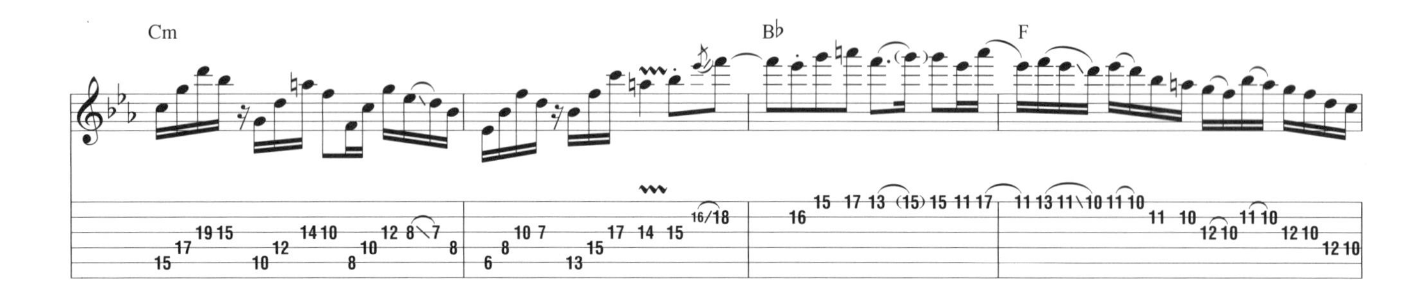

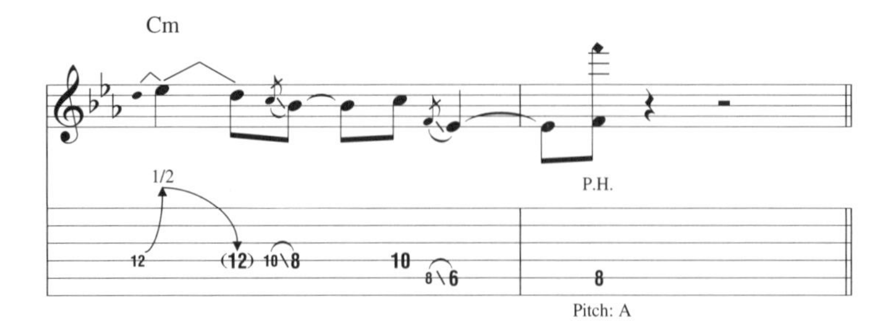

Notice that, again, the key signature used here indicates C minor (three flats). Even though we're adding a natural sign to every A that's played, the three flats in the key signature make it clear to the performer that C is the tonic.

Those are really the only two modes besides Ionian and Aeolian that are consistently used. You will occasionally see a song in a Lydian mode (Joe Satriani and Steve Vai are good examples of this, as is the theme song from "The Simpsons"), but it's a rarity in comparison.

How Do You Tell Borrowed Chords from a Modal Progression?

This is a good question, and the line can certainly be blurred between the two. Generally, if the song is exclusively using chords from the mode (Dorian or Mixolydian, for example) and no others, then you'd call it a modal progression. If a song uses chords from the major or minor scale that contradict the modal chords, then you'd label the chords that don't fit as borrowed chords.

For example, let's say you're in the key of C, and you have the following progression:

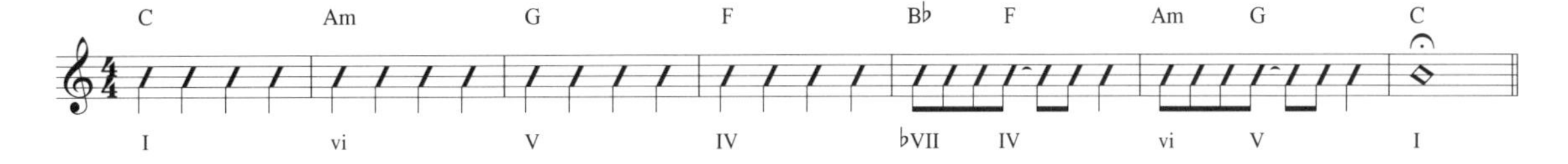

The only non-diatonic chord to C major is the B♭ chord. However, we also have a V chord (G) in the progression, which contains the note B♮. We can't call this a modal progression because all of the chords don't belong to one mode. Therefore, the song is in C major, and the B♭ would be called a borrowed chord (♭VII).

As another example, let's say you're in C minor with this progression:

TRACK 52

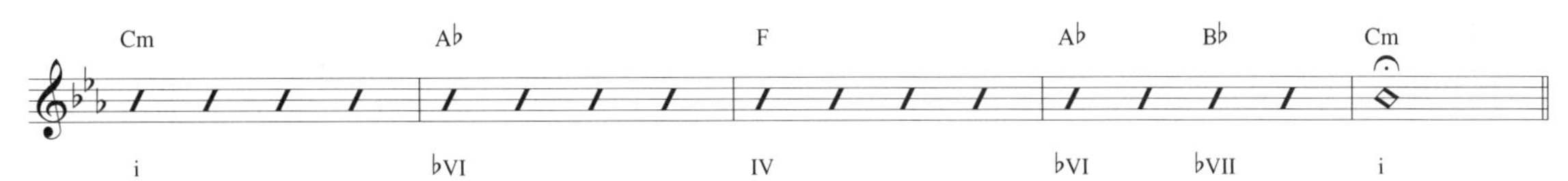

Again, try as you may, you won't be able to fit all of these chords into one mode. The Cm, A♭, and B♭ chords fit within the minor mode, but the F chord doesn't. Therefore, it can't be a modal progression, so we'd say the progression is in C minor and the F chord (IV) is borrowed.

Let's close out with a few more licks that venture into keys other than C.

Example 5 takes place over a B Dorian progression and makes use of some rhythmically imitative phrasing.

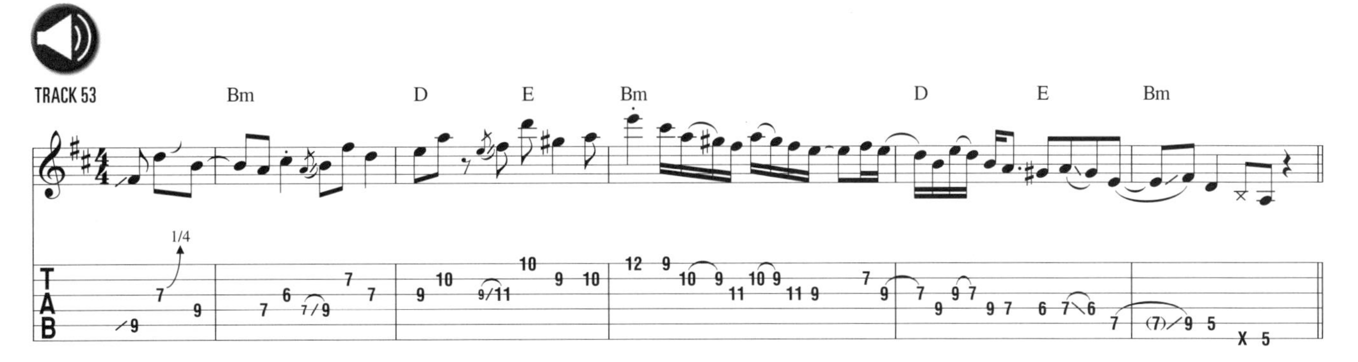

In example 6, we're playing F Mixolydian over a I–vi–v–IV–I progression. Note how the chord tones are carefully targeted on the sustained chords.

Example 6

TRACK 54

F Dm Cm B♭ F

Check out the bluesier side of Mixoydian with this phrase, in example 7, which draws from the D Mixolyian mode. The abundance of the chromatic grace notes does much to enhance this feel.

Example 7

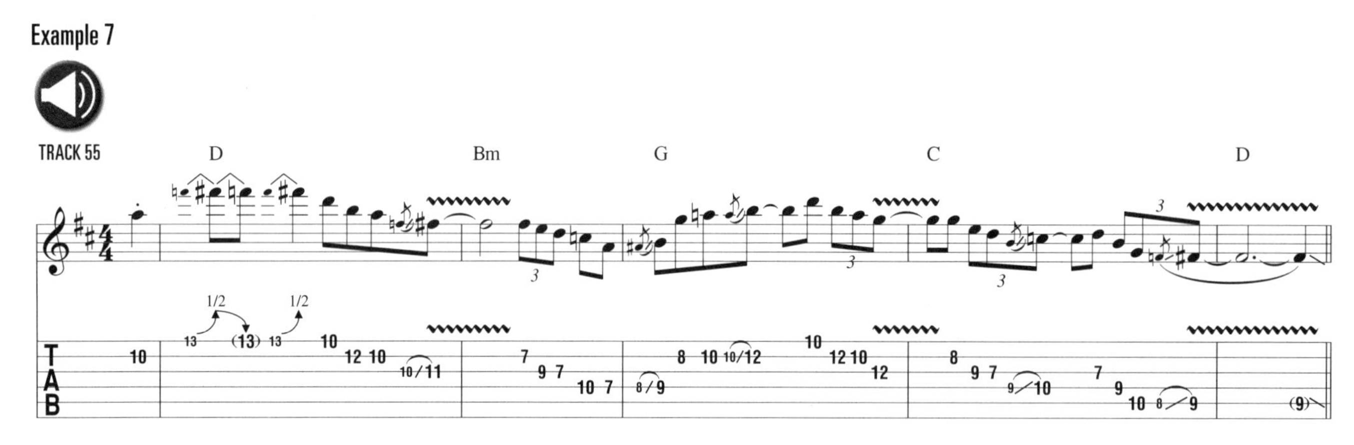

WHAT YOU LEARNED:

- How to harmonize the Mixolydian and Dorian modes.
- How to determine if a song is using a modal progression.
- Mixolydian and Dorian are the most commonly used modal progressions (aside from Ionian and Aeolian).
- One tell-tale sign of a Mixolydian progression is a major I chord and a ♭VII chord.
- One tell-tale sign of a Dorian progression is a minor i chord and a IV chord.

CHAPTER 8: SEVENTH CHORDS AND EXTENDED HARMONY

Triads make up a large portion of chords we use, but there are others that are common as well. In this chapter, we'll take a look at seventh chords and extended harmony. We've briefly touched upon seventh chords in previous chapters. Now let's examine them more closely.

SEVENTH CHORDS

Whereas triads contain only three different notes, *seventh chords* contain four different notes. Now that you understand how triads are built, seventh chords should seem like the logical next step. We build them by continuing to stack yet another 3rd on top of the triad.

If we stack another 3rd on top of our diatonic triads in the key of C, for example, we'll end up with several types of seventh chords:

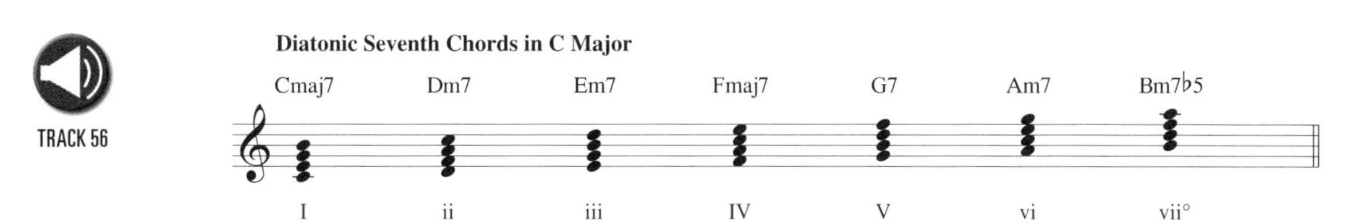

Notice that the Roman numerals haven't changed because all the chord functions are still the same. They're just a little dressier as seventh chords. We see four different types of seventh chords within the diatonic scale: *major seventh* (maj7), *minor seventh* (m7), *dominant seventh* (7), and *minor seventh flat five* (m7♭5). Again, this is the diatonic seventh chord formula for any major key: maj7 (I), m7 (ii), m7 (iii), maj7 (IV), 7 (V), m7 (vi), and m7♭5 (viiø)*.

* This (ø) is the symbol for *half-diminished*, which is another name for minor seventh flat five.

Let's look at each type with C as the root so we can see the formula for each one. First is a major seventh (maj7), which is spelled 1–3–5–7. This is a major triad with a major 3rd stacked on top. Another way to say it is a major triad with a major 7th interval (from the root) added. Here's Cmaj7:

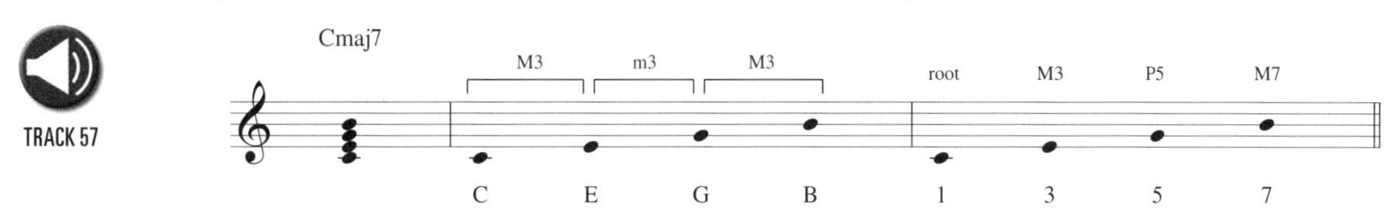

Next let's look at the dominant seventh (7), which is spelled 1–3–5–♭7. It's the same as a major seventh, but the top note (7th) has been lowered to a minor 7th interval. Here's C7:

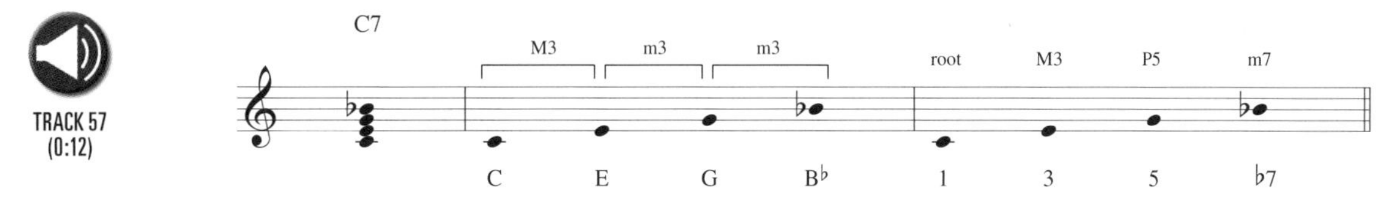

Now for a minor seventh (m7), which is spelled 1–♭3–5–♭7. Compared to the major seventh, it has a lowered 3rd and a lowered 7th. Here's Cm7:

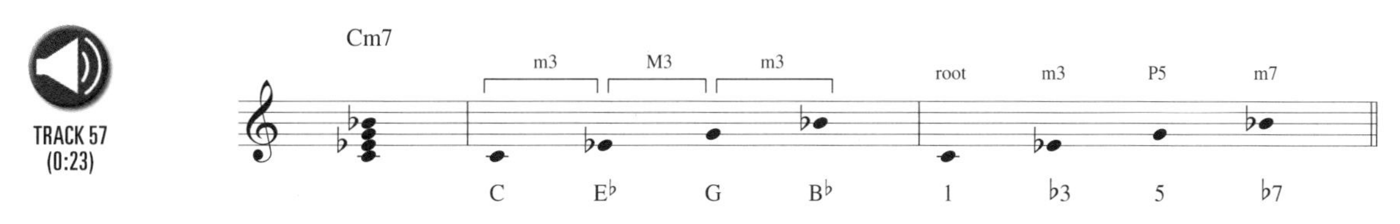

And now here's the minor seventh flat five (m7♭5), or half-diminished, chord. Compared to the major seventh, it has a lowered 3rd, lowered 5th, and lowered 7th. Here's Cm7♭5:

TRACK 57
(0:34)

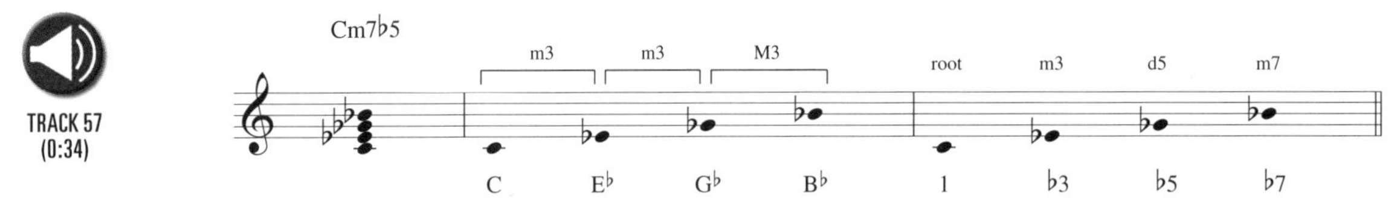

These tones (7ths) are another possibility to consider when soloing. Depending on the chord (major sevenths in particular), you may not want to completely resolve your lines on them, but they're nice to highlight occasionally for a bit more color. Let's hear how this sounds.

In example 1, we've got a I–vi–V–IV progression in D with two seventh chords: Bm7 and Gmaj7. Notice how the 7th of Bm7, which is an A note, is a relatively stable note compared to the 7th of Gmaj7, F♯, which would draw a bit more attention if held for an extended period of time. Things like this are really more of a personal preference; experiment to find your own preferences.

Example 1

TRACK 58

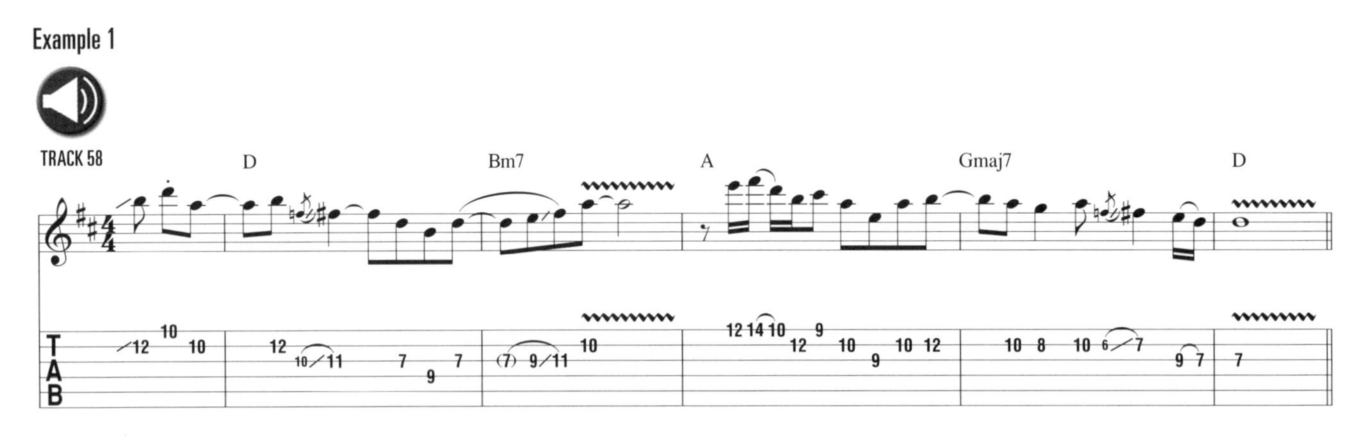

Example 2, in F, uses a tonic major seventh chord (Fmaj7) as well as a V7 (C7).

Example 2

TRACK 59

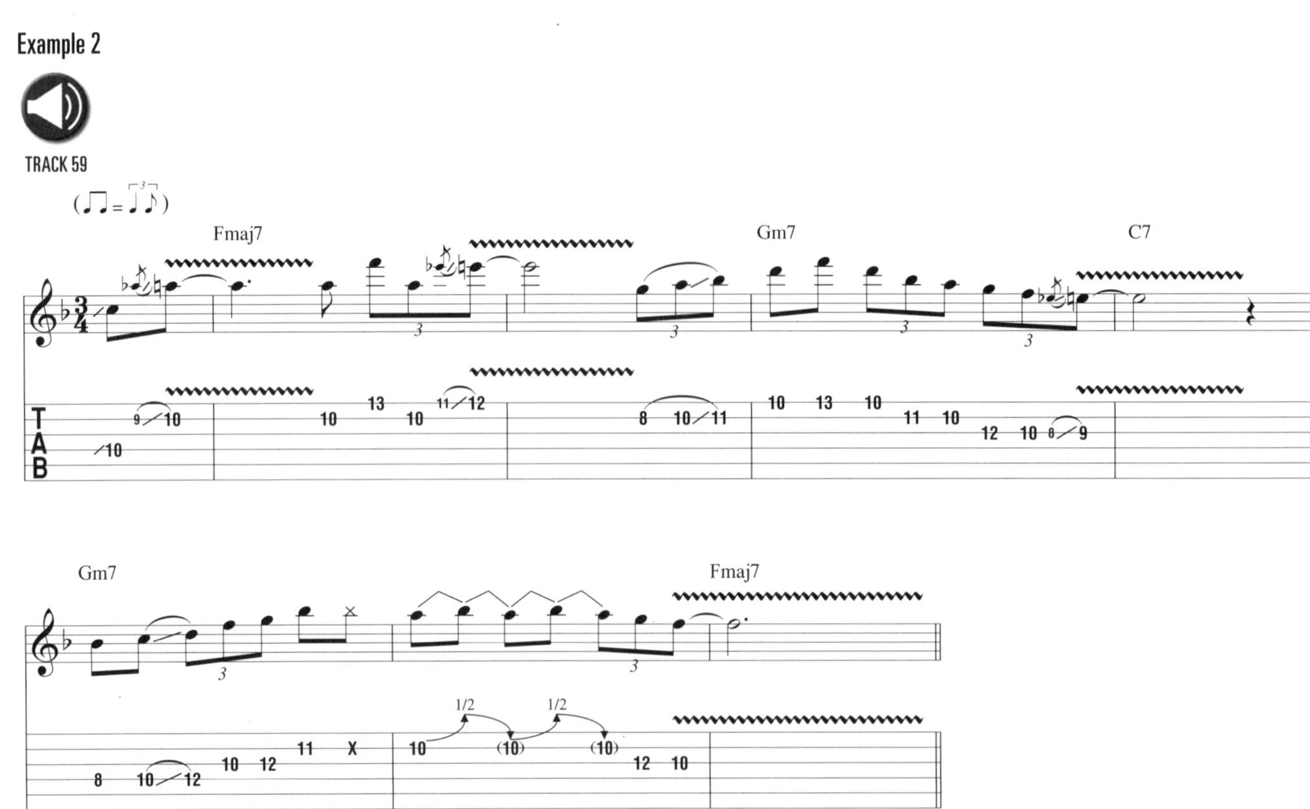

What About Non-Diatonic Chords?

Pretty much everything we've covered with regards to non-diatonic chords applies to seventh chords too. This means that, instead of a IV chord being a major seventh, it could be a dominant seventh, for example. It also means that we could see our non-diatonic chords turned into seventh chords. For example, in the key of C, a II chord (V/V) could be a D7 instead of just a D. Or a borrowed B♭ chord (♭VII) could appear as a B♭maj7 or even a B♭7.

Each one of these examples presents their own challenges when soloing. Sometimes, the fact that they're seventh chords won't require any additional adjustment. In other words, the same scale (D Mixolydian) you use for a D chord (II) in the key of C would work equally well over a D7. This is because the 7th of D7 is C, and therefore it doesn't add any additional conflicts to the scale.

A B♭maj7 chord (♭VII) in the key of C could also be handled by the same scale used to handle a B♭triad: C Mixolydian. Again, this is because the 7th of B♭maj7, A, is contained within that C Mixolydian mode. A B♭7 chord in the key of C, however, would be a different story. It's still a ♭VII chord, but the 7th of B♭7 is A♭, and A♭ is not contained within C Mixolydian. For this type of chord, you'd need another type of scale, which we'll look at in Chapter 10.

Let's take a look at a few more examples using non-diatonic seventh chords that can still be covered with the scales and modes we've learned this far. Example 3 is built from a I–V–IV–♭VII progression in G, using Fmaj7 as the ♭VII chord. As with the ♭VII triad, the tonic Mixolydian mode (G Mixolydian) will still cover this chord nicely since the 7th of Fmaj7 (E) is contained within that mode.

Example 3

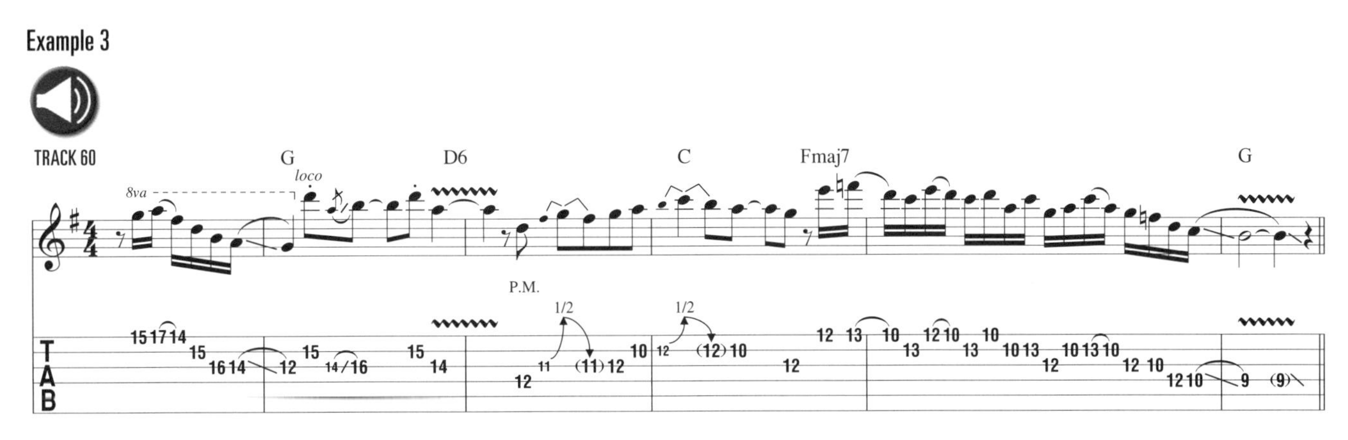

Example 4 is a funky example using a I7 (B7) and a IV7 chord (E7). For this, we'll switch between each chord's respective Mixolydian mode: B Mixolydian over B7 and E Mixolydian over E7.

Example 4

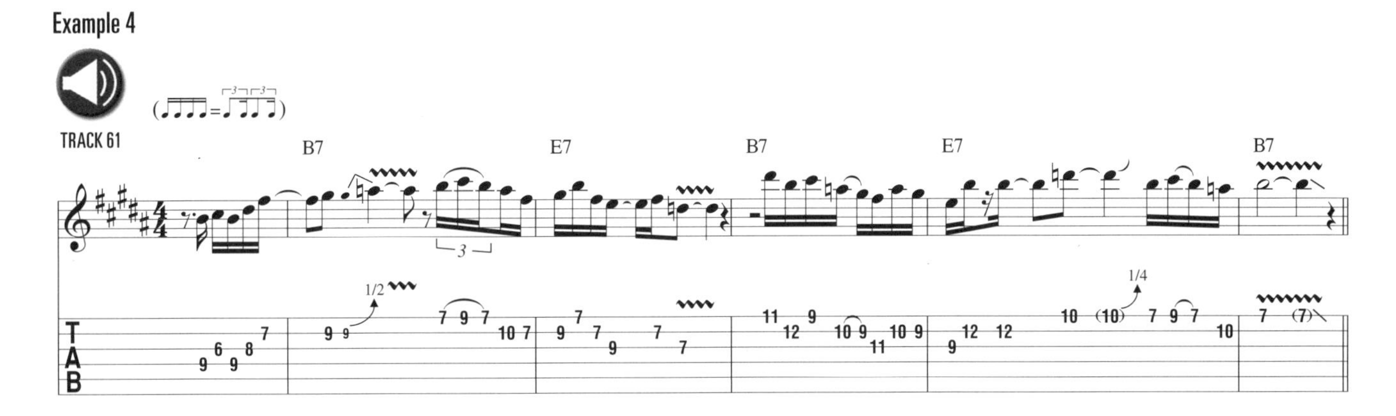

Example 5 will require you to really put the thinking cap on. We're in D minor here. Along with a im7 chord (Dm7), we also move through a ♭III7 chord (F7), ♭VI (B♭), and then a V7 chord (A7). This requires three different scales. D minor (or D minor pentatonic) will handle the Dm7 and B♭ chords, but we'll use F Mixolydian over F7 and D harmonic minor (or A Phrygian dominant) over the A7.

Example 5

TRACK 62

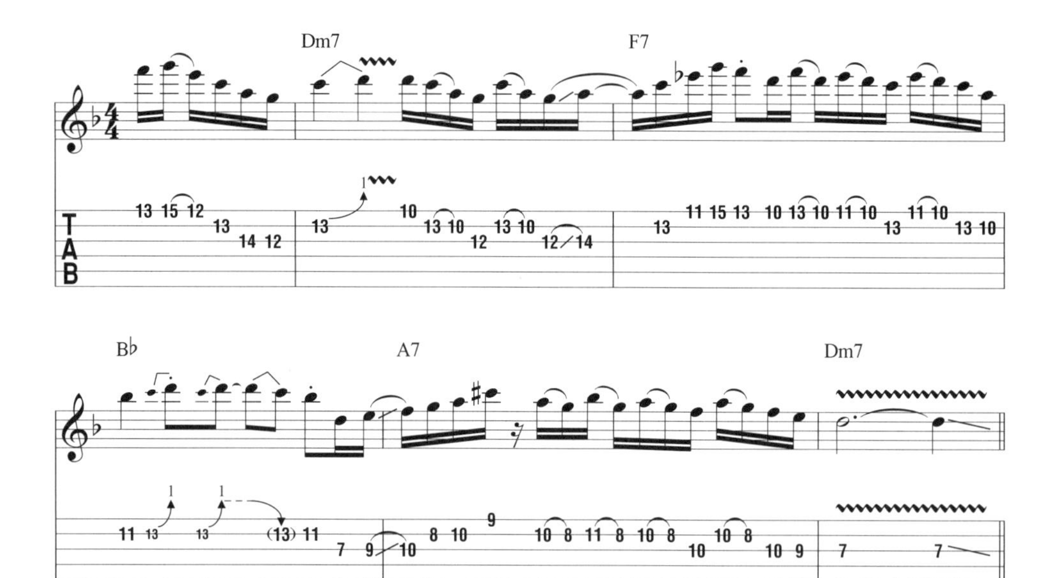

Phrasing Tip: Resolution by Step

Take another look at example 5 closely. Notice that when resolving from the dominant chords (F7 and A7), our line moved by a step (i.e., half or whole step) to a chord tone of the following chords. In each instance, we move from the dominant chord's 3rd to the following chord's root: A to B♭ when moving from F7 to B♭, and E to D when moving from A7 to Dm7. This ♭7th-to-3rd resolution is also very common.

Here's a little exercise to try out this technique. Pick a V–I progression, like G7 to C. Then play each chord tone of the dominant chord and look for the closest chord tone of the I chord, like this:

TRACK 63

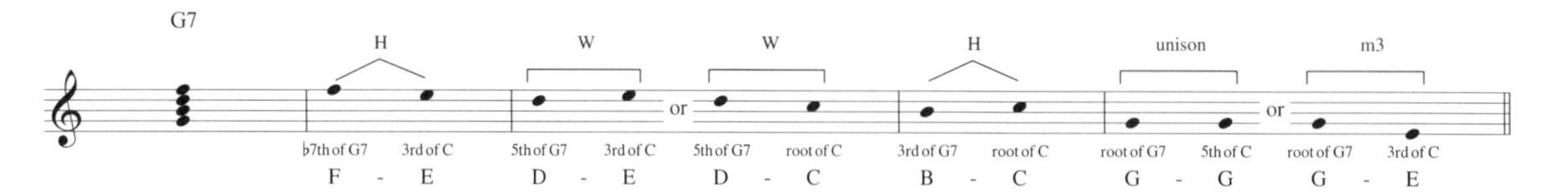

You can see that, in most instances, a chord tone always lies either a half step or a whole step away. In this instance, the nearest chord tone of the I chord (besides its unison) is the 3rd, which is a minor 3rd interval. Keep your ears open for this device being used in the other licks in this book and the solos of your favorite players.

EXTENSIONS

Beyond seventh chords, we can still continue the process of stacking 3rds to get what we call *extensions*, or *extended harmony*. In a seventh chord, we stacked 3rds three times to get the root, 3rd, 5th, and 7th. With extended chords, we continue to stack yet more 3rds on top of that.

Stacking one more 3rd on top of a 7th gives us what we call the 9th. It's the same as the 2nd, only an octave higher, so we call it a 9th. For example, here's our Cmaj7 chord again:

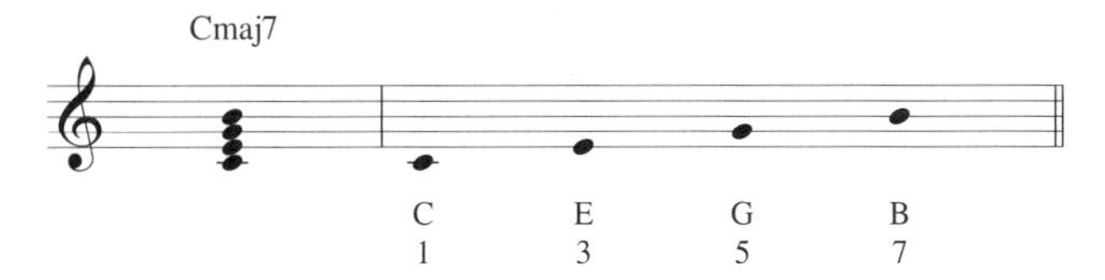

The 7th of the chord is B. What's a 3rd above B? It's D. So when we stack a D on top, we get a Cmaj9 chord.

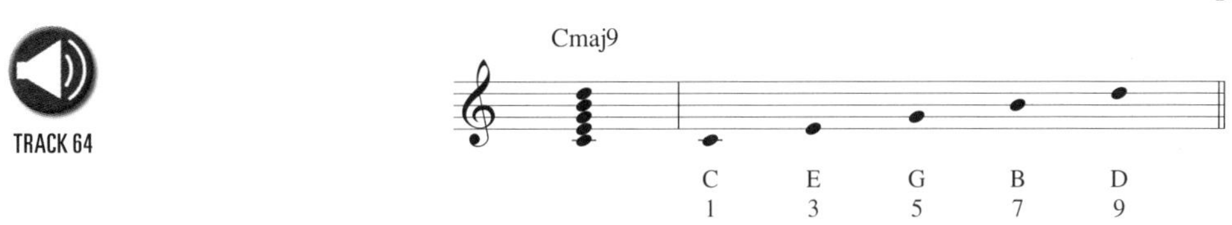

Why do we call it a 9th instead of a 2nd? The basic rule is this: If the chord contains a 7th, then you call it a 9th. If it doesn't contain a 7th, you call it a 2nd. The above is a ninth chord because the 7th (B) is present. It's a Cmaj9 chord because it contains a major 3rd (E) and a major 7th. Just as with seventh chords, we can alter notes to get different types of ninth chords:

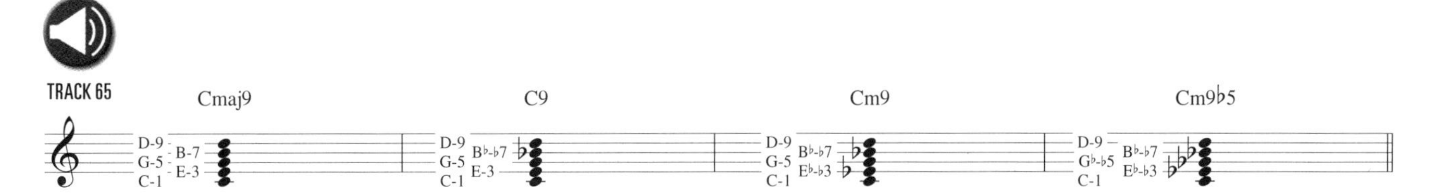

It's beyond the scope of this book to fully cover extensions because it's an expansive topic and quite a big can of worms. (You can continue stacking more 3rds to get eleventh chords and even thirteenth chords.) Suffice it to say, these are other options to consider when soloing. Extensions such as the 9th, 11th, and 13th of a chord tend to sound better when played in the higher registers so they don't muddy up things by rubbing too closely to the root, 3rd, 5th, etc. However, this is by no means a rule, so feel free to experiment with them.

Another thing to keep in mind is that we (guitarists, especially) rarely play these chords (or seventh chords, for that matter) as they're shown here—stacked vertically—because it's often just not possible on the guitar. We usually rearrange the order of the notes into more playable voicings. They're presented this way to make it easier to visualize the process of stacking 3rds. You can find many useful voicings for all these types of chords by picking up a good chord reference book, such as the *Hal Leonard Picture Chord Pocket Guide*.

Also realize that you don't necessarily have to be playing over a ninth chord to highlight the 9th in your melodies. (By the same token, you don't need to be playing over seventh chords to highlight the 7ths.) You could even superimpose a major 9th sound over just a major triad by including the 7th and 9th in your line. It's helpful to learn the chords because it'll help get the sound of the harmonies in your ear. But when soloing, the use of all of these notes is at your discretion.

Example 6 demonstrates this idea over a I–vi–IV progression in C. Over the I chord, we're playing the B and D notes at the peak of our run, creating a Cmaj9 sound over the C triad.

Example 6

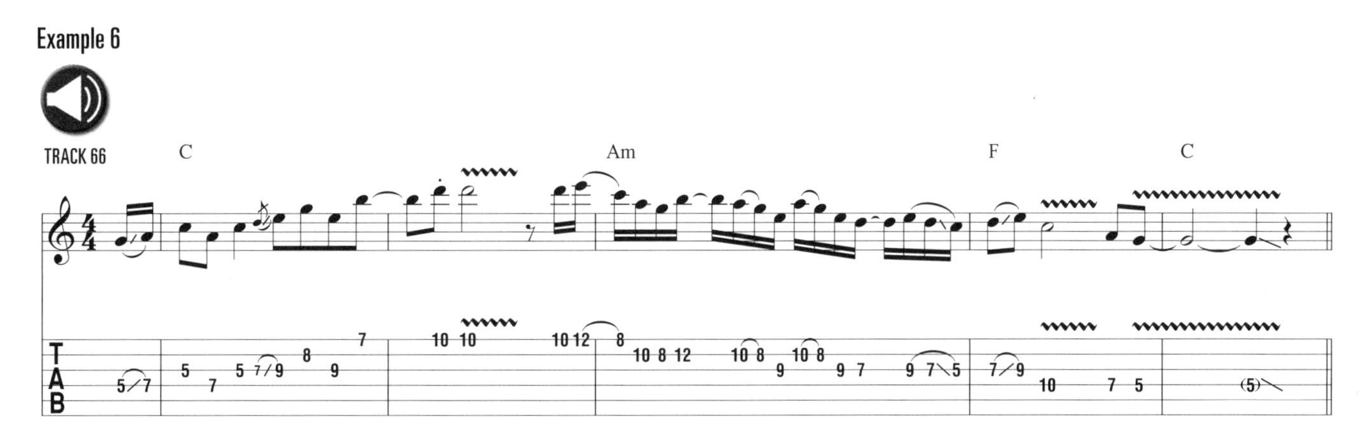

Here's another one: In example 7, we're playing over a i-chord vamp in D minor. After a few fairly standard pentatonic phrases, we play a colorful line that suggests a Dm9 sound.

Example 7

TRACK 67

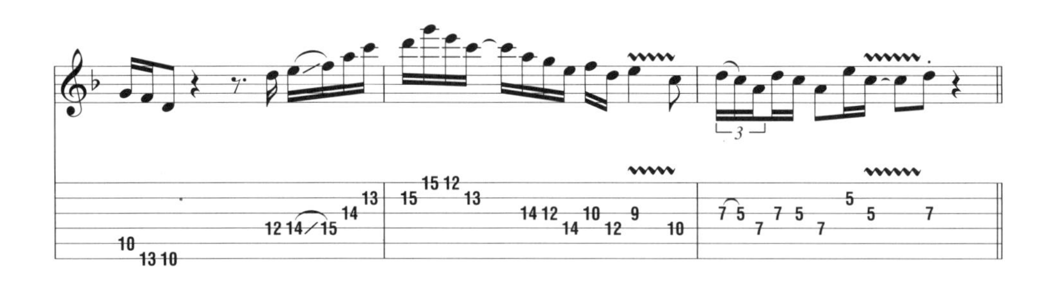

WHAT YOU LEARNED:

- By stacking another 3rd on top of a triad, we create **seventh chords**.
- There are four types of diatonic seventh chords: **major seventh** (maj7), **minor seventh** (m7), **dominant seventh** (7), and **minor seventh flat five** (m7♭5).
- Non-diatonic chords can appear as seventh chords and may require an alternate scale choice, depending on whether the 7th is contained within the mode or not.
- **Phrasing Tip:** It's common to resolve your phrases by a step when moving from a dominant chord to another chord up a 4th.
- We can continue to stack 3rds on top of seventh chords to make ninth, eleventh, and thirteenth chords, sequentially.
- These 7ths and extensions (9ths, 11ths, and 13ths) can be accented as color tones when playing lead—extensions that are sustained for any period of time normally sound better in higher registers.

CHAPTER 9: THE BLUES

Now that you've spent all this time learning conventional theory (remember: they're conventions, not rules!), it's time to look at one of the most defiant of all styles: blues. It's not really that bad, but there are definitely plenty of exceptions happening in the style with regards to scale/chord relationships that need some attention.

HARMONY

The first unconventional trait in blues deals with harmony. In a typical *12-bar blues* (the most common blues form), three chords are used: I, IV, and V. However, *all three* of these chords are typically dominant seventh chords. A normal 12-bar blues progression in C would look like this:

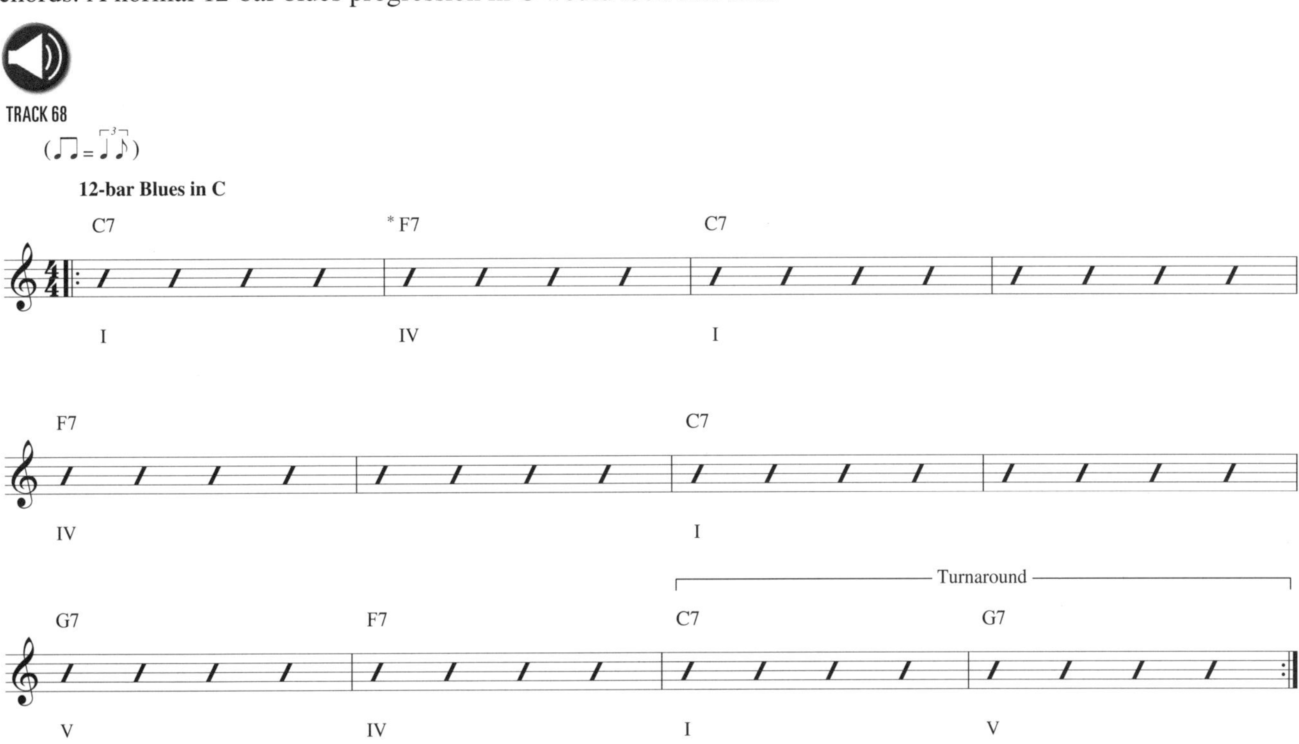

* Alternatively, measures 1–4 can remain on the I chord.

This is known as the "quick change" version of the 12-bar blues and is probably the most common. Another variation is the "slow change" version, in which measures 1–4 contain only the I chord. Measures 11–12 are known as the *turnaround*, which sets up the progression for another chorus (another time through the 12-bar form).

There are many variations on this basic 12-bar blueprint, but this is probably the most ubiquitous of all blues progressions and is therefore a great place to start.

SCALE CHOICES

Now let's look at what to play over the form; we have several options. Again, we'll work mostly in the key of C here to make it easier to see the different scale applications, but be sure to transpose these ideas to all chords.

Option 1: Mixolydian or Major Pentatonic Relative to Each Chord

Since the matching mode for a dominant seventh chord is the Mixolydian mode, it's only logical to assume that we can play each chord's matching Mixolydian mode through the form. This is certainly true and, though it may not be the most common approach (in straight blues or blues-rock styles), it's a valid approach that can produce some very melodic, if slightly jazzy, results.

Example 1 demonstrates this approach, using C Mixolydian over the I chord (C7), F Mixolydian over the IV chord (F7), and G Mixolydian over the V chord (G7). Note that, in measures 5–6 over the IV chord (F7), I'm actually thinking C minor pentatonic. This is still keeping with our strategy, because the notes of C minor pentatonic (C–E♭–F–G–B♭) are contained within F Mixolydian (**F**–**G**–A–**B♭**–**C**–D–**E♭**).

Example 1

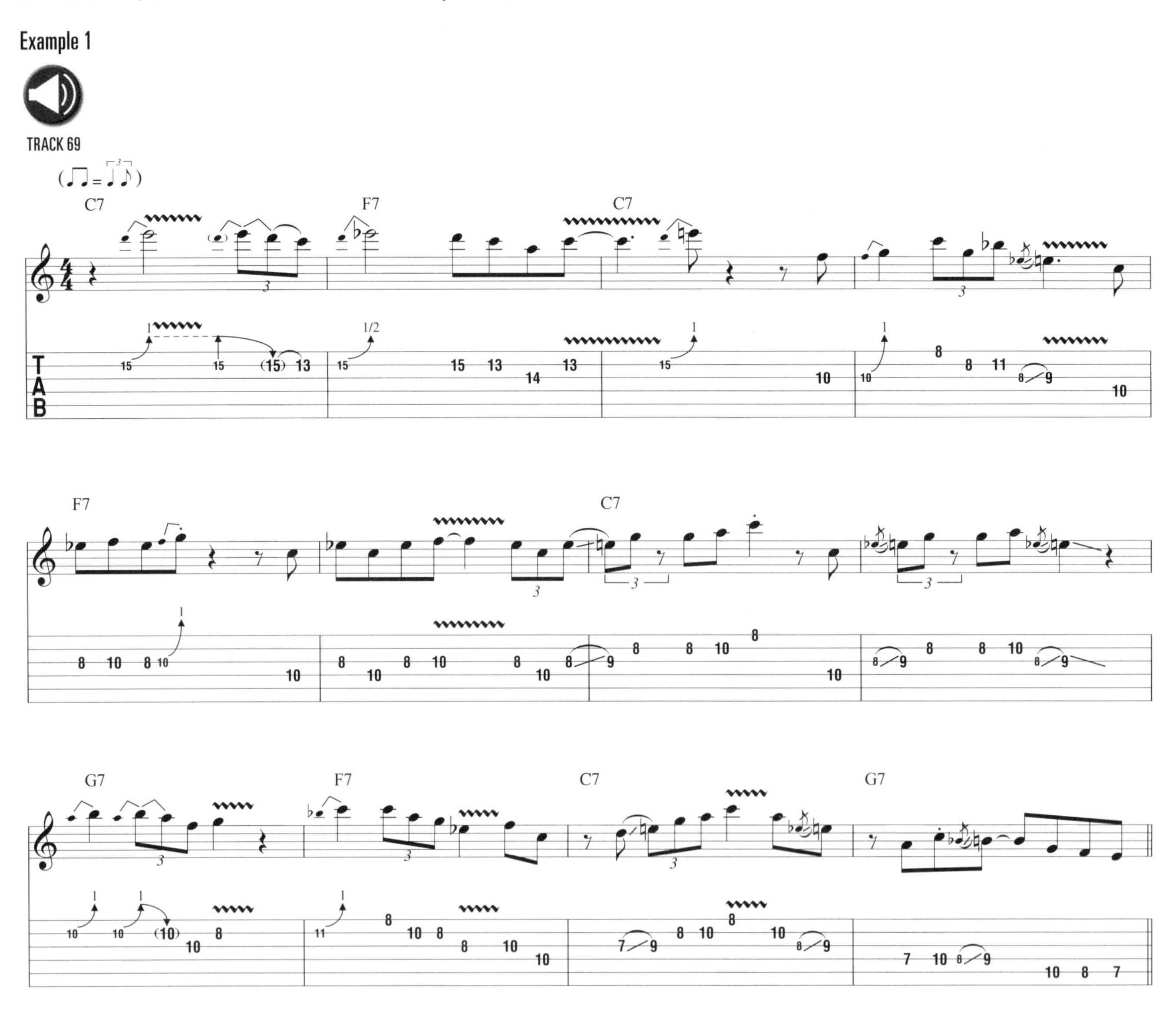

If we can play Mixolydian for each chord, then it stands to reason that we can play the matching major pentatonic for each chord as well, since the major pentatonic scale (1–2–3–5–6) is contained within the Mixolydian mode (**1**–**2**–**3**–4–**5**–**6**–♭7). This will have a brighter sound than the Mixolydian mode and is a bit easier to work with, as all of the notes are relatively "safe" to land on. (The Mixolydian mode, by comparison, contains the 4th degree, which can sound awkward if not resolved properly.) Example 2 demonstrates this approach with C major pentatonic over I, F major pentatonic over the IV, and G major pentatonic over the V.

Example 2

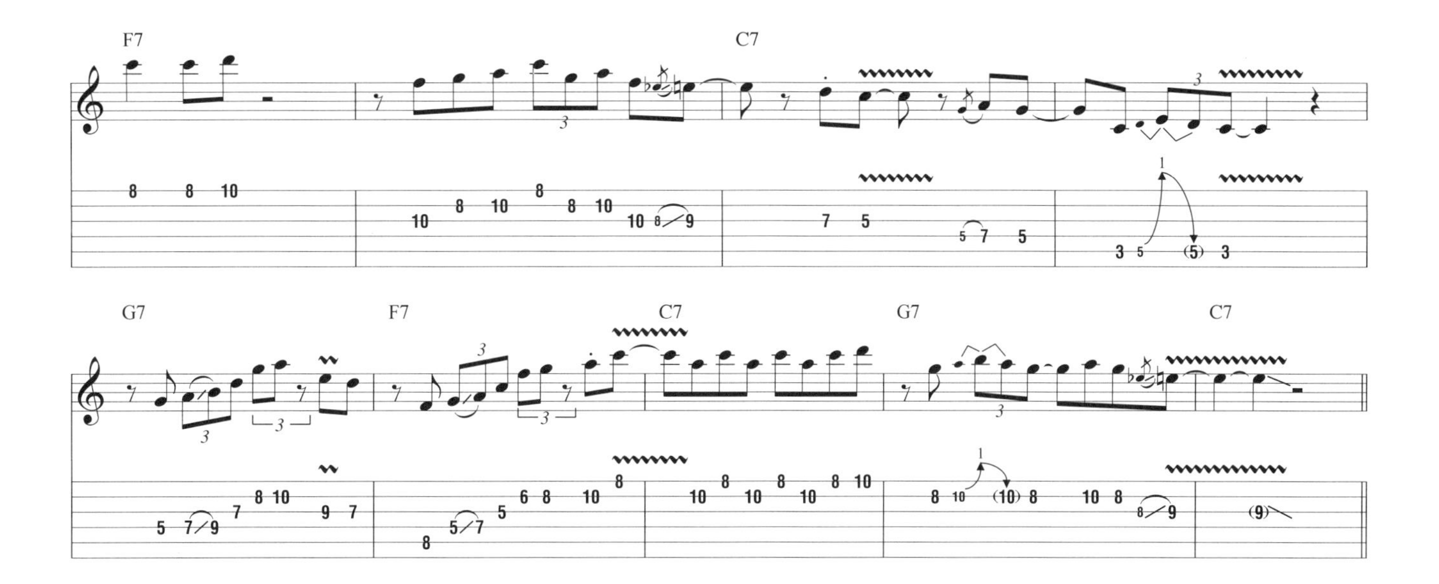

Both of these approaches (matching Mixolydian or major pentatonic relative to each chord) are in keeping with the philosophy we've worked with throughout the book so far—i.e., making intelligent note choices based on chord tones. However, there's another way of playing over a blues progression that's considerably more common. And that is …

Option 2: The Tonic Blues Scale

The *blues scale* is basically a minor pentatonic scale with one added chromatic note between the 4th and 5th degrees. So its formula is 1–♭3–4–♯4 (♭5)–5–♭7. Here's the C blues scale and the most common two-octave fingering pattern, which is based on our C minor pentatonic scale, Shape 2, in eighth position.

C Blues Scale

TRACK 71

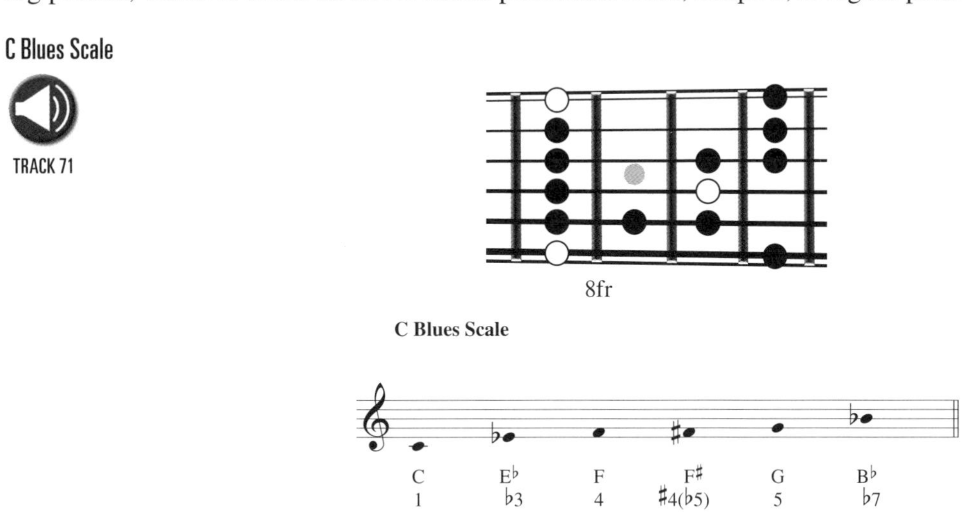

We can use this one scale to solo over the whole 12-bar blues in C. But, wait a minute. The blues scale contains a *minor 3rd*, and a C7 chord contains a *major 3rd*—what kind of rubbish is this? Playing a minor scale over a major chord? Yep! Believe it or not, our ears have grown to accept this sound over the years. It's a much meaner sound than the Mixolydian/major pentatonic approach.

Rather than concentrating on making intelligent note choices based on chord tones, with this approach we're thinking more about creating and resolving tension by moving away from and back to the root. By root, it can actually be the root of the scale (in this case, C) or the roots of the chords (C, F, and G).

Certain notes, such as the ♭3rd (E♭) and 4th (F), will create a good deal of tension when played over a tonic C7 chord. Generally speaking, you probably don't want to sustain these notes (especially the E♭) for long periods of time over the C7 chord with nothing happening. In other words, holding those notes may sound less dissonant if you treat them with some liberal vibrato or a gradual bend, for instance. The more you play around with this approach, the more you'll become adept at ways to use this tension and resolve it. By the same token, those same two notes (E♭ and F) will sound much more stable over the IV chord (F7) because they're both contained within the chord. It's these types of relationships that you'll learn to recognize the more you practice playing the blues scale over a 12-bar form.

Make It Cry!

The blues is all about expression, and one of the most expressive tools we have on the guitar is the bend. In blues guitar, you'll see bends of all types: whole-step bends, half-step bends, and *microtonal* bends (quarter-step bends)—i.e., ones that fall "in between the cracks" of two other notes. You'll especially see these types of bends on the ♭3rd and ♭7th degrees. Pay attention to the following examples to hear these in action.

Example 3 demonstrates how this approach may sound with a more laid-back approach. We're using the C blues scale over the whole 12-bar form. Notice how we still target certain notes of the scale over specific chords (i.e., the note G over the V chord, G7).

Example 3

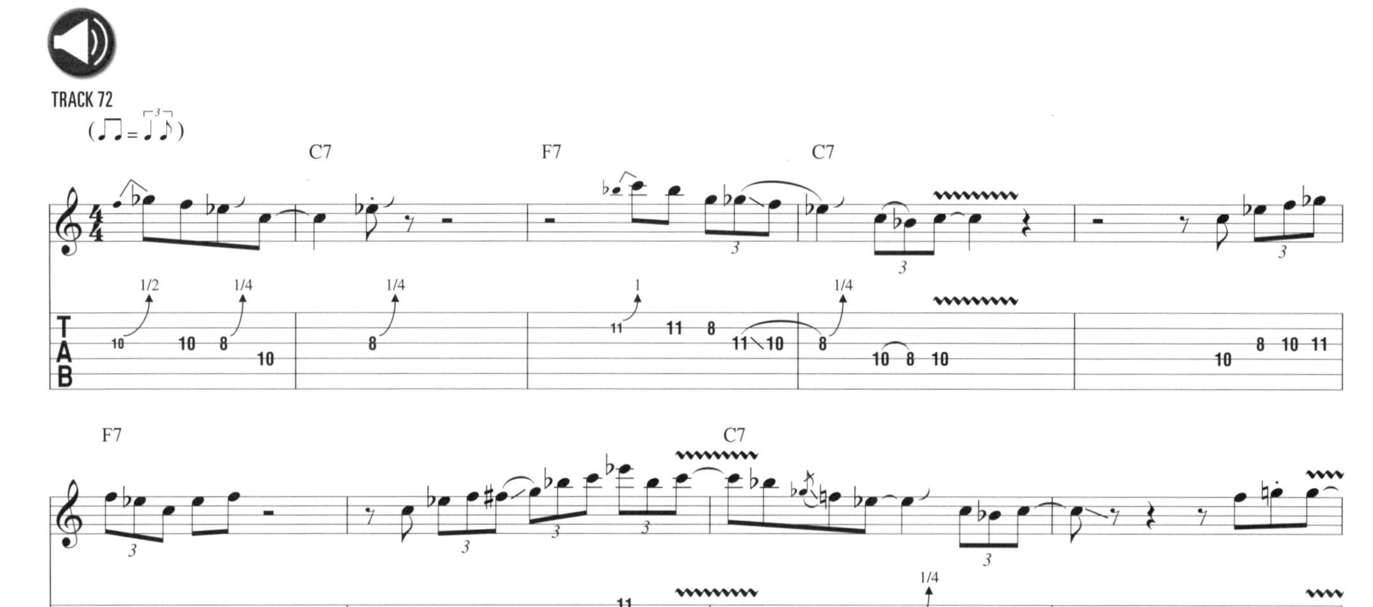

In example 4, we hear a much more aggressive approach with the same scale. This approach is really all about conviction. Really dig in and let the guitar have it!

Example 4

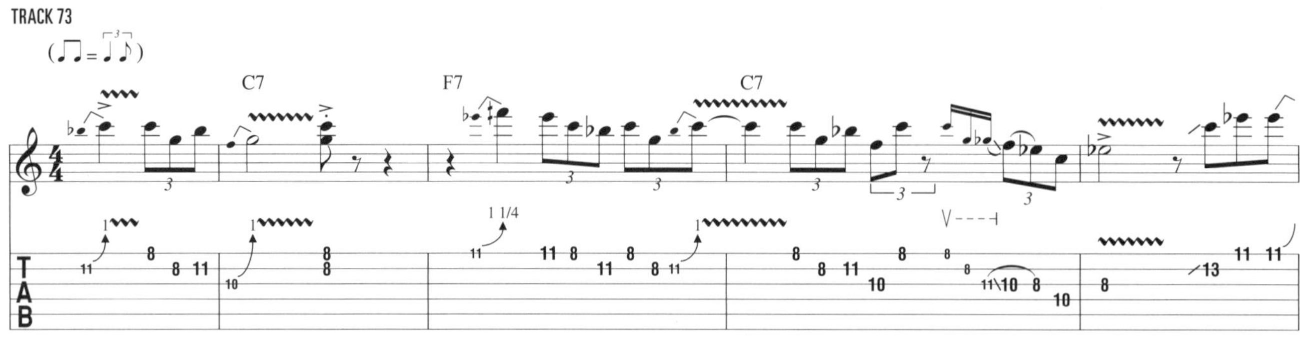

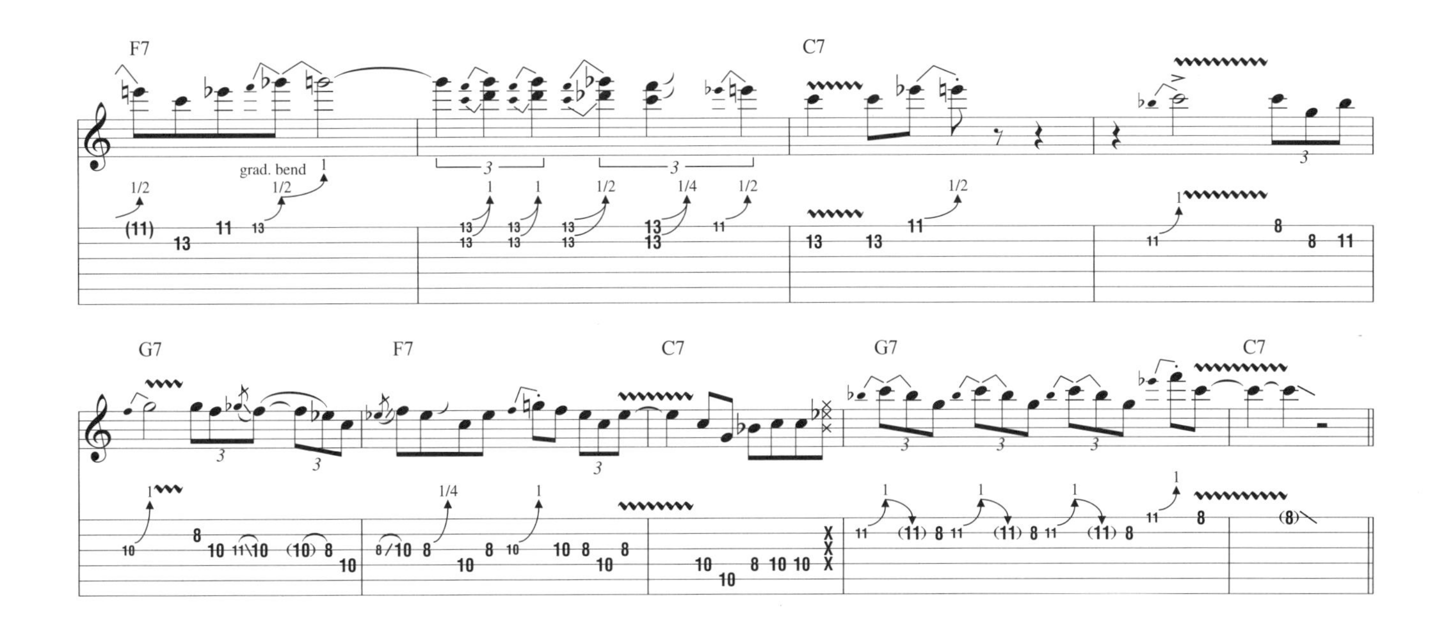

Option 3: Mixing Tonic Major Pentatonic and Minor Pentatonic/Blues Scale Sounds

Yet a third approach deals with switching between the tonic major pentatonic and minor pentatonic scales (or blues scale). This is sort of a combination of Option 1 and Option 2.

- Over the I chord (C7), you'd play C major pentatonic.
- Over the IV chord (F7), you'd play C minor pentatonic or C blues (because the E♭ fits well with the dominant F7 chord).
- Over the V chord (G7), you'd play either C major pentatonic or C minor pentatonic (minor pentatonic is probably more common).

Example 5 demonstrates this approach, using C major pentatonic over the V chord (G7). Notice that this sounds much sweeter than examples 3 and 4—very reminiscent of B.B. King.

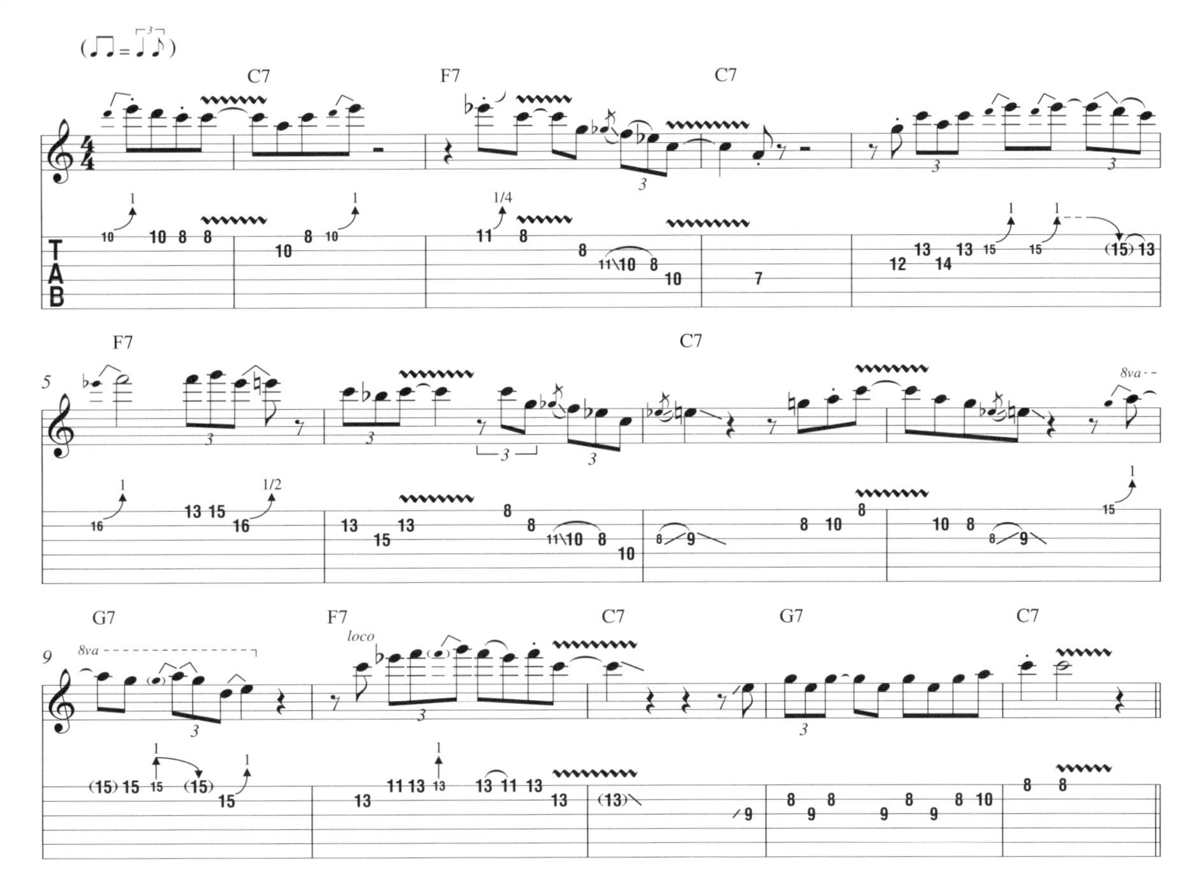

In example 6, we're using the C blues scale over the V chord. This makes for a tougher sound than example 5. As measures 1–8 contain the same solo as example 5, only measures 9–12 are written out here. (Refer to example 5, then jump to example 6 when you reach measure 9.)

Example 6

TRACK 75

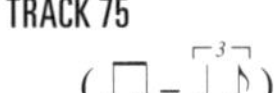

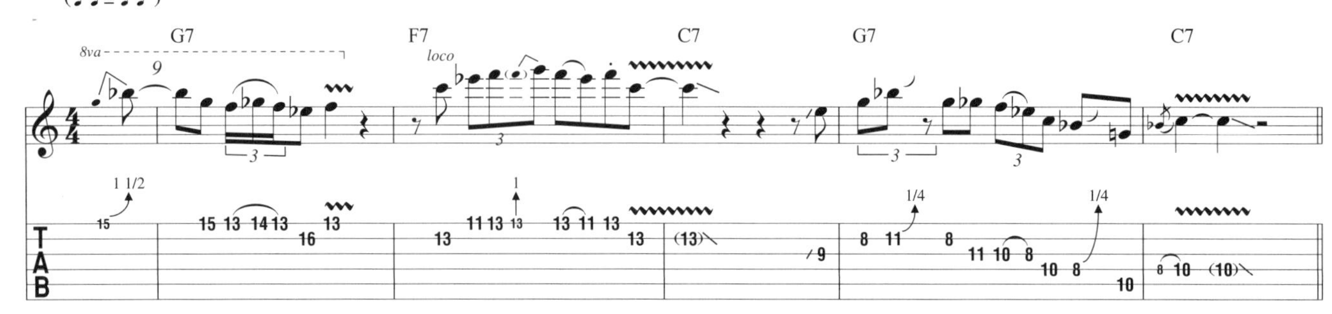

Phrasing Tip: Take a Breather and Get Some Rest

As guitar players, we have a tendency to fill up every second of the music with something. But when you listen to horn players, you'll notice that there are periods of silence (rests) in their phrases. This is a matter of necessity for them; they have to breathe. We can take a tip from them on this matter and start using this concept ourselves.

Try consciously breathing along with what you play. Take a breath and exhale as you play a phrase. When you run out of air, stop playing. Don't start playing again until you take another breath. Eventually, you'll learn to wrap up your ideas and resolve your lines as you run out of breath. Once you've practiced this technique enough, you'll begin to naturally incorporate rests into your lines without having to think about it. Listen to the examples in this chapter specifically for this idea. It can really help lend your solos direction and purpose.

SCALE SUMMARY: DOMINANT BLUES

When we consider all the different options listed for each chord, this is what we get. We've included one extra possibility: the minor pentatonic built off the root of the V chord when playing over the V chord (in C, this would be G minor pentatonic over G7). This isn't quite as common as the rest of the approaches, but it is used on a regular basis.

- C7 (I chord): C Mixolydian, C major pentatonic, C minor pentatonic, C blues.
- F7 (IV chord): F Mixolydian, F major pentatonic, C minor pentatonic, C blues.
- G7 (V) chord): G Mixolydian, G major pentatonic, G minor pentatonic, C major pentatonic, C minor pentatonic, C blues.

In actual practice, any and all of these choices may be combined in one solo. Examples 7 and 8 demonstrate two possibilities with this approach.

Example 7

TRACK 76

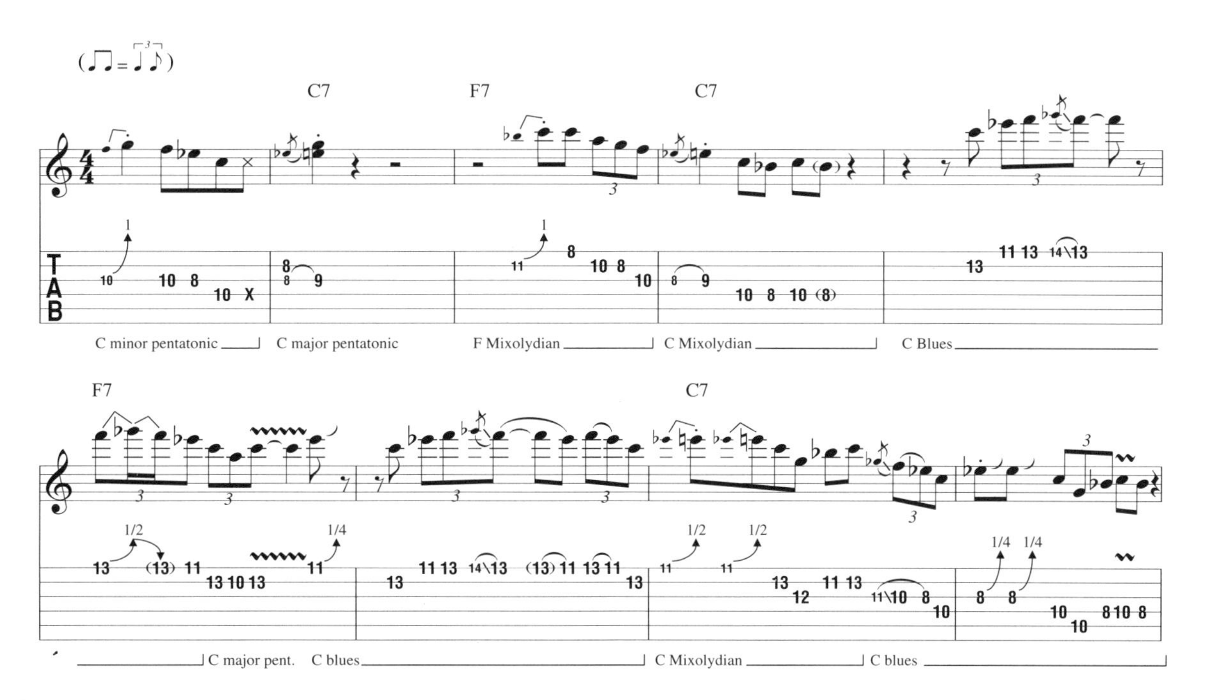

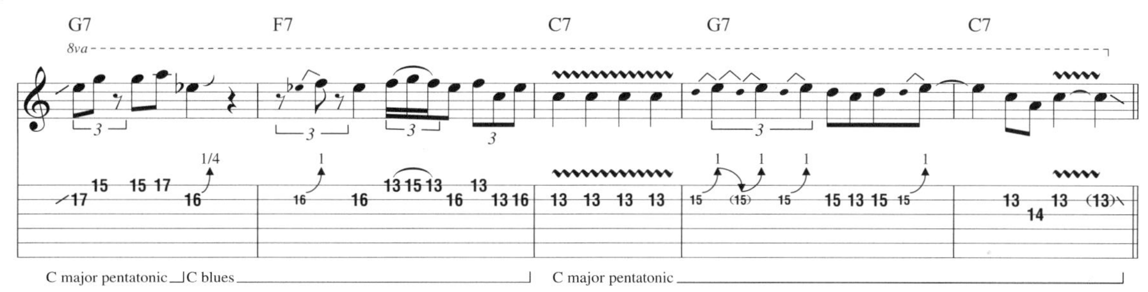

Example 8

TRACK 77

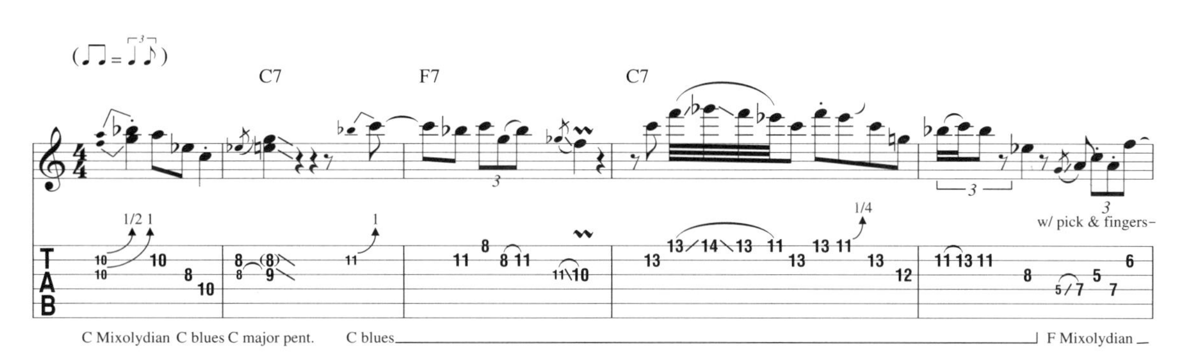

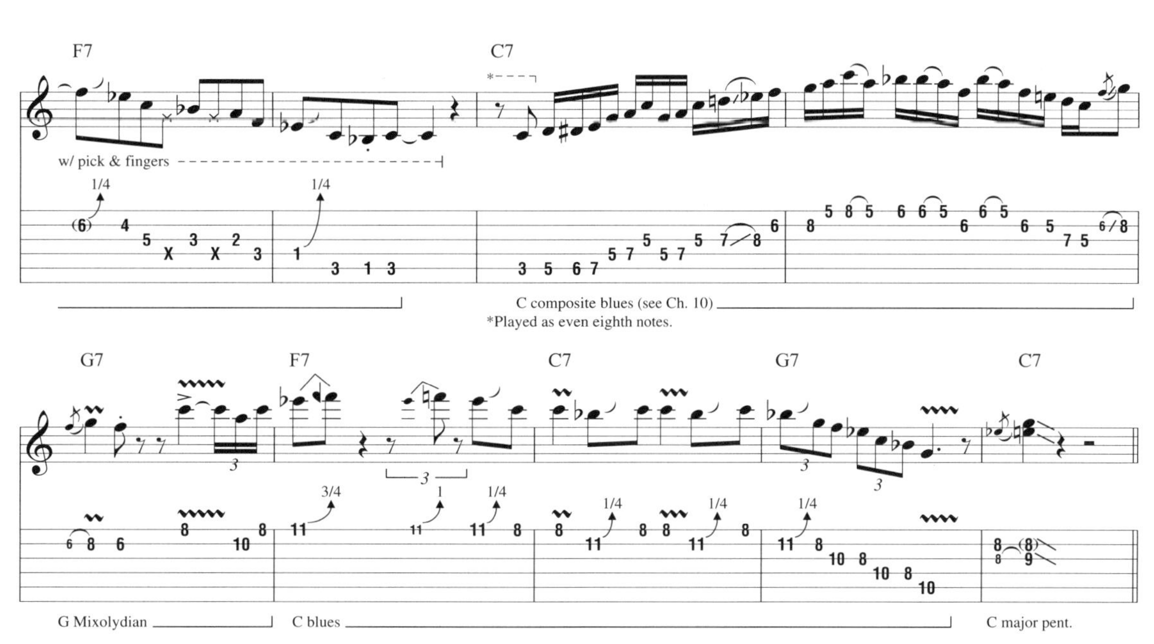

Why Not the Matching Minor Pentatonic of the IV Chord?

If we can play the matching minor pentatonic scales for the I and V chords, why can't we do the same for the IV chord? In other words, in our C blues, why can't we play F minor pentatonic over F7? Well, there's no law that says you can't. However, it's normally not done.

The only real problem lies with the ♭3rd of the F minor pentatonic scale: the A♭ note. This note is just a bit too foreign to the C blues tonality and ends up sounding kind of sour. Try it, and you'll hear what I'm talking about.

MINOR BLUES

The minor blues uses a different harmonic set than a dominant blues. It also commonly uses four different chords instead of just three. Here's a typical C minor 12-bar blues progression:

TRACK 78

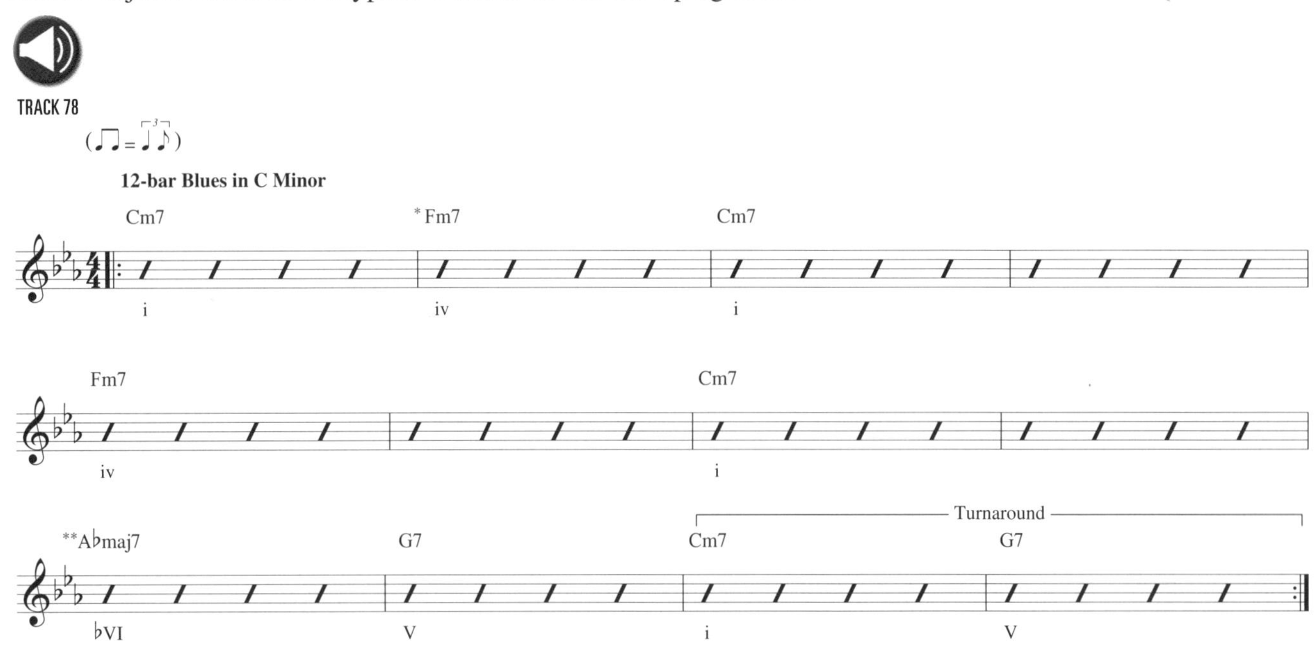

* Alternatively, measures 1–4 can remain on the i chord.
** This can also appear as a dominant seventh chord (A♭7).

Notice that, while the basic 12-bar form is intact, the prominent difference (from the dominant blues) lies in measures 9–10. In a minor blues, we move from ♭VI to V instead of from V to IV.

SCALE SUMMARY: MINOR BLUES

Typically, there aren't as many scale options employed for the minor blues. This is because, where we use both major and minor versions of a few scales in a dominant blues, we don't do that in a minor blues. Here are the most common scales played over a minor blues:

- Cm7 (i chord): C minor pentatonic, C blues, C minor, C Dorian*.
- Fm7 (iv chord): F minor pentatonic, C minor pentatonic, C blues.
- A♭maj7 (♭VI chord): C minor pentatonic, C blues, C minor (if A♭7 is used, another scale option would be A♭ *Lydian dominant*, which is covered in Chapter 10).
- G7 (V chord): G minor pentatonic, C minor pentatonic, C blues, C harmonic minor.

* C Dorian would technically be a non-diatonic scale because its 6th tone, A♮, is not contained within the key of C minor. However, it's commonly employed over a i chord—especially in blues or jazz-blues styles.

Again, we have the option of simply playing the tonic minor pentatonic or blues scale over the entire progression, and it's certainly used often. Example 9 demonstrates this approach.

Example 9

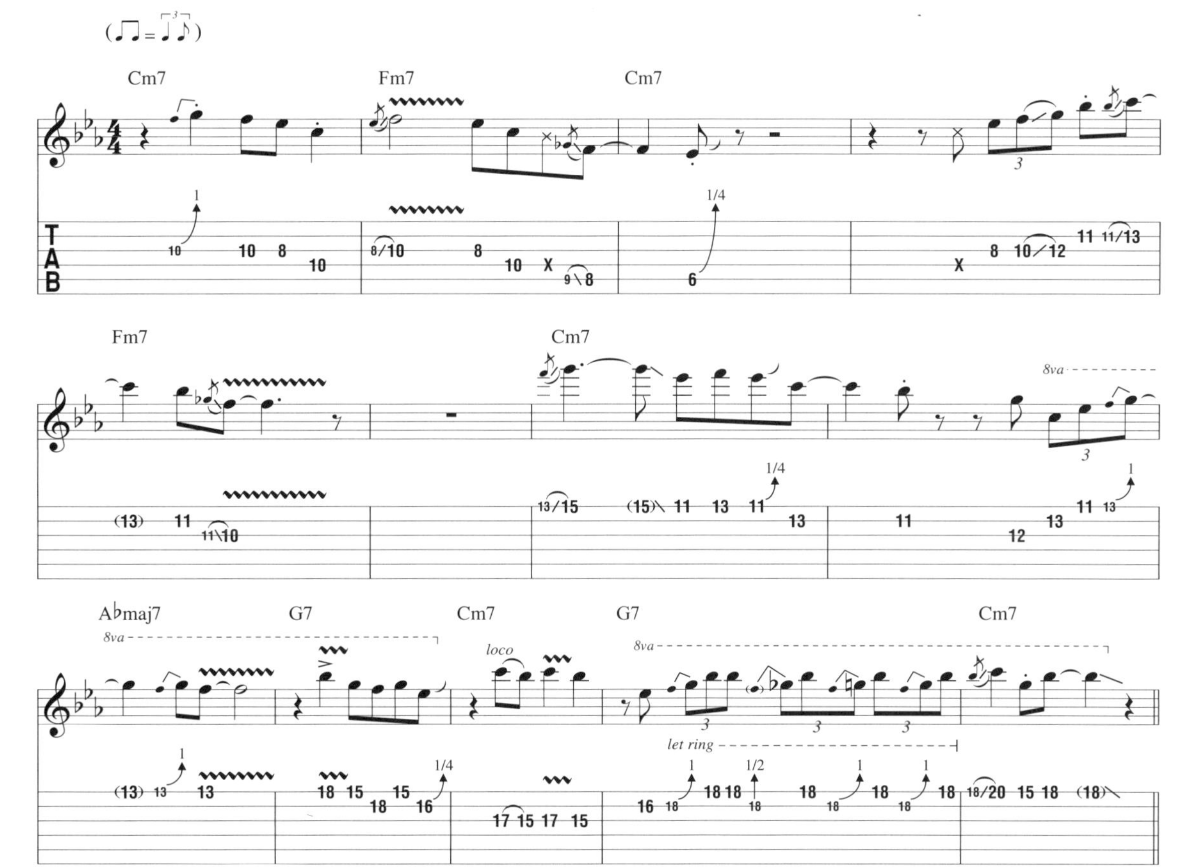

We can also pick and choose our scales depending on the chords. Example 10 demonstrates how this might sound.

Example 10

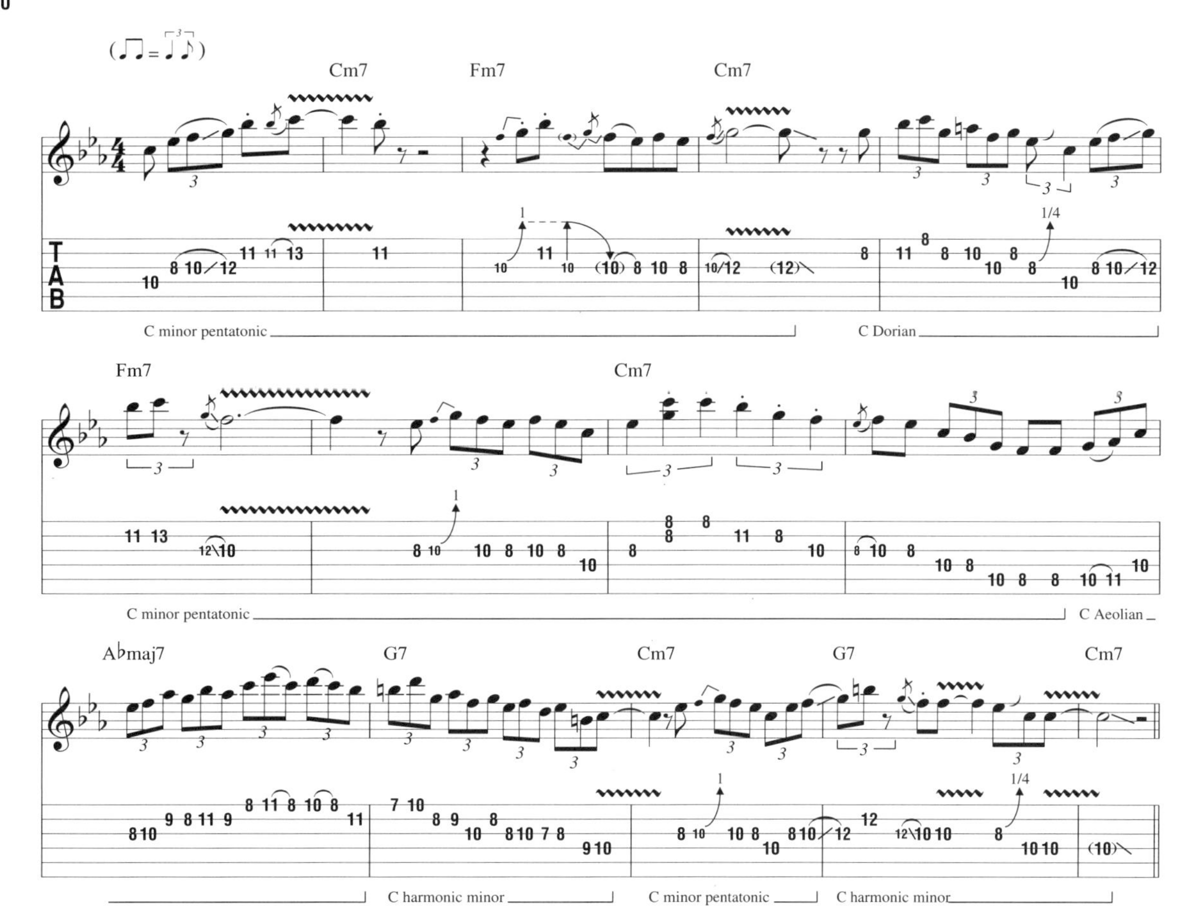

There are just about as many variations in a minor blues as there are in a dominant blues, but this is plenty to get you started. You'll also notice that the phrasing strategy when using only the tonic minor pentatonic/blues scales will be different in a minor blues, because the ♭3rd degree is actually a chord tone of the tonic chord. This means, among other things, that you can use this note as a point of resolution rather than a point of tension.

Try to make it a habit to practice playing over both types of blues progressions. Many players are well-versed in a standard (dominant) blues but have a little trouble with minor blues because they're not as familiar with them. The minor blues is a slightly different animal and, therefore, requires specific attention.

WHAT YOU LEARNED:

- A standard (dominant) 12-bar blues is built upon three chords: I, IV, and V.
- A minor 12-bar blues is built upon four chords: i, iv, ♭VI, and V.
- The seventh chord (instead of the triad) is the standard harmony in blues.
- There are several scale choices available when playing over a standard blues—most interesting is the fact that you can play a tonic minor pentatonic or blues scale (with a minor 3rd) over a dominant chord.
- There are several scale choices available when playing over a minor blues.
- Soloing over a blues form is often about creating tension and releasing it.
- **Phrasing Tip:** Incorporate rests into your lines and allow the music to breathe.

CHAPTER 10: OTHER SCALES AND ADVANCED APPLICATIONS

So far, we've looked at many different types of chords and the scales that are commonly used to play over them. We've developed a strong foundation in chord/scale theory and should be able to confidently handle most of the musical situations we encounter. However, there still are many other scale options available. Some of these are simply used to get different sounds, and some of them are required to play over specific non-diatonic chords that we haven't encountered thus far. In this chapter, we'll look at examples of each.

THE MAJOR/MINOR MIX

As we learned in Chapter 9, we're able to use not only the tonic major pentatonic, but also the tonic minor pentatonic and blues scale when playing over a standard 12-bar blues, even though the chords are dominant sevenths, which contain a *major 3rd*. However, this anomaly is not limited to the 12-bar form. The influence of the blues is far-reaching, and this major/minor mix of tonic scales is something that we see in many other styles of music—especially rock, country, pop, and jazz.

In other words, we can add this option to our scale arsenal when using the key-center approach to play over a major key chord progression. As with the 12-bar blues, experience will teach you how to best use and resolve the tension created with the minor pentatonic and blues scale when used in this fashion. Let's take a look at a few examples.

In example 1, we've got a typical I–V–vi–IV progression in C that repeats. The first time through the progression, we're using the C major pentatonic scale and/or C major scale (C Ionian mode). The second time through, we switch to the C blues scale. Note the change in character.

Example 1

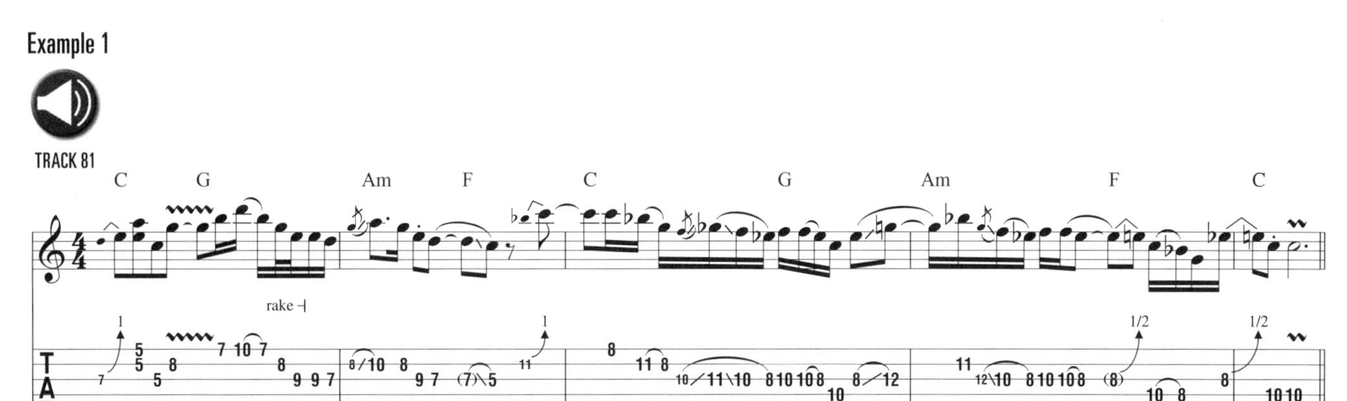

The above example was distinctly broken up neatly into two parts, but in practical application, things are usually not that tidy. Example 2 takes place over the same progression, but we're mixing the scales throughout in a way that's more typical.

Example 2

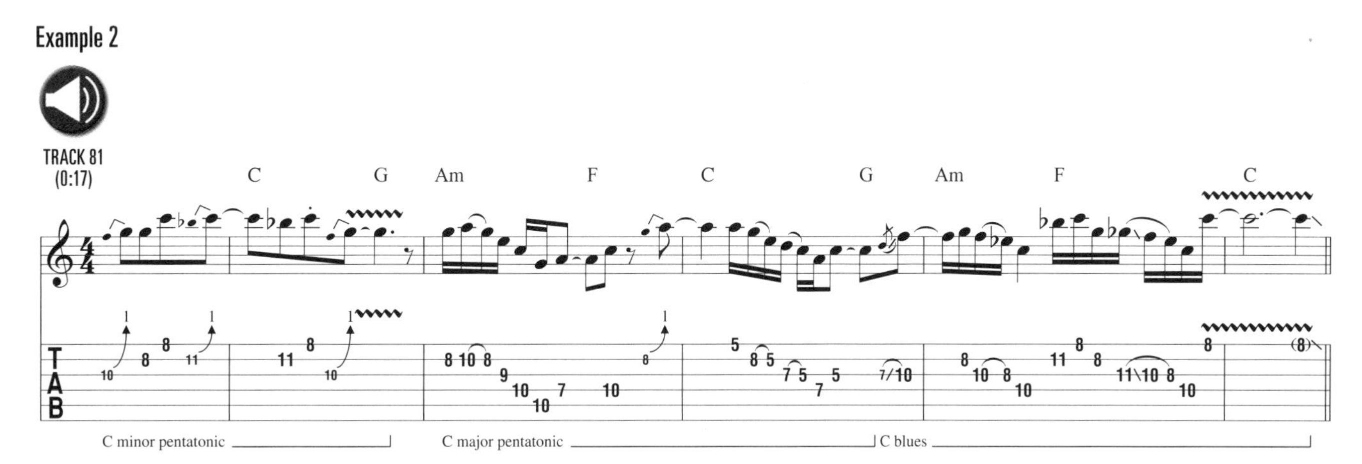

This device is particularly useful when you're playing over a vamp that contains only one or two chords. You can hear a beautiful demonstration of this concept throughout Stevie Ray Vaughan's "Lenny." The solos take place over nothing but a I–IV vamp in E, but Stevie skillfully mixes the E major pentatonic and the E blues scale to keep things interesting. Example 3, which takes place over an E–A progression, is in the spirit of "Lenny."

Example 3

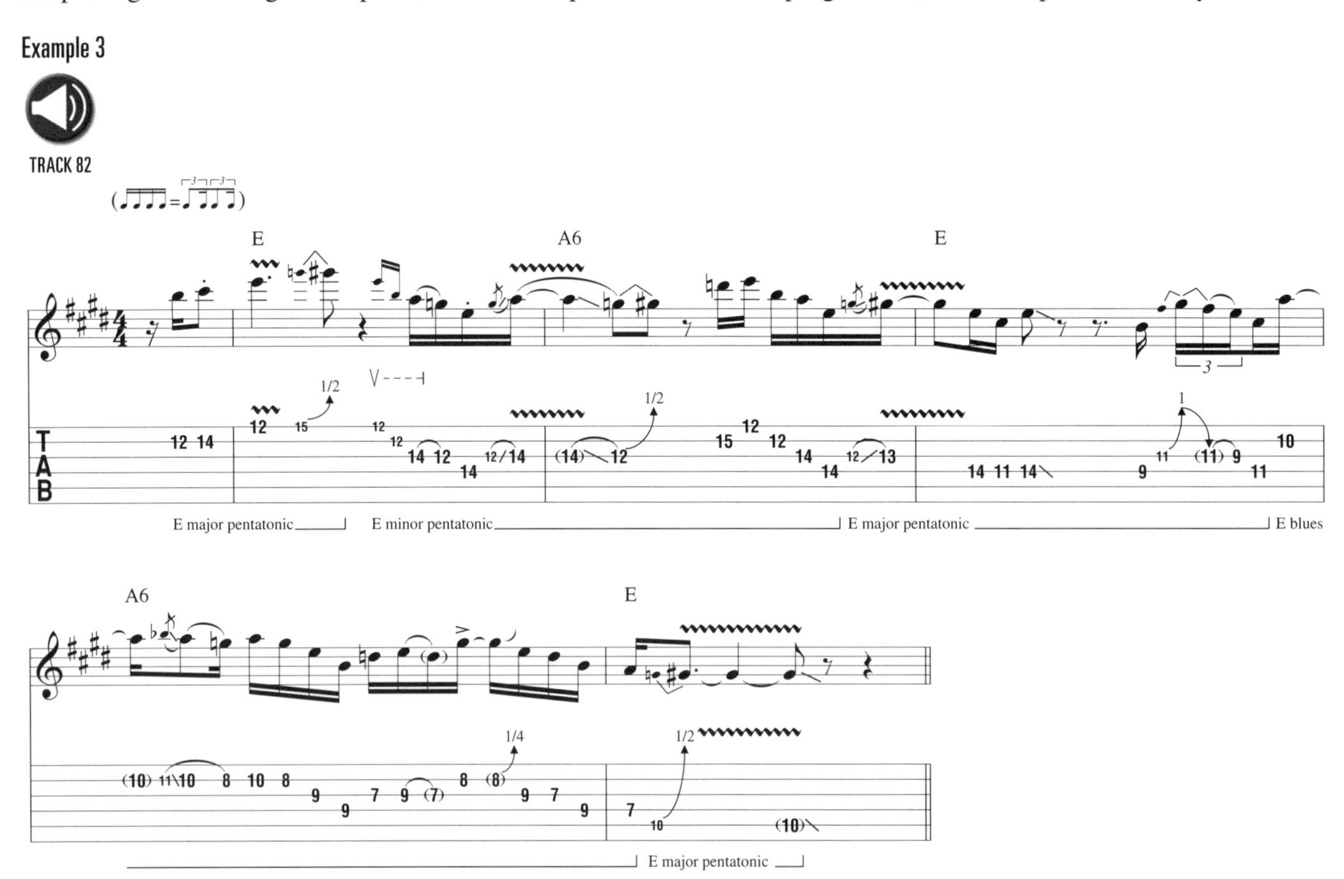

In example 4, we're playing over nothing but a G7 chord. To keep things interesting, though, we're mixing G Mixolydian and G blues scale ideas throughout. Notice, again, that we don't make it a habit of landing on the tart ♭3rd (B♭) and just sitting there; that note is normally used as a tension builder within the contour of a longer line. When we do resolve the phrases, we're usually doing so with our chord tones (G, B, D, or F).

Example 4

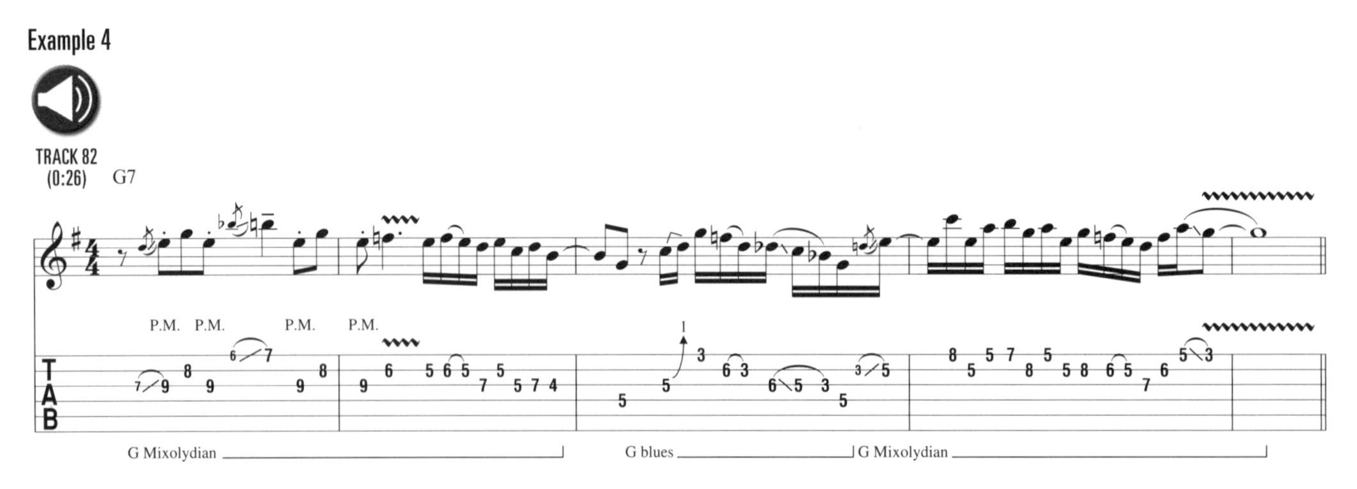

This concept opens up a whole new slew of sounds, some of which can sound pretty colorful. Example 5 takes place over the same G7 vamp, but here we're deliberately mixing up the different scales within each lick. In example 4, we were thinking of one scale for a few beats and then thinking of another one for the next few beats, whereas here we're combining the notes from the different scales all into one "super scale" that actually contains 9 different notes: G–A–B♭–B–C–D♭–D–E–F. This is sometimes referred to as the *composite blues scale.* You can think of it as a combination of a G major pentatonic (G–A–B–D–E) and a G blues scale (G–B♭–C–D♭–D–F).

Example 5

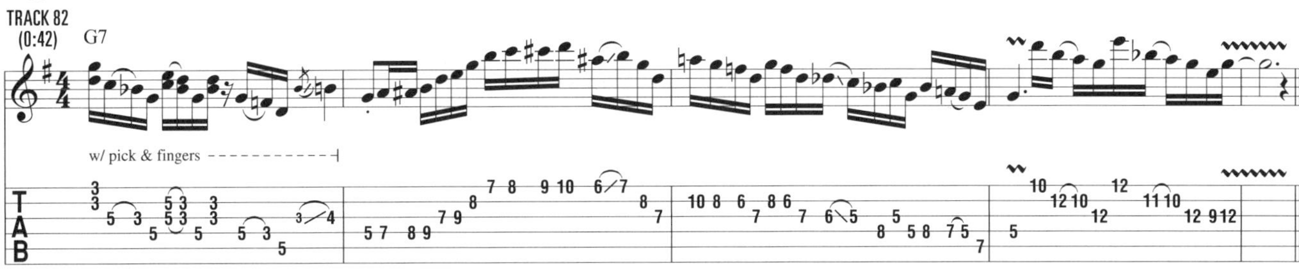

When you consider all these options, you'll find that it's hard to get bored playing over a major key progression!

One Way and Not the Other?

Again, this major/minor mix concept usually only goes one way—i.e., when playing in a minor key, the major 3rd-based scales just tend to sound wrong. There is one main exception to this and that deals with *superimposition*. To superimpose means to play a scale over a chord that normally wouldn't be associated with it. This is our one chance to get away with playing a major 3rd over a minor chord.

If we have a minor i chord that moves to a iv chord, for instance, we have a root movement that's up a 4th. In the key of C minor, for instance, this would be Cm up to Fm. Well, what we can do is temporarily treat the i chord (Cm) as a secondary dominant and think C7 instead of Cm. (We saw this same idea in Chapter 6, only we were dealing with a major key.) In this case, we'll actually be superimposing a dominant sound over a minor chord. So we'll be playing C Phrygian dominant (F harmonic minor) over Cm. Example 6 demonstrates how this might sound.

Example 6

There are a few things to keep in mind with this concept:

- The superimposition is normally brief—i.e., it normally occurs a beat or two before moving to the new chord. Notice that we played C minor until beat 3 of measure 2.
- This approach normally works best in a functional line, meaning it resolves smoothly to a chord tone of the new chord.
- It's usually best to use this device sparingly. It can lose its effectiveness if it becomes predictable.

A great spot to try this is in measure 4 of a minor blues. Check out the play-along track in the appendix and try it out.

THE MELODIC MINOR SCALE

Earlier we learned that we can alter the natural minor scale by raising its 7th tone to create the harmonic minor scale. We also learned that a popular mode of the harmonic minor is its fifth mode, which is called Phrygian dominant.

Another common altered minor scale is the *melodic minor scale*. It's constructed by raising both the 6th and 7th degrees of a minor scale. It can also be viewed as a major scale with a lowered 3rd. Its formula is 1–2–♭3–4–5–6–7. Here's the C melodic minor scale and a common two-octave fingering pattern:

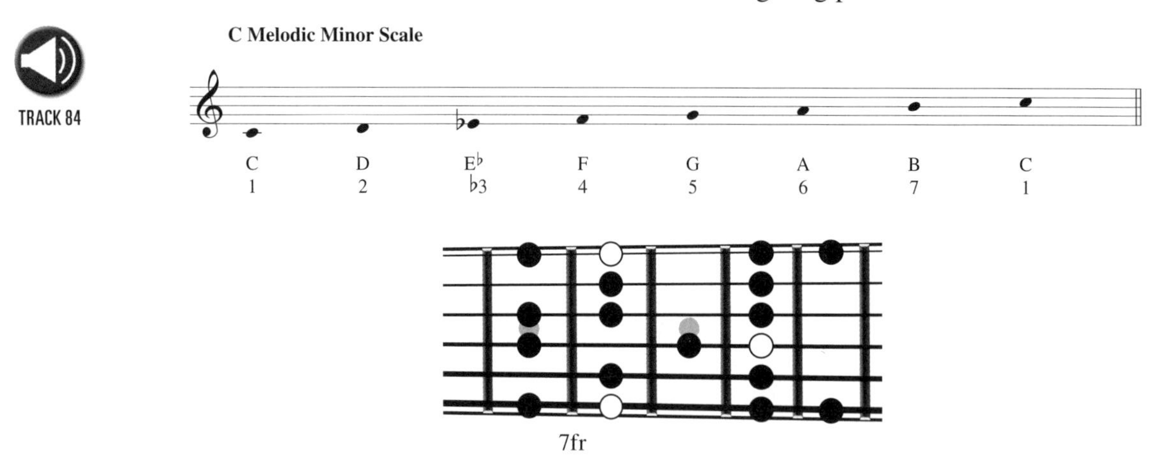

The melodic minor scale has several uses, especially in jazzier styles. Let's take a look at a few.

Application 1: Tonic Minor Scale

One such use is over a tonic minor chord to provide extra color. In example 7, we have a single-chord vamp on Dm7. Here, we're mostly using D Dorian, but we throw in a few D melodic minor (D–E–F–G–A–B–C♯) phrases for color. Even though the C♯ of D melodic minor technically clashes with the C of the Dm7 chord, it's accepted by the ear if used briefly.

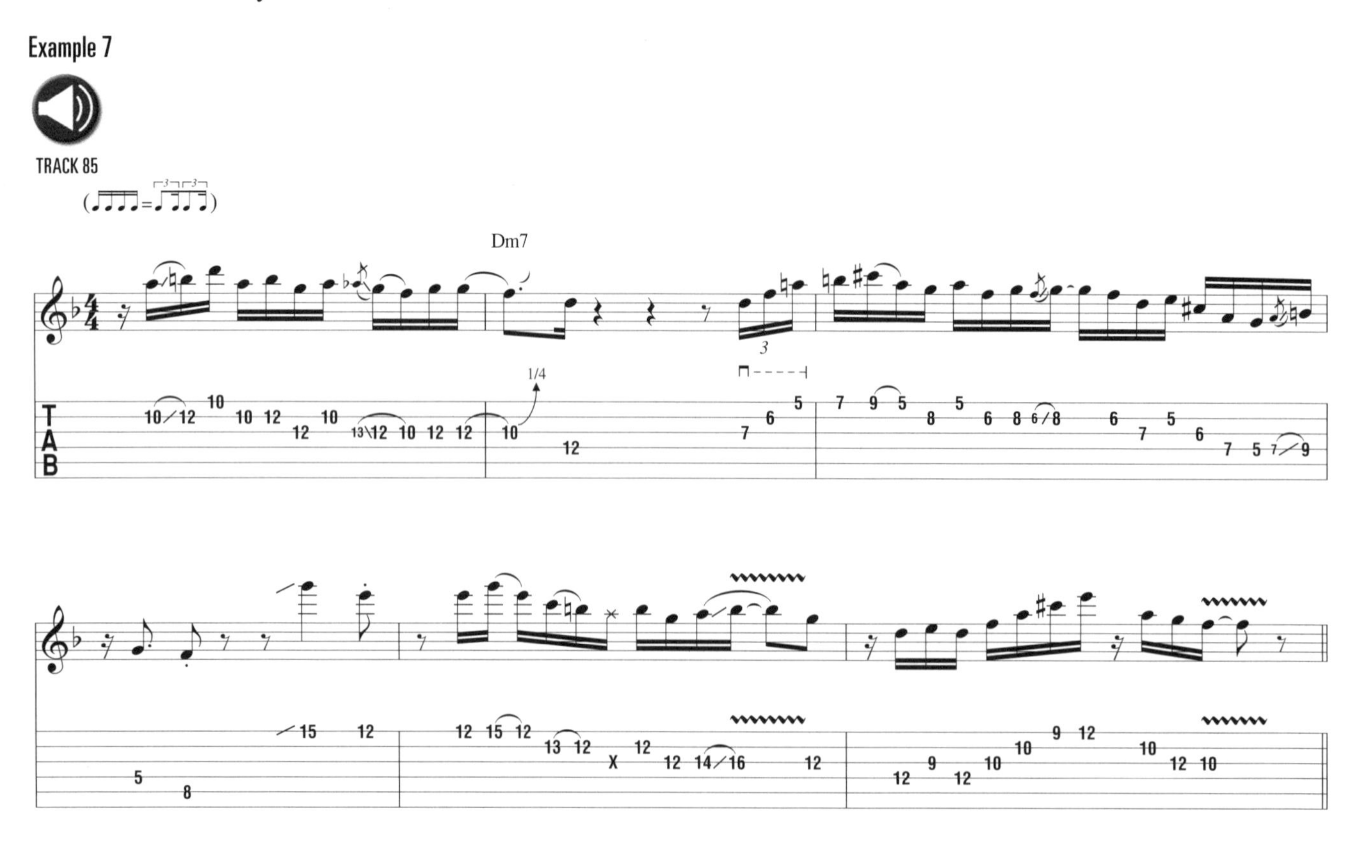

Application 2: Handling Specific Non-Diatonic Chords

This is where you need to put your thinking cap back on. Just as we used the fifth mode of the harmonic minor scale (Phrygian dominant) to play over a dominant chord that resolves to a minor chord, we can use modes of the melodic minor to play over certain chords. One such mode is the fourth mode, which is known as *Lydian dominant*. If we have a C melodic minor scale, for instance, then the fourth mode would be F Lydian dominant.

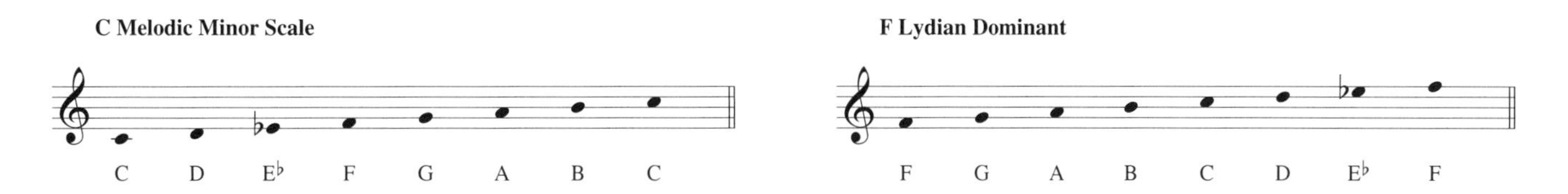

The formula for Lydian dominant is 1–2–3–♯4–5–6–♭7. From this, we can see how it got its name. It's just like a Lydian mode with a ♭7th degree, like a dominant chord. Now that we know the scale's intervallic formula, we can build one from any root. Here's D Lydian dominant and a common two-octave fingering pattern:

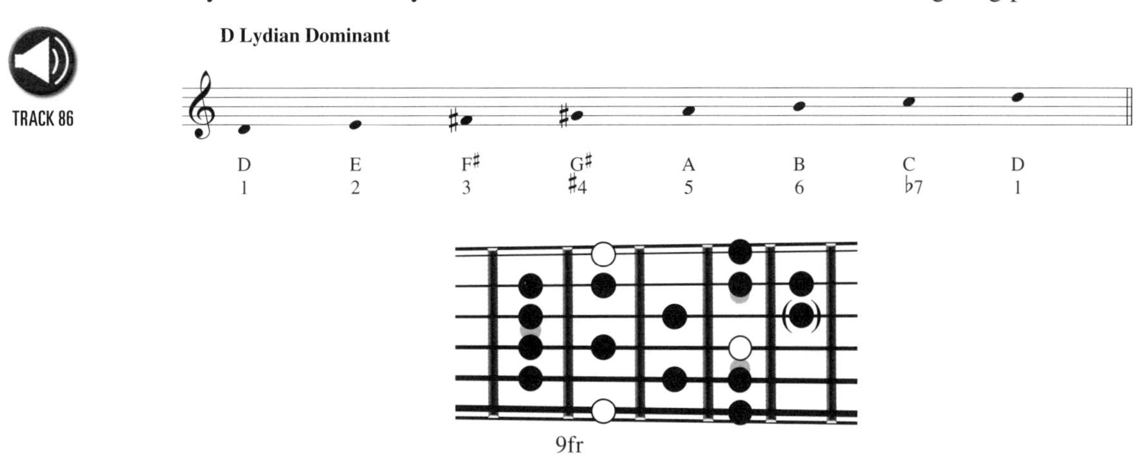

Lydian dominant is a great scale choice to use when you have a dominant chord built off a root note that doesn't appear in the tonic major scale. For example, let's say you have a I–vi–IV–♭VII progression in E, but the ♭VII chord appears as a D7 instead of just a D triad. Example 8 demonstrates this. We handle the first three chords with the E major scale and switch to D Lydian dominant over the D7 chord.

Example 8

In example 9, we have a I–♭III–IV–I progression in C: C–E♭9–F9–C. We begin with C major pentatonic over C, use E♭ Lydian dominant for the E♭9, and move to F Mixolydian over F9, resolving to the 3rd (E) of C the first time and the root the second time.

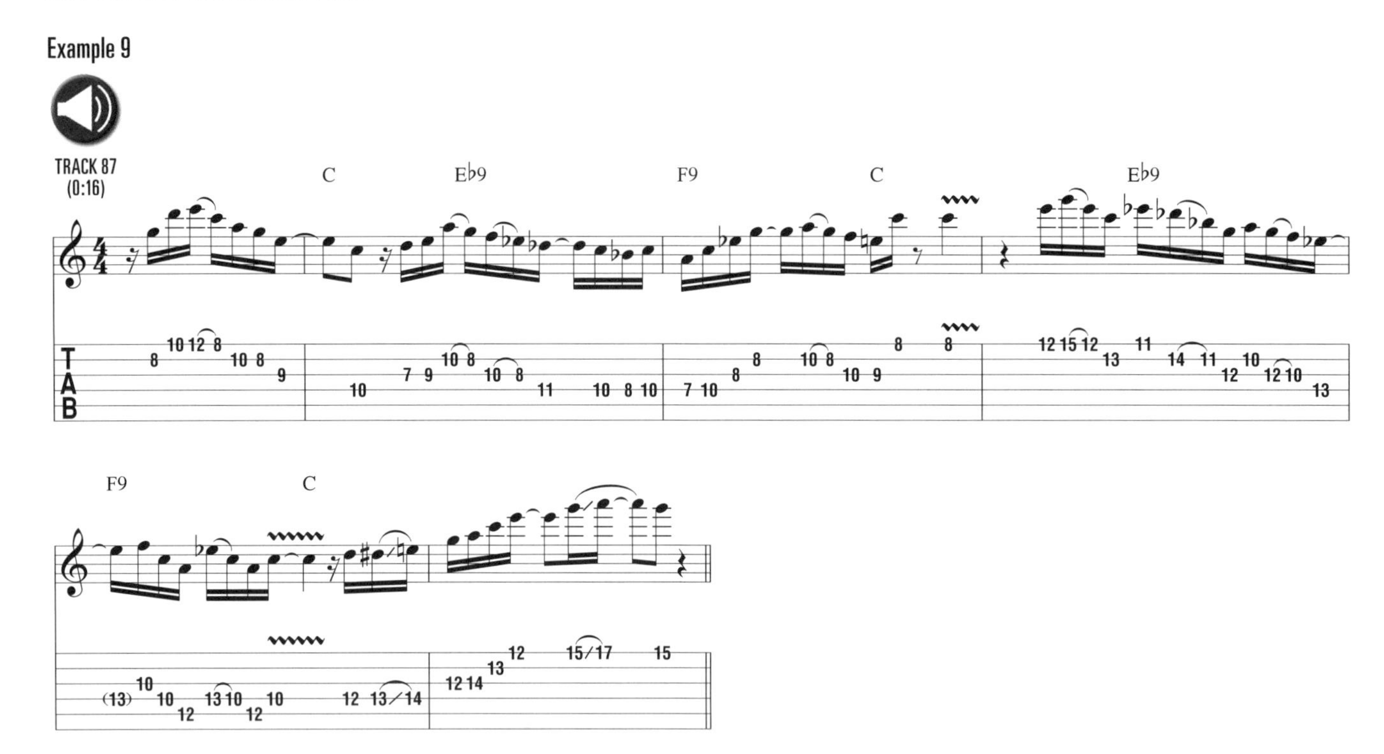

In minor keys, Lydian dominant has a place for non-diatonic chords as well. However, as opposed to major keys, these are often built from roots that lie within the scale.

Example 10 takes place over a i–iv–♭VI–V progression in A minor: Am7–Dm7–F7–E7. After using the A blues scale to handle the first two chords, we switch to F Lydian Dominant for the F7 chord and E Phrygian dominant for E7.

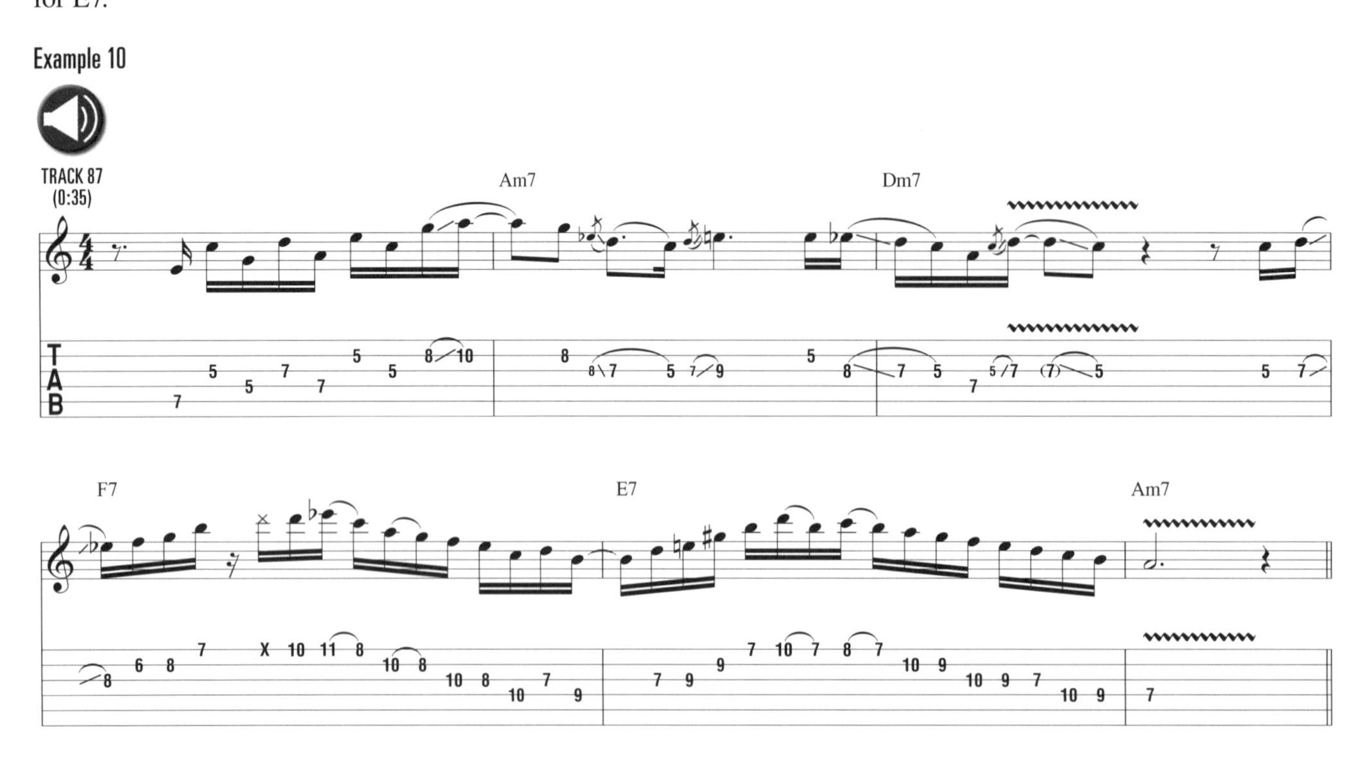

Here's a list of non-diatonic seventh chords in major and minor keys for which the matching Lydian dominant scale is commonly used:

Major key: ♭II, ♭III, ♭VI, and ♭VII.

Minor key: ♭II, IV, and ♭VI.

Application 3: Getting Altered Sounds

Our final application of the melodic minor scale deals with getting altered sounds. An *altered* dominant chord is one in which the 5th and/or 9th (if the 9th extension is present) have been either raised or lowered by a half step. Let's look at a typical C9 voicing:

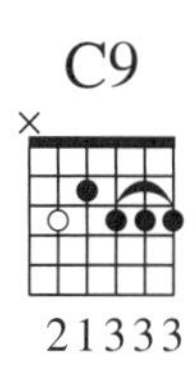

This chord is voiced, low to high, 1–3–♭7–9–5. If we raise the 5th on top by a half step, we get an altered chord; in this case, it's a C9♯5:

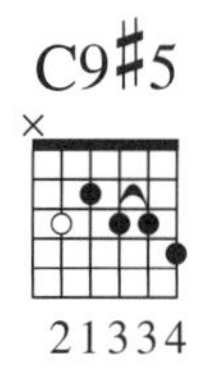

If we look at all the possibilities of altering the 9th and/or 5th of this C9 chord, we'll end up with eight altogether. In the first four chords, either the 5th or the 9th is altered. In the last four, both the 5th and the 9th are altered.

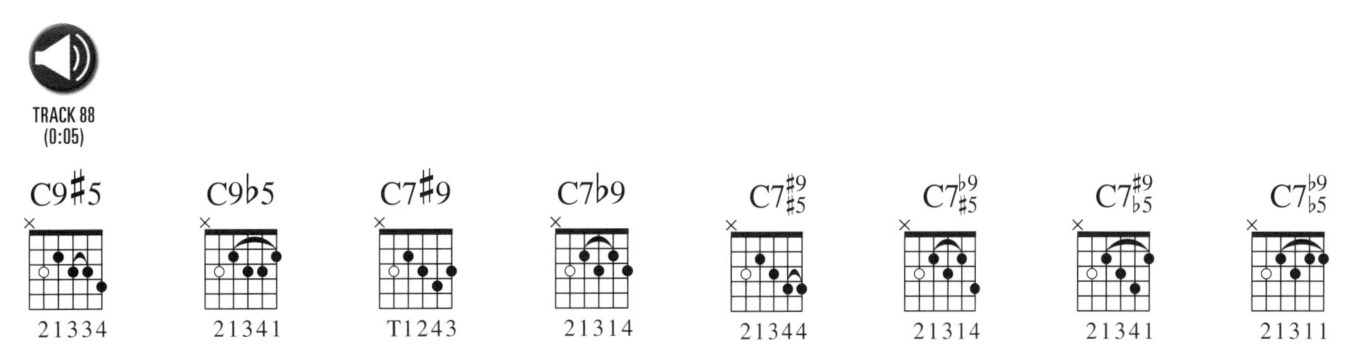

We started with a ninth chord to show all these possible alterations, but you can also alter the 5ths of seventh chords, resulting in 7♯5 or 7♭5 chords. Needless to say, these are all non-diatonic chords that need special scale treatment, and the modes of the melodic minor scale are especially helpful in this regard.

LYDIAN DOMINANT

Another use for Lydian dominant is on a functioning dominant chord that resolves to a major chord, such as the V chord of a major key. In the key of C, the V chord would be G7. If this were to be changed to a G7♭5 chord (sometimes notated as G7♯11), Lydian dominant would be a perfect fit. In fact, you can play Lydian dominant over an unaltered V chord in a major key if you just want to get a different sound. The dominant chord with a ♭5 is just tailor-made for the scale because of its ♯4th (same note as ♭5th) degree.

Example 11 demonstrates this with a I–IV–V progression in C: C6–Fmaj7–G7♭5–C. (A *sixth chord* is simply a major triad with an added 6th tone; C6 is spelled C–E–G–A.) After using the C major scale for C6 and Fmaj7, we use G Lydian dominant over the G7♭5 chord.

Example 11

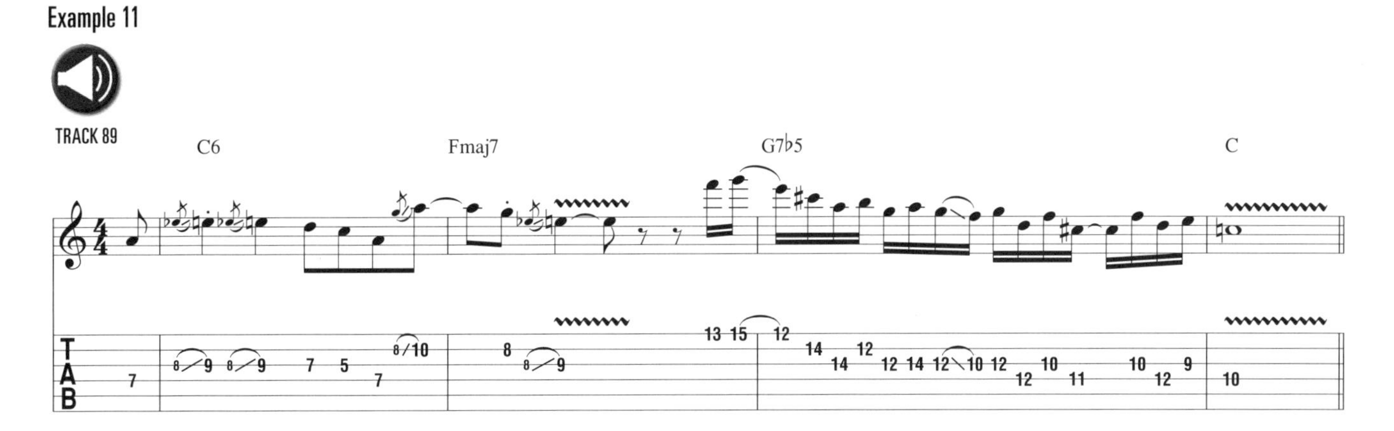

SUPER LOCRIAN

Another useful mode of the melodic minor is known as *Super Locrian*. This is the seventh mode of melodic minor. If we have a C melodic minor scale, for instance, the seventh mode would be B Super Locrian.

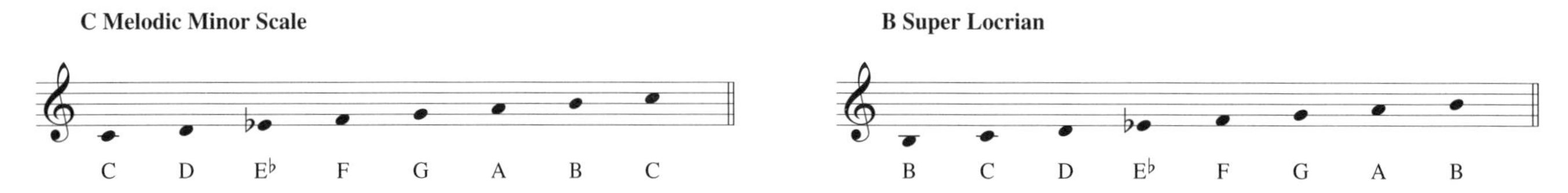

Its scale formula is 1–♭2–♭3–3–♯4–♯5–♭7. You may also see this called the *altered scale* or the *half- diminished/ half-whole tone scale*. This is the scale of choice when playing over a functioning (i.e., it resolves up a 4th) altered dominant chord—specifically one with an altered 5th and 9th, such as a 7♭9♯5 or a 7♯9♭5. Here's a common two-octave fingering pattern for C Super Locrian:

TRACK 90

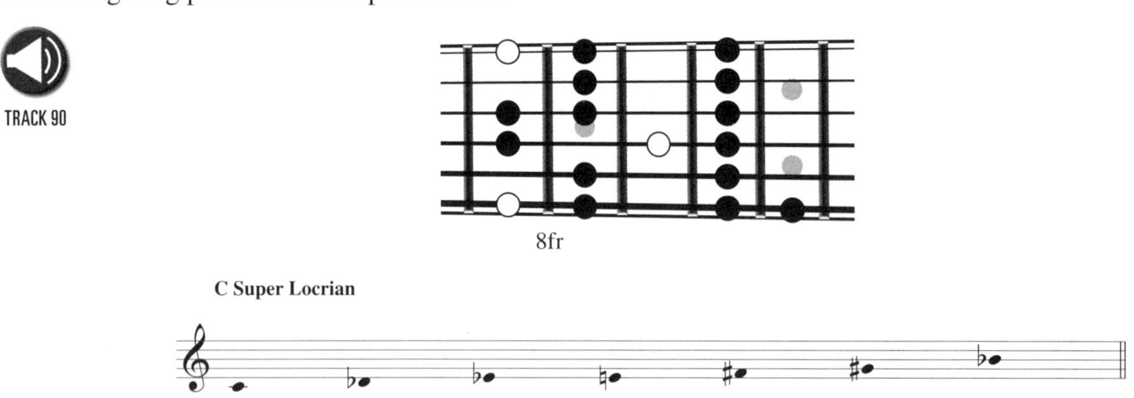

Example 12 is a funk-fusion groove in F with a I–V–I progression: F9–C7♯9♯5–F9. Over the F9, we're using the F composite blues scale (F major pentatonic and F blues combined), and over the C7 altered chord, we're playing C Super Locrian.

Example 12

TRACK 91

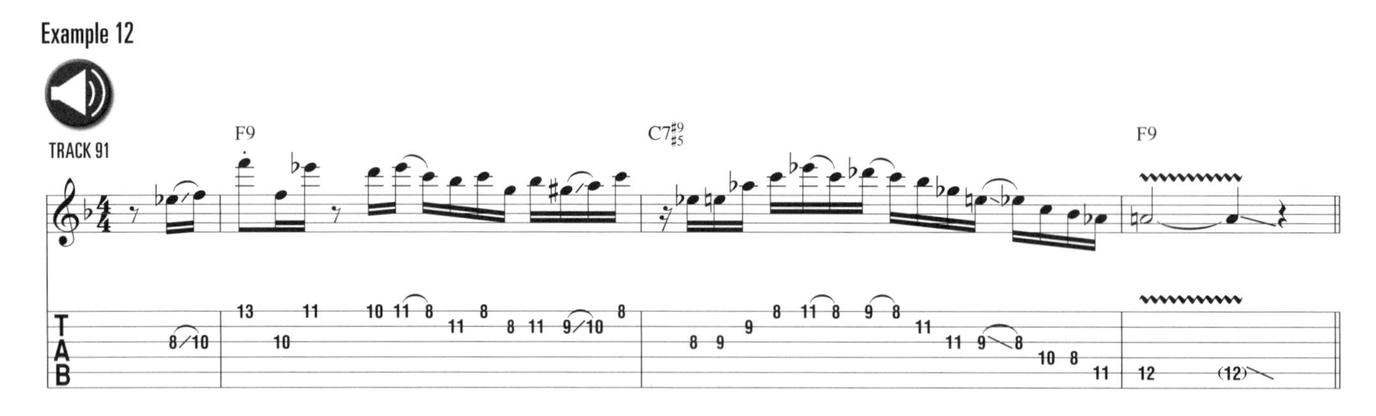

Example 13 is the same thing, only we're using a i–V–i progression: Fm9–C7♯9♯5–Fm9. We're playing F Dorian over the tonic Fm9 chord, and again using C Super Locrian over C7♯9♯5.

Example 13

TRACK 91 (0:13)

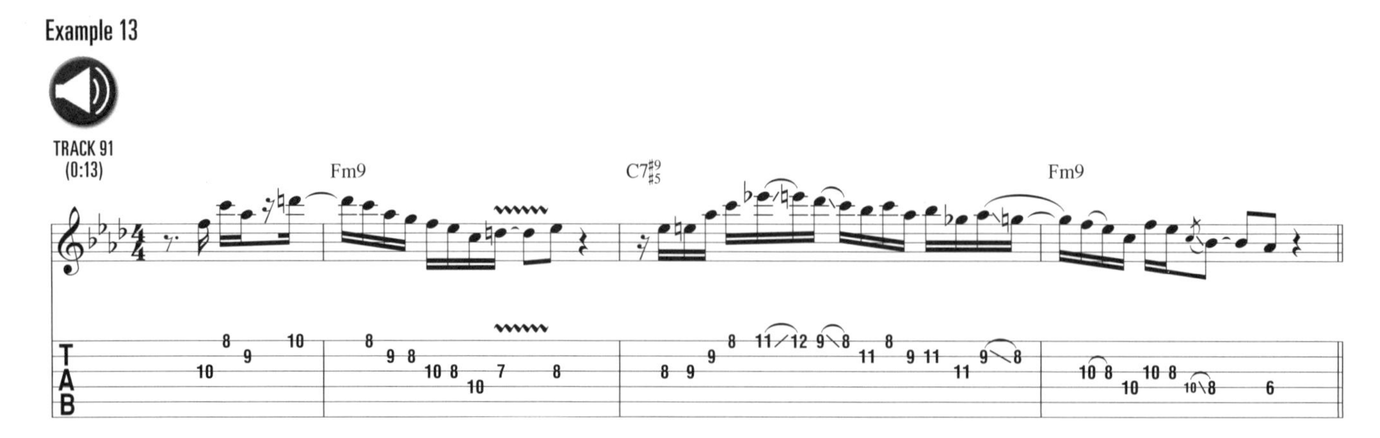

Things aren't always so neat and tidy in actual practice. This means that, for instance, sometimes players will use the Super Locrian scale, even over an unaltered dominant chord. In this case, you're simply superimposing an altered sound, similar to our earlier example of using Phrygian dominant over a minor chord. At moderate to fast tempos, this is usually not a problem. If you're playing a slow, pretty ballad, however, the clashing notes would be more conspicuous. Therefore, on slower tempo songs, it may be helpful to discuss with your band members how the dominant chords will be treated.

WHAT YOU LEARNED:

- You can mix the tonic major pentatonic and blues scales when playing over a major key progression to get a bluesier sound.
- The combination of the major pentatonic and blues scales is called the **composite blues scale**.
- Though the composite blues scale doesn't work as well in minor keys, you can **superimpose** a dominant sound over a minor chord that's resolving up a 4th by playing Phrygian dominant.
- The **melodic minor scale** (1–2–♭3–4–5–6–7) is like a minor scale with a raised 6th and 7th, and its modes are helpful in getting more useful sounds as a soloist. The melodic minor can be used over the tonic i chord for a brighter sound.
- The fourth mode of melodic minor, **Lydian dominant**, can be used for playing over non-diatonic seventh chords in major and minor keys.
- An **altered dominant** chord is one whose 5th and/or 9th has been raised or lowered by a half step.
- Lydian dominant and the seventh mode of the melodic minor, **Super Locrian**, can be used for playing over altered dominant chords and/or superimposing altered sounds over standard dominant chords.

CHAPTER 11: FULL SOLO EXAMPLES

It's time to put everything together into four full-length solos that are designed to illustrate just about all the concepts we've covered. Within each transcription, Roman numeral analysis is provided so you can see the harmony at work. Just below each example's introduction, each scale is noted measure-by-measure, along with any specific chord/scale theory concept, if applicable. If any of these concepts are foggy, the page numbers are supplied so you can go back and refresh your memory.

Example 1 is a 12-bar blues in A. I've packed a bunch of different strategies in this one, so be sure you're familiar with everything that's being used and why.

Meas. 1: A maj. pent. (pg. 63)
Meas. 2: D Mixolydian (pg. 63)
Meas. 3–4: A Mixolydian (pg. 63)
Meas. 5: D maj. pent. (pg. 63)
Meas. 6: A blues (pg. 65)
Meas. 7: A Mixolydian (pg. 63)
Meas. 8: A comp. blues (pg. 74)
Meas. 9: A maj. pent. (pg. 67)
Meas. 10: D Mixolydian (pg. 63)
Meas. 11–12: A comp. blues (pg. 74)

Example 1

TRACK 92

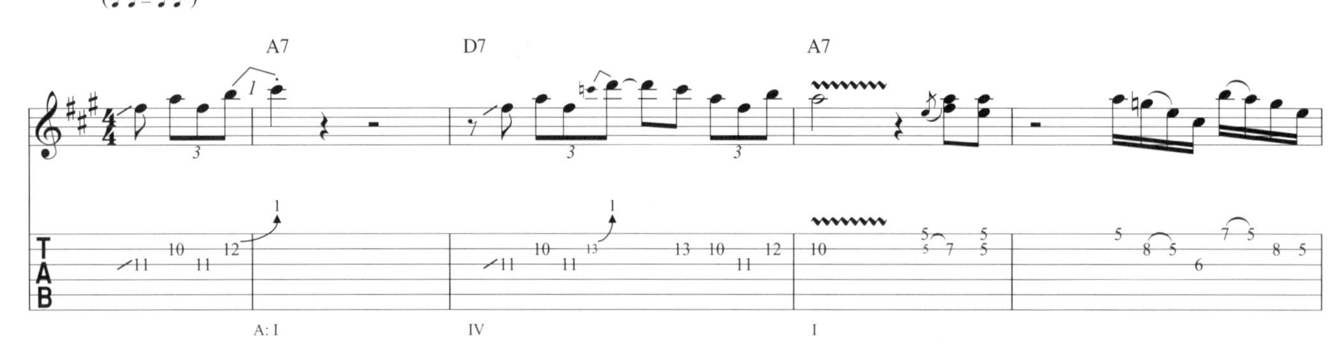

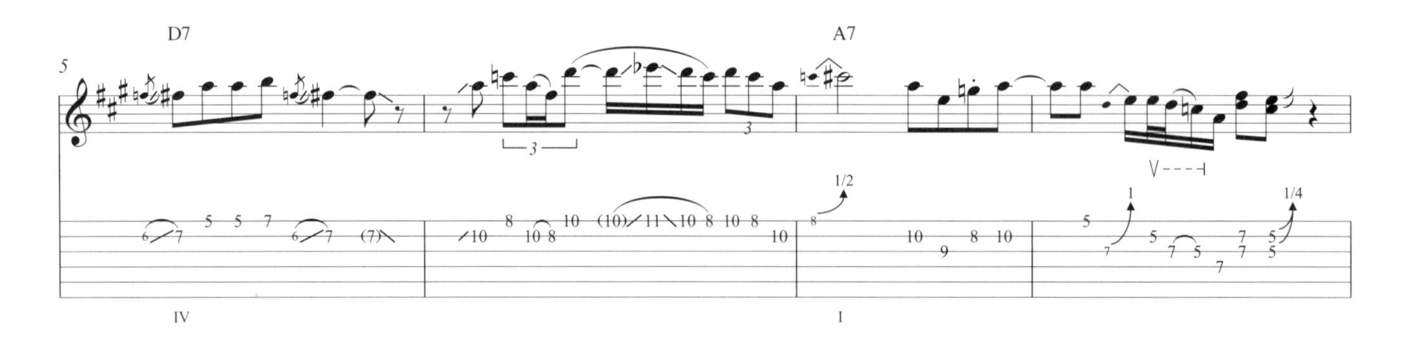

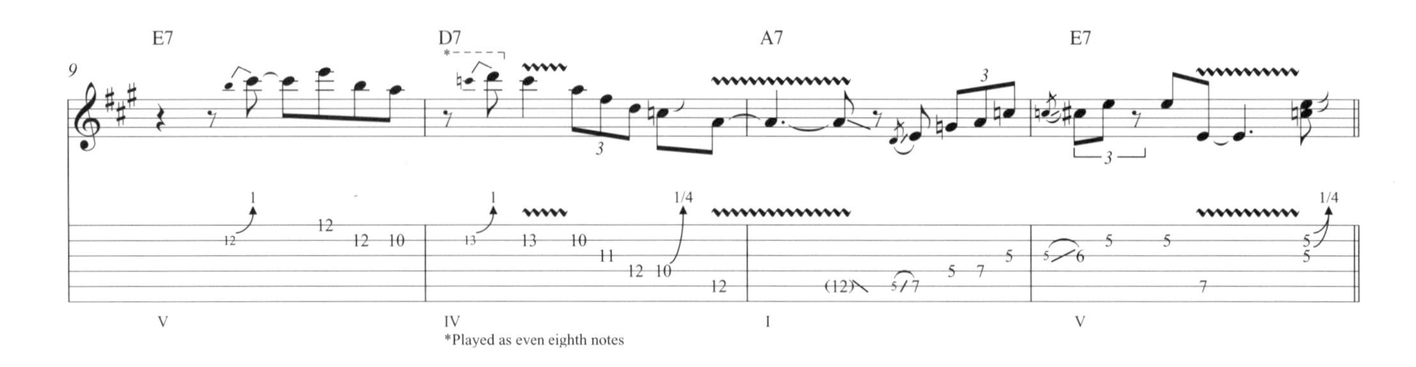

Example 2 is a rock tune in the key of C. We've got several different non-diatonic chords sprinkled throughout, over which we make use of different scales.

Meas. 1–2: C Mixolydian (pg. 42)
Meas. 3: F Mixolydian (pg. 68)
Meas. 4: C maj. pent. (pg. 25)
Meas. 5: C Mixolydian (pg. 48)
Meas. 6–8: C comp. blues (pg. 74)
Meas. 9: C min. pent. (pg. 48)
Meas. 10–11: C blues (pg. 73)
Meas. 12: C comp. blues (pg. 74)
Meas. 13: C min. pent. (pg. 48)
Meas. 14: C blues (pg. 73)
Meas. 15–17: G comp. blues (pg. 68, 74)

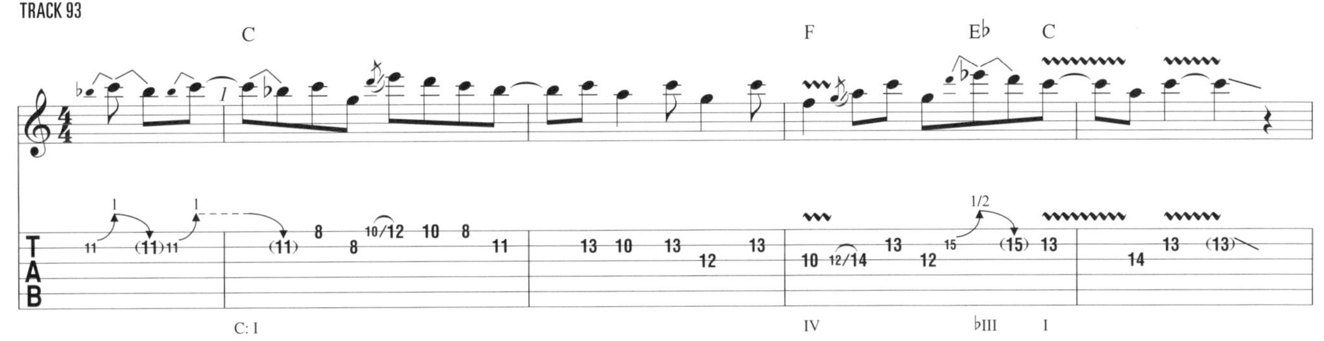

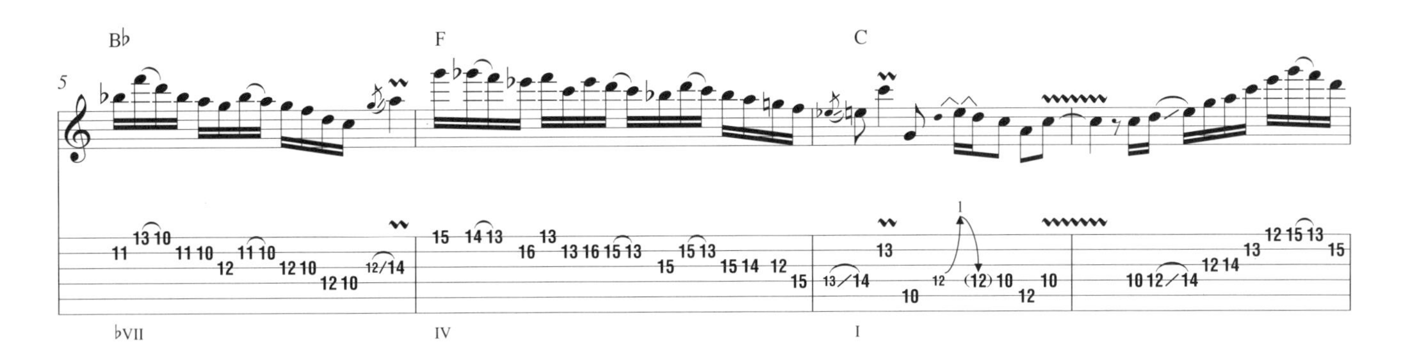

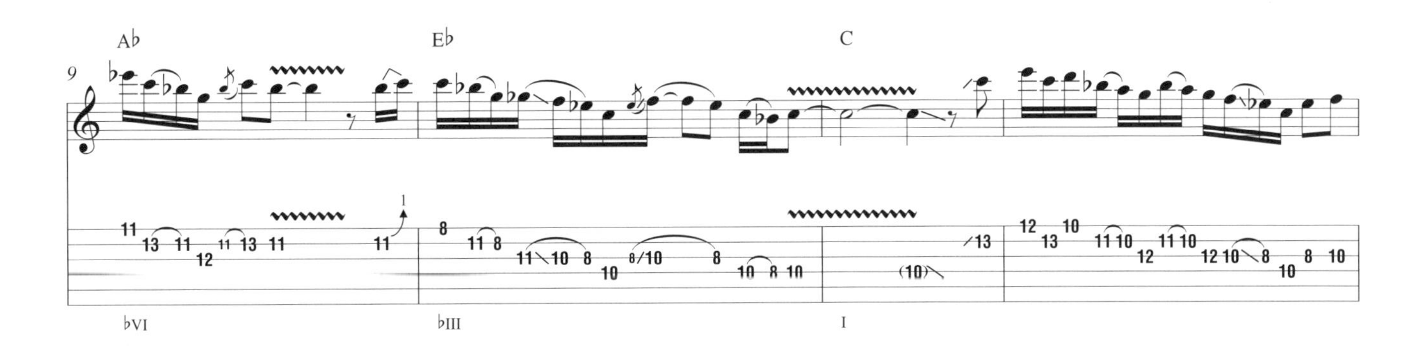

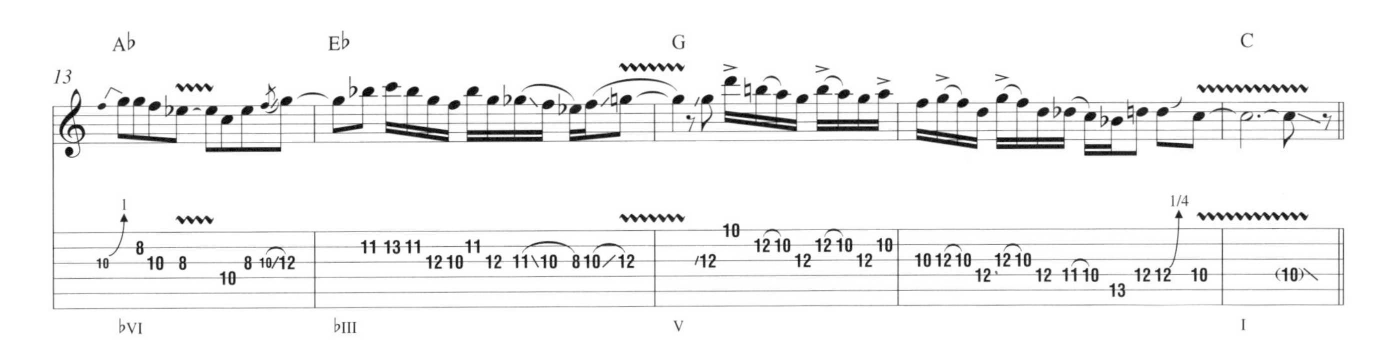

In example 3, we have a jazzy, bluesy progression in D minor that contains non-diatonic chords as well.

Meas. 1–3: D min. pent. (pg. 70)
Meas. 4: D Dorian (pg. 50)
Meas. 5–6: D Aeolian (pg. 28)
Meas. 7–8: D min. pent. (pg. 28)
Meas. 9–11: B♭ Mixolydian (pg. 44)
Meas. 12: F Lydian Dominant (pg. 79)
Meas. 13–14: B♭ Mixolydian (pg. 44)
Meas. 15: F maj. pent. (pg. 25)
Meas. 16.5: D harm. min. (pg. 50)

Example 3

TRACK 94

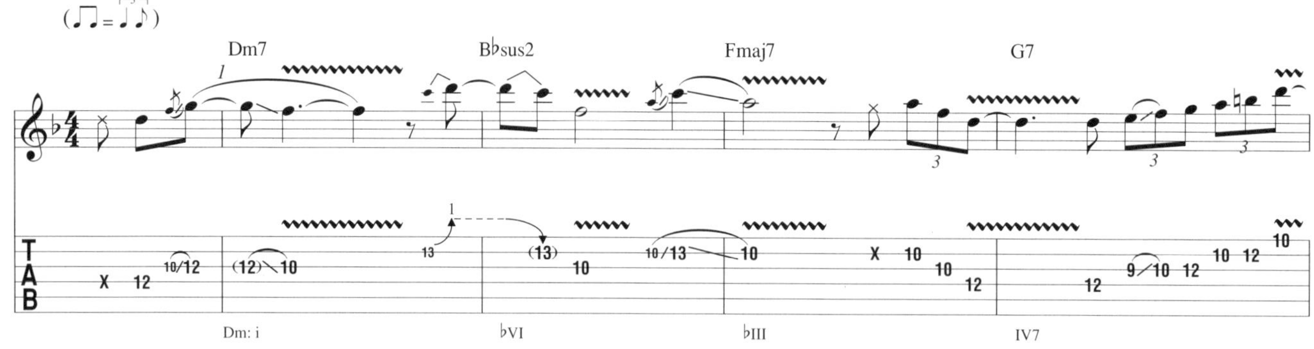

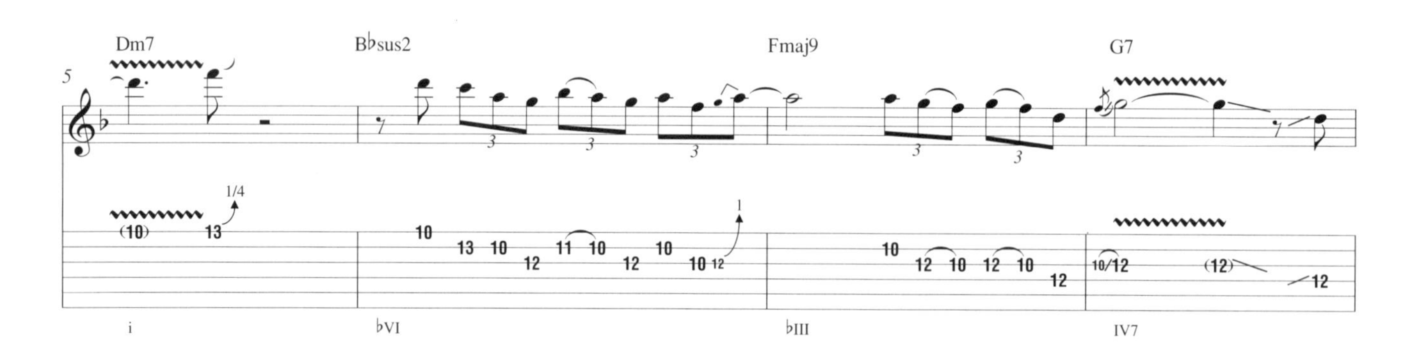

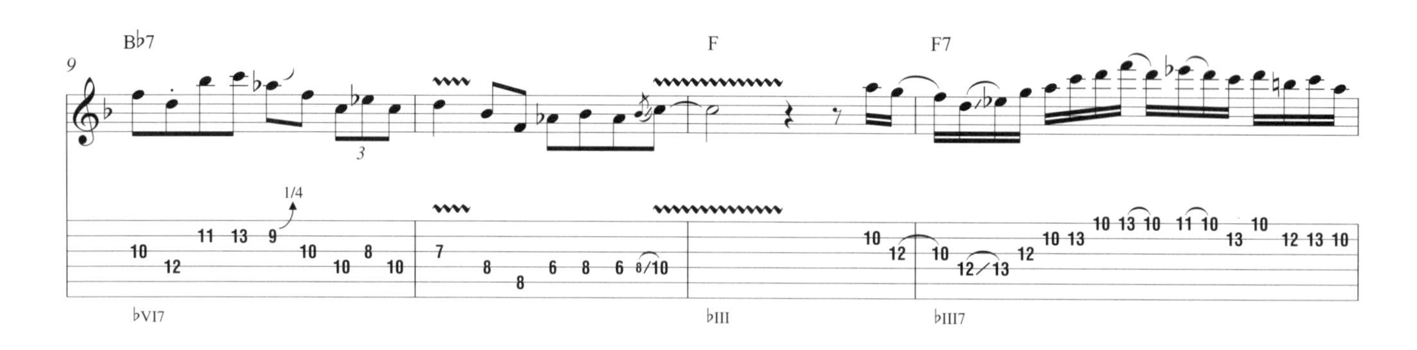

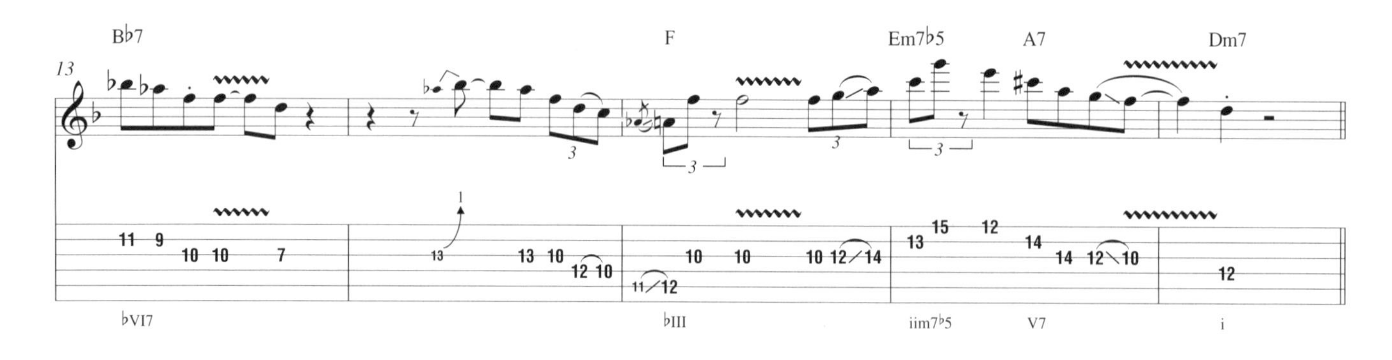

Finally, the funky example 4 begins with an extended vamp on a single dominant chord: F9. Afterwards, it unfolds into a Steely Dan-style progression filled with twists and turns. We basically change keys to E minor in measure 9 and remain there until measure 13, where the B♭maj7 chord begins to guide us back to the home key of F.

Meas. 1: F maj. pent. (pg. 63)
Meas. 2: F Mixolydian (pg. 63)
Meas. 3–8: F comp. blues (pg. 74)
Meas. 9: E blues (pg. 70)
Meas. 10: E mel. min. (pg. 76)
Meas. 11–12.5: E blues (pg. 70)
Meas. 12.5: C Mixolydian (pg. 63)
Meas. 13: F Ionian (pg. 30)
Meas. 14: D mel. min. (pg. 76)
Meas. 15–16.5: F maj. pent. (pg. 25)
Meas. 16.5: C Super Locrian (pg. 80)
Meas. 17: F Mixolydian (pg. 63)

Example 4

TRACK 95

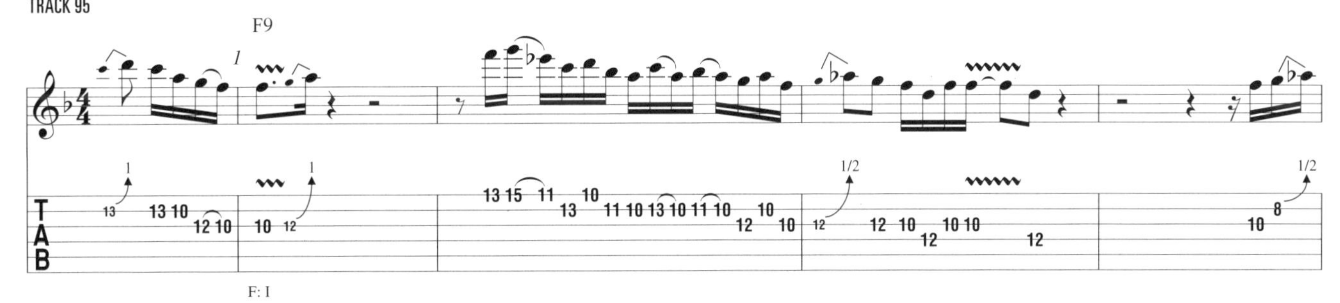

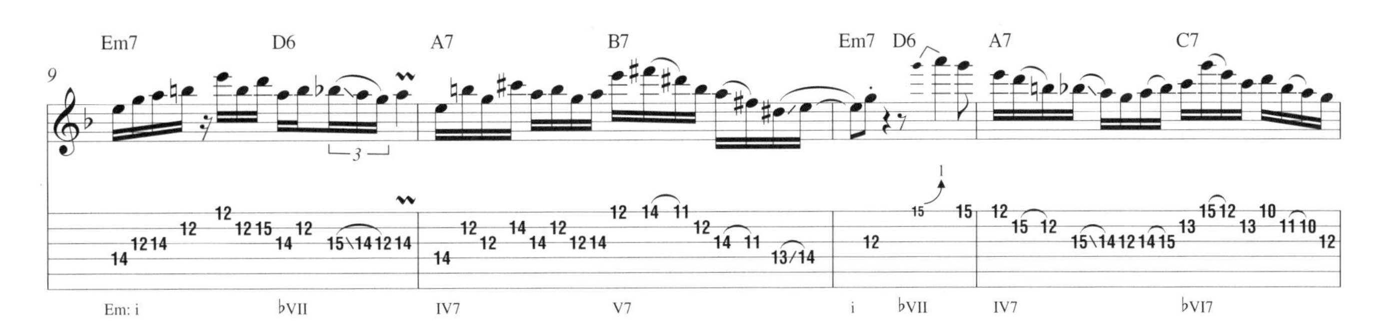

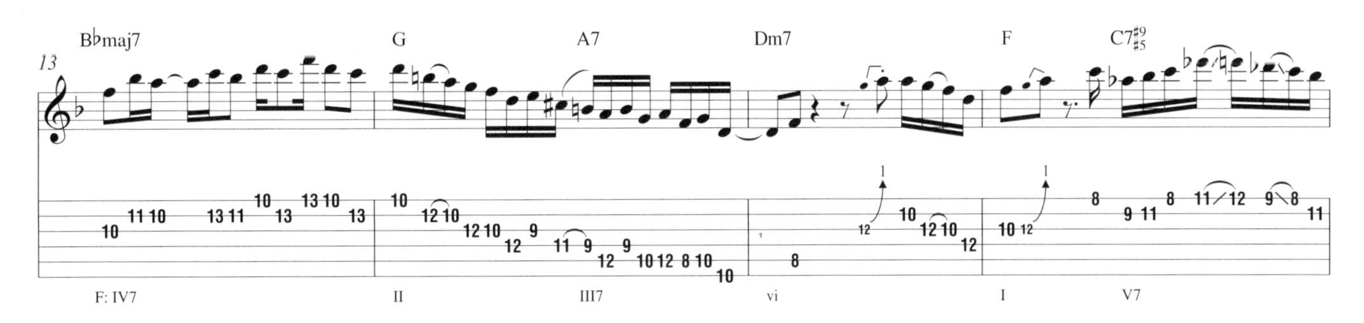

CONCLUSION

Well, that wraps it up. We've come a long way and covered a bunch of ground, so be sure to re-read the sections that are a little foggy. There's a lot of information to absorb, and it will probably take a good while before you're able to assimilate it all and apply it at the drop of a hat. Familiarity with these concepts comes with practice and experience. Keep your ears open and always *listen* to what you play. Many times, this act alone makes the difference between something musical and something mechanical.

There's still much more to learn, which is what makes the study of music such a rewarding journey. Here are some recommendations for further study:

- **Learn Melodies:** This is a big one. Lots of people don't realize it, but the simple act of learning a melody can do wonders for your improvising. It helps you make important scale/chord connections automatically, helps you keep your place within the form, and gives you ideas with which to play around.
- **Sing!:** Lots of people say they can't sing. Certainly some people have more of a natural gift for it than others. But for a musician, there's simply no better way to train your ear than to practice singing what you play and vice versa. You'll learn to link your ear with your hands much quicker, in my opinion, and who knows ... you may end up enjoying it, and it will only make you more marketable as a player.
- **Listen to Other Instruments:** This is a great way to gather new ideas. The licks that a pianist plays, for instance, are idiomatic to that instrument. Learning a solo played by another instrument for the guitar can be an eye-opening (and ear-opening) experience.
- **Set Short-Term Goals:** Setting goals keeps you focused on improving and trying new things as opposed to falling into the same old predictable patterns.
- **Play with Other Musicians:** Interaction with other players is incredibly inspiring in many ways. And you'll pick up things from others simply because they have a different way of looking at music than you do.

Be sure to check out the appendixes that follow. All of the scales we looked at are shown in five different shapes each, covering the entire neck. There are also play-along tracks of common progressions and more. Good luck!

APPENDIX A: SCALE REFERENCE

This appendix contains all the scales covered in this book, presented with C as the root. Be sure to practice them in all keys.

> NOTE: The "Shape" numbers system used with these scales is not a standard in the guitar community; many people have their own way of organizing and cataloging scale shapes on the neck. This is just the method that makes sense to me. What I call "Shape 1," others may call "Shape 2" or another name altogether. This is why I've also included the chord form from which they're based, as this information can be agreed upon by everyone.

Here are the five moveable major chord forms on which these scale shapes are based. These are all derived from open chord forms, and are voiced with C as the root.

G-form

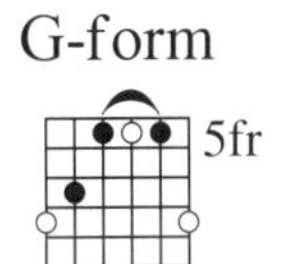

E-form

D-form

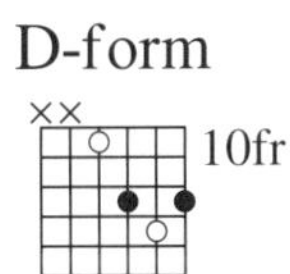

C-form

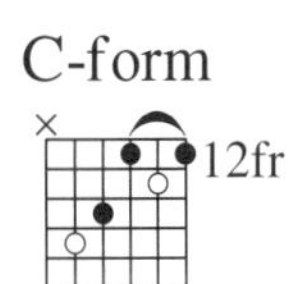

A-form

C MAJOR SCALE (IONIAN)

Shape 1 (G-form)

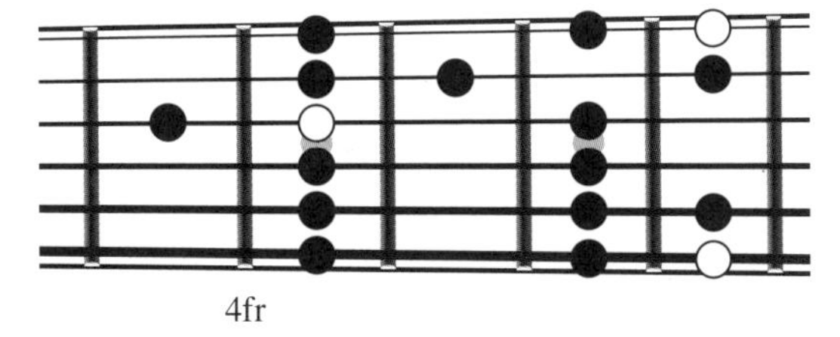

Shape 2 (E-form)

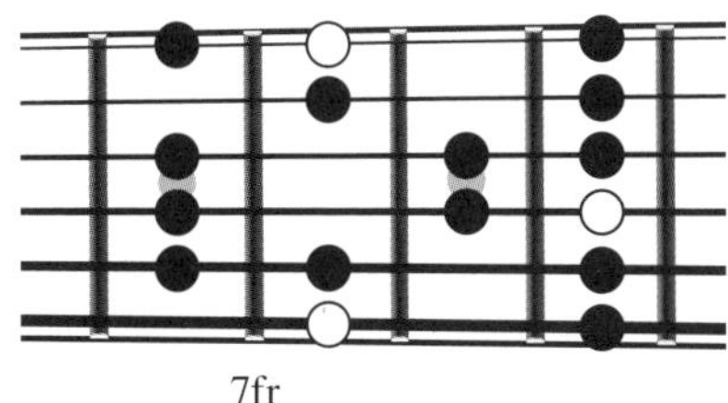

Shape 3 (D-form)

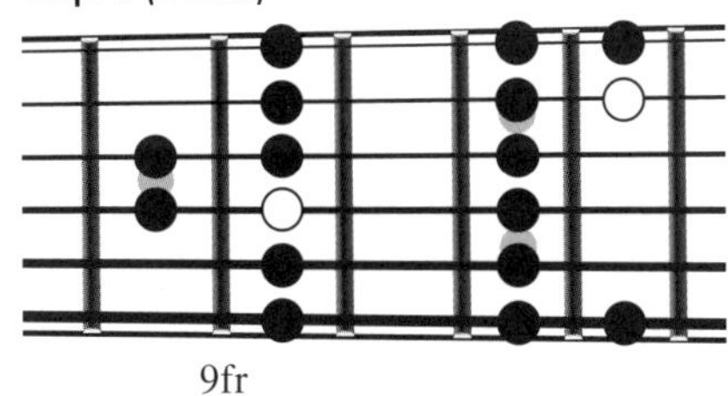

Shape 4 (C-form)

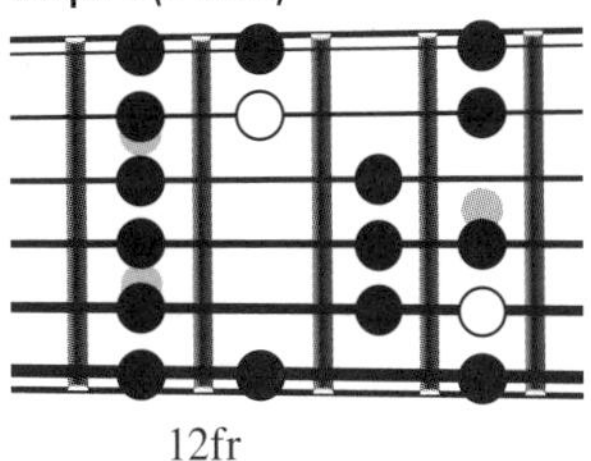

Shape 5 (A-form)

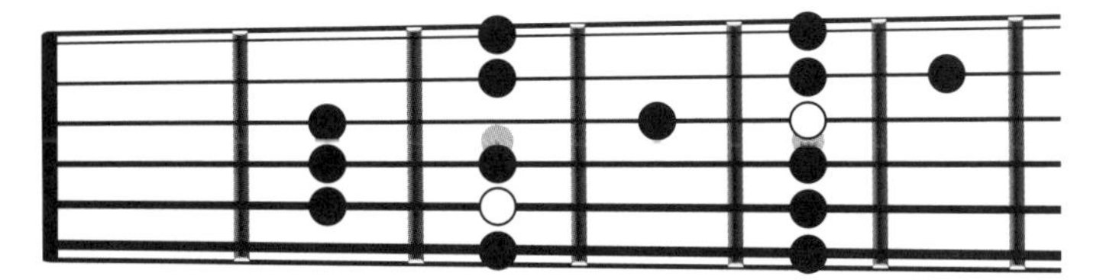

C MAJOR PENTATONIC SCALE

Shape 1 (G-form)

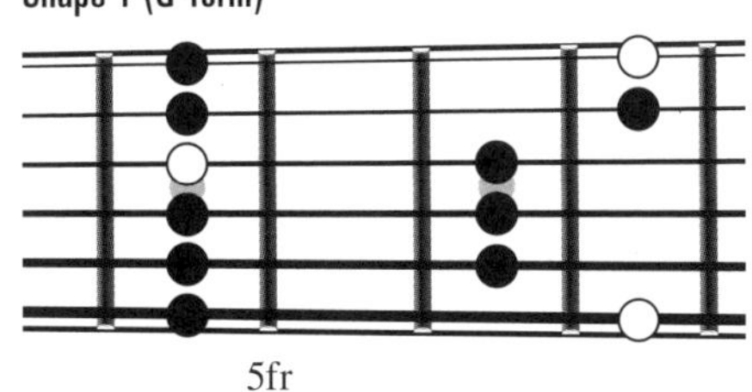

Shape 2 (E-form)

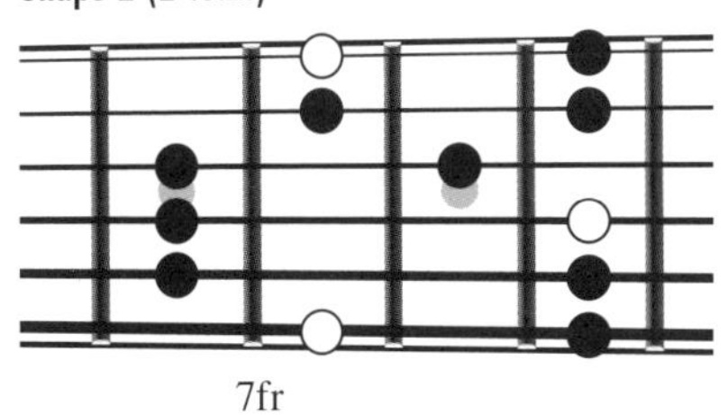

Shape 3 (D-form)

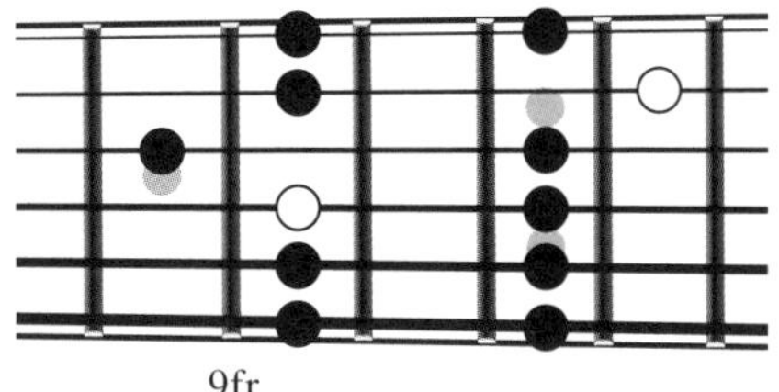

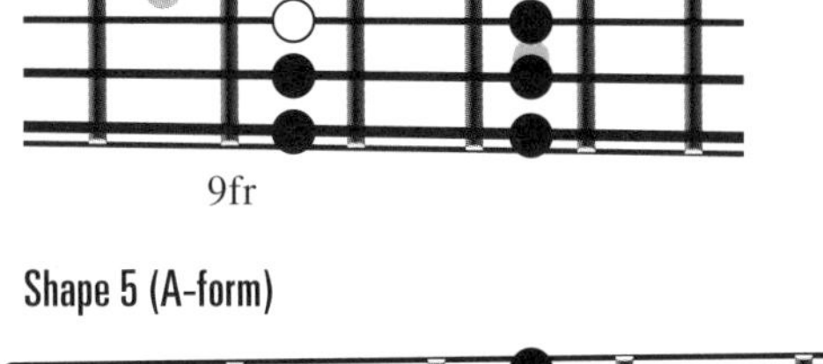

Shape 4 (C-form)

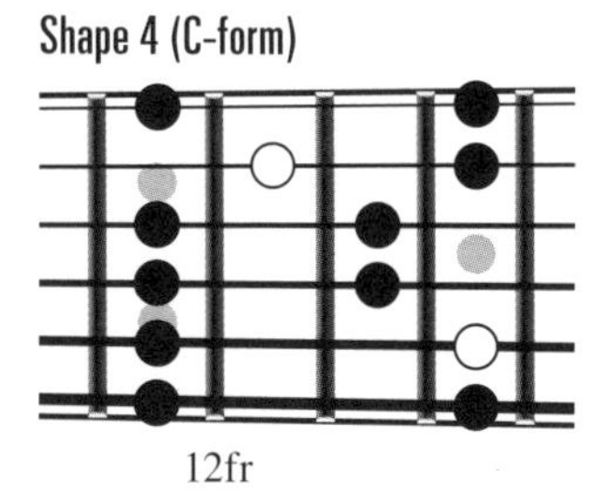

Shape 5 (A-form)

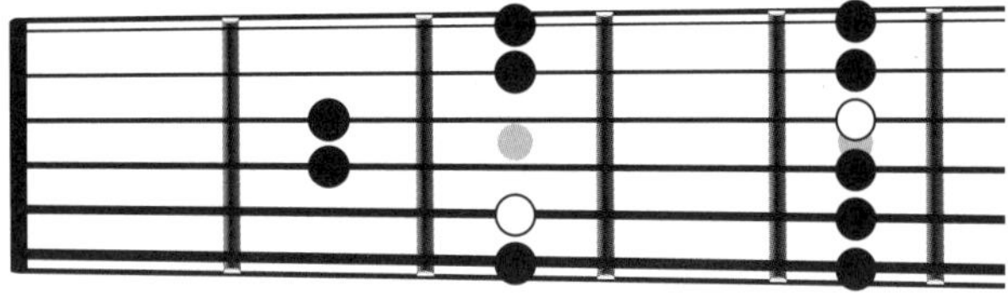

C MINOR SCALE (AEOLIAN)

Shape 1 (G-form)

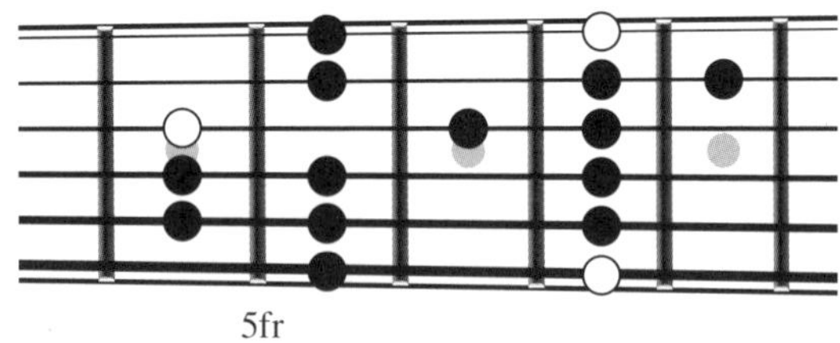

Shape 2 (E-form)

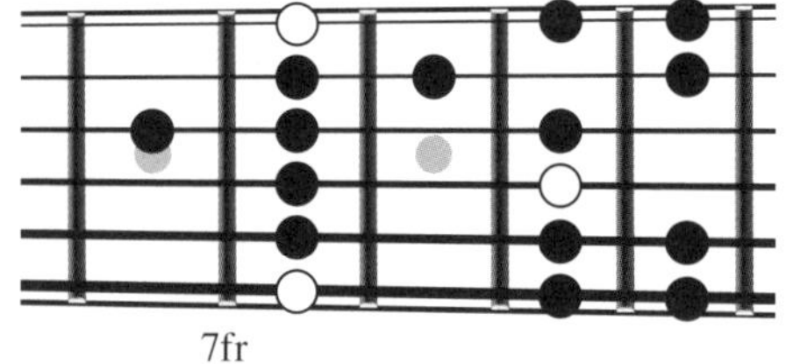

Shape 3 (D-form)

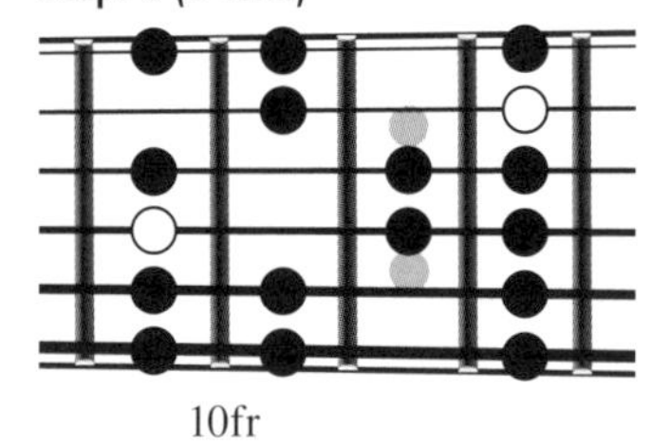

Shape 4 (C-form)

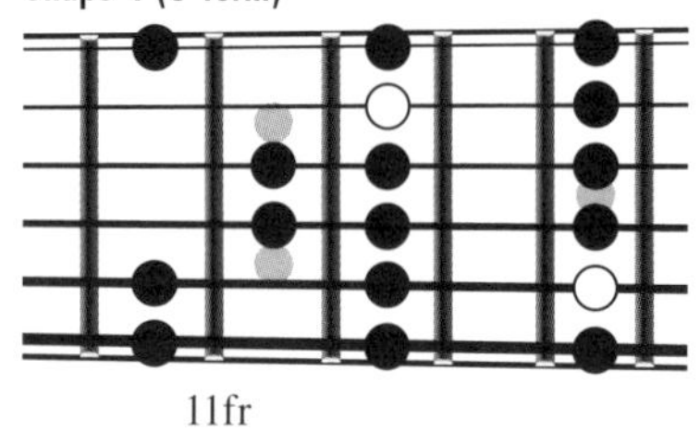

Shape 5 (A-form)

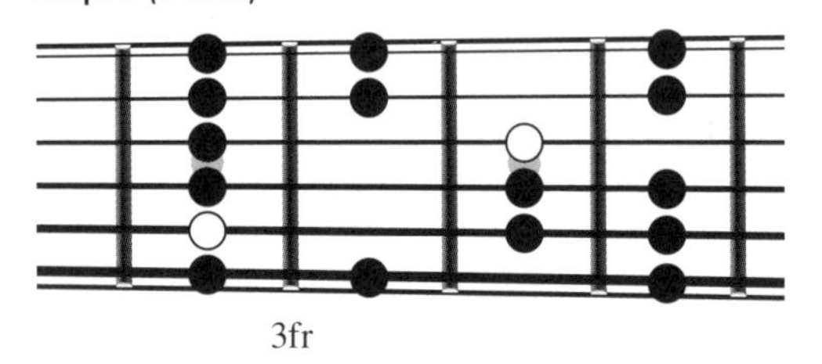

C MINOR PENTATONIC SCALE

Shape 1 (G-form)

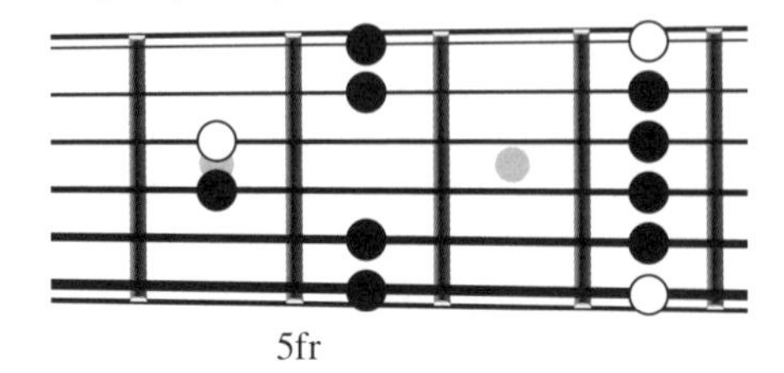

Shape 2 (E-form)

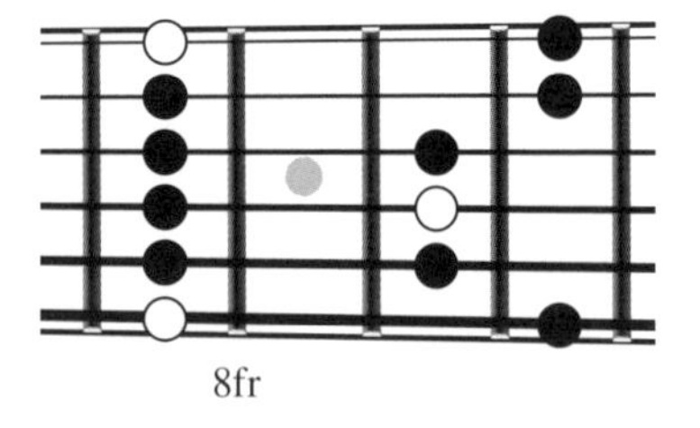

Shape 3 (D-form)

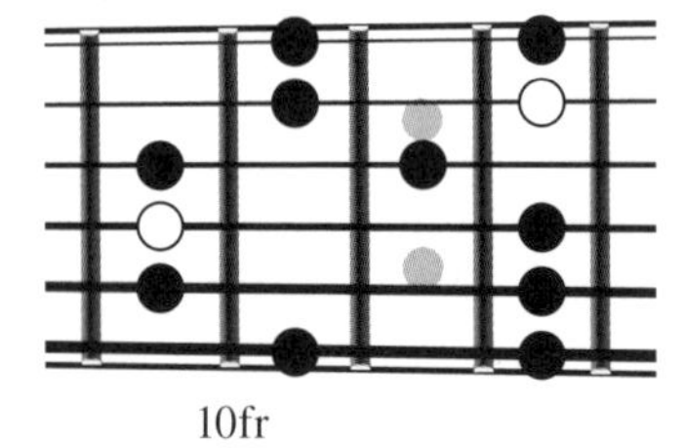

Shape 4 (C-form)

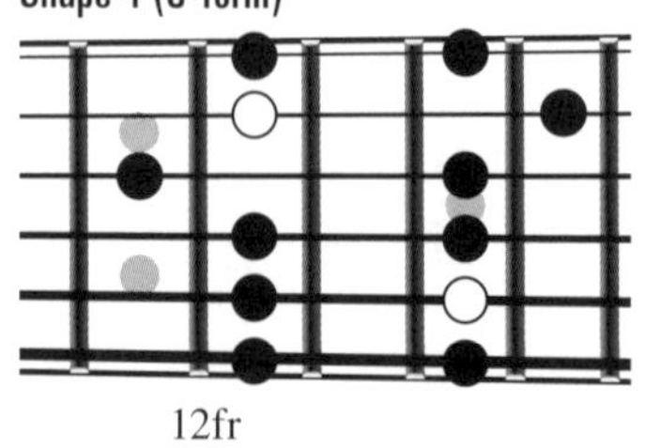

Shape 5 (A-form)

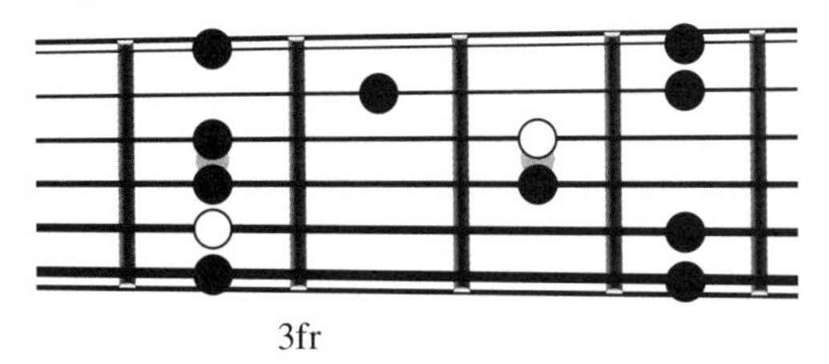

C BLUES SCALE

Shape 1 (G-form)

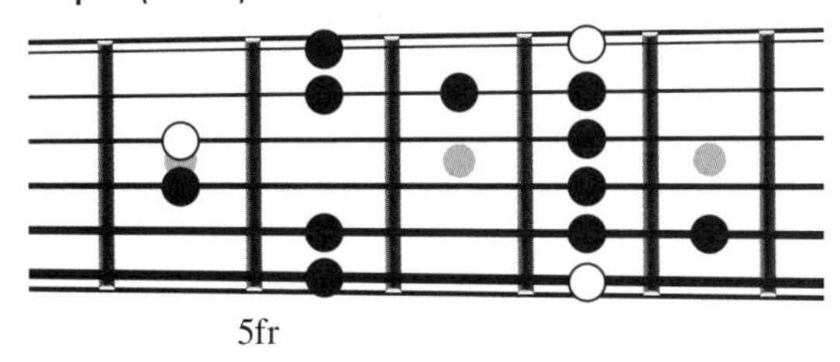

Shape 2 (E-form)

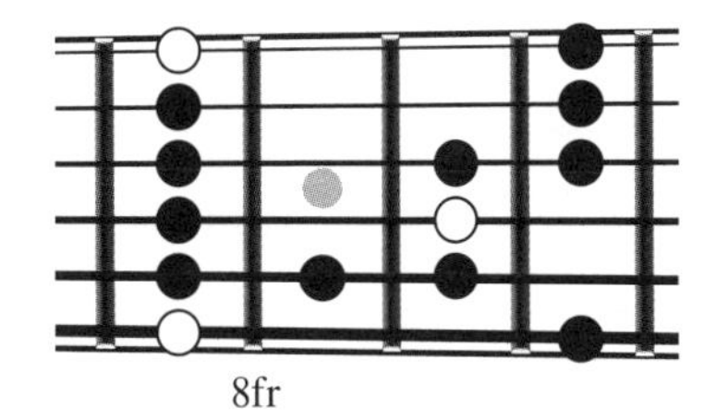

Shape 3 (D-form)

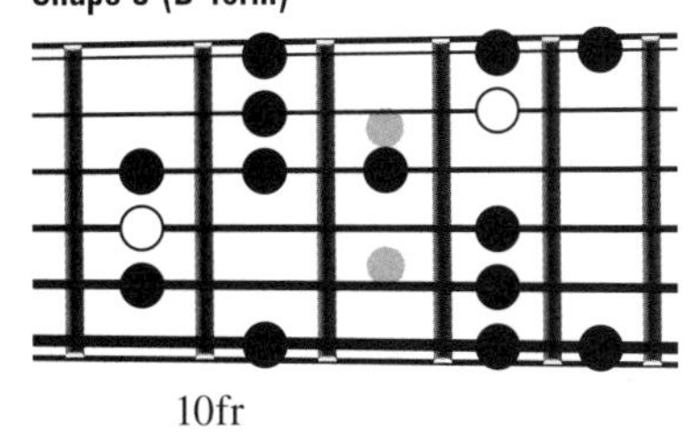

Shape 4 (C-form)

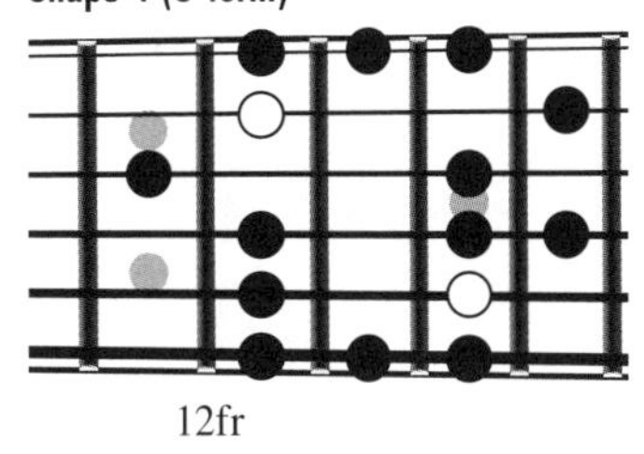

Shape 5 (A-form)

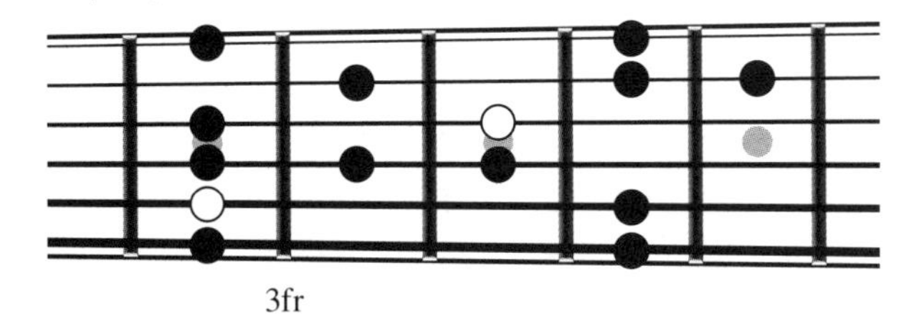

C DORIAN

Shape 1 (G-form)

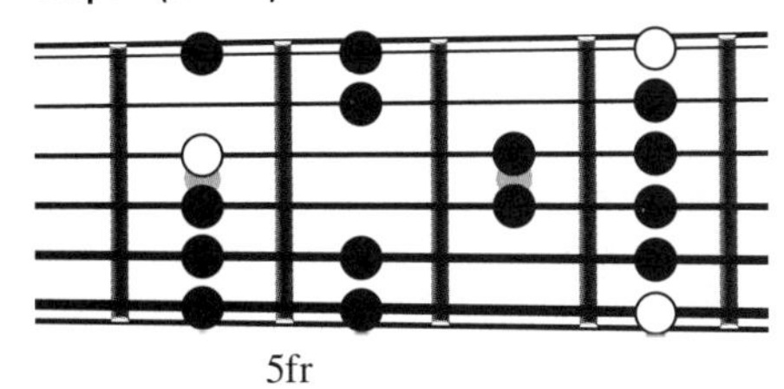

Shape 2 (E-form)

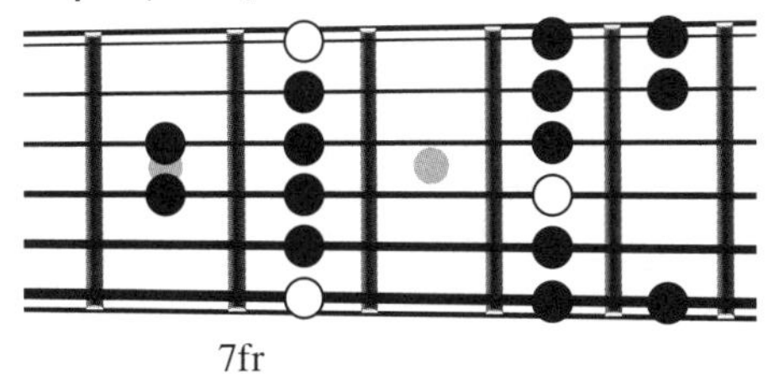

Shape 3 (D-form)

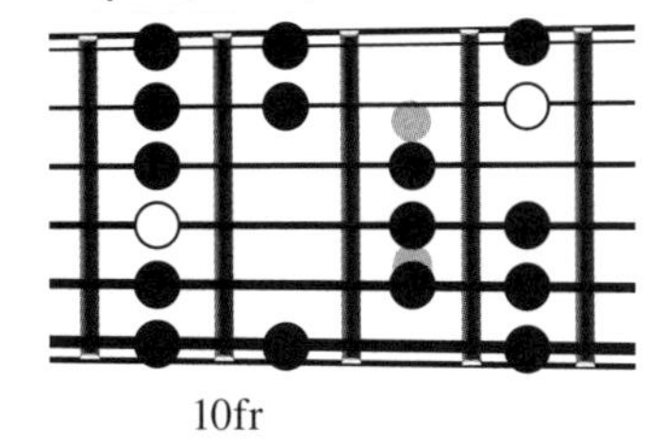

Shape 4 (C-form)

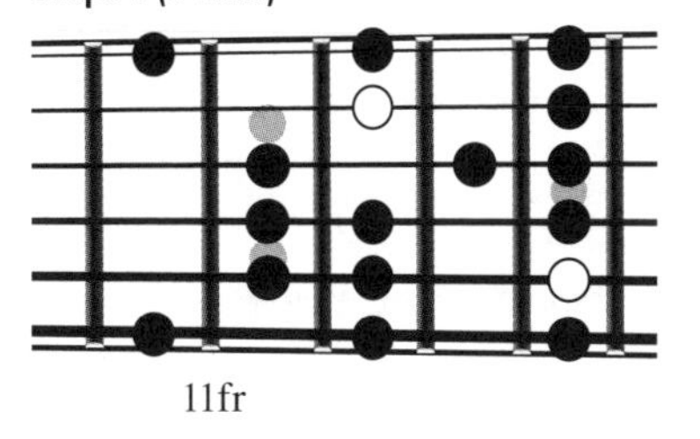

Shape 5 (A-form)

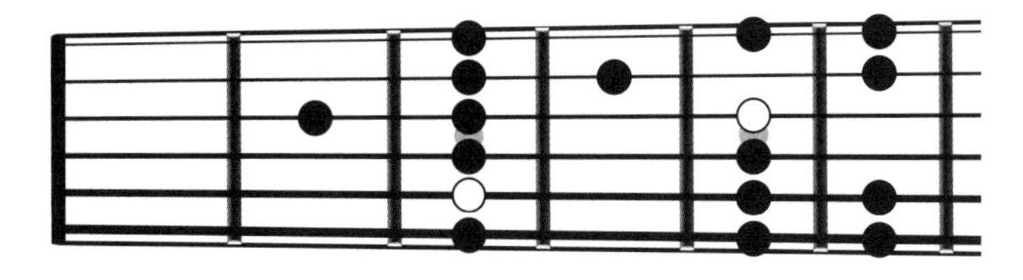

C PHRYGIAN

Shape 1 (G-form)

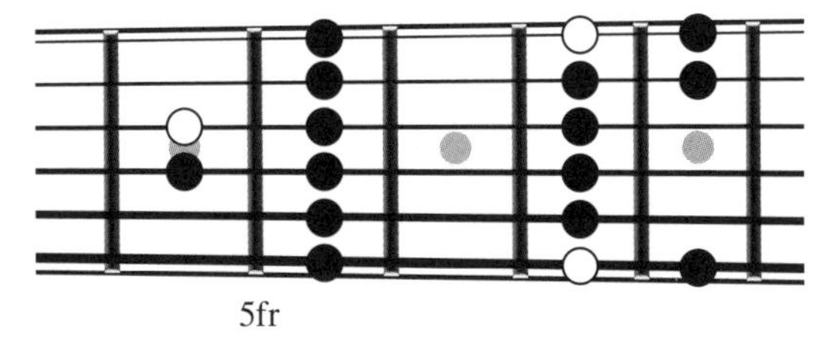

Shape 2 (E-form)

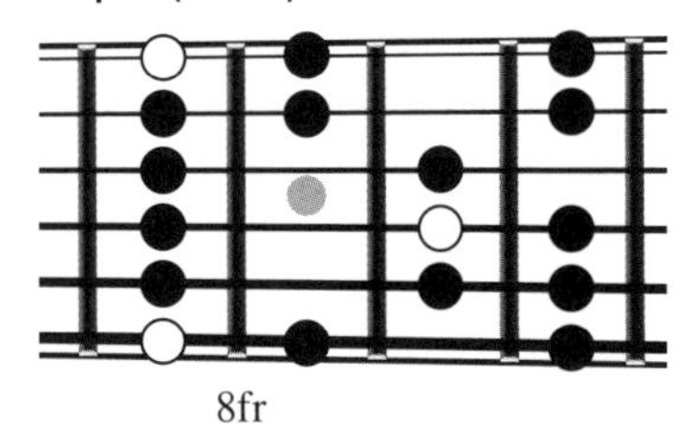

Shape 3 (D-form)

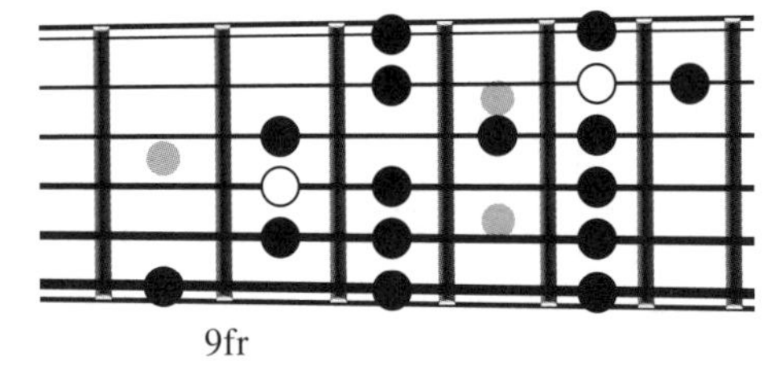

Shape 4 (C-form)

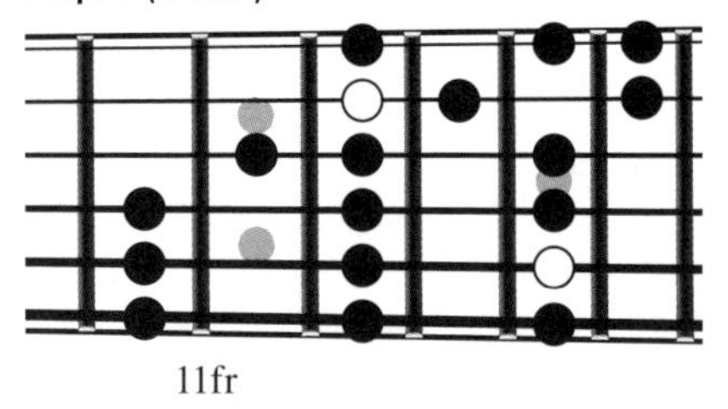

Shape 5 (A-form)

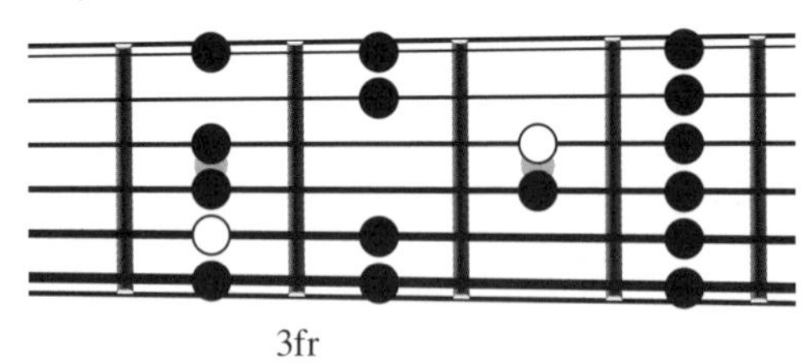

C LYDIAN

Shape 1 (G-form)

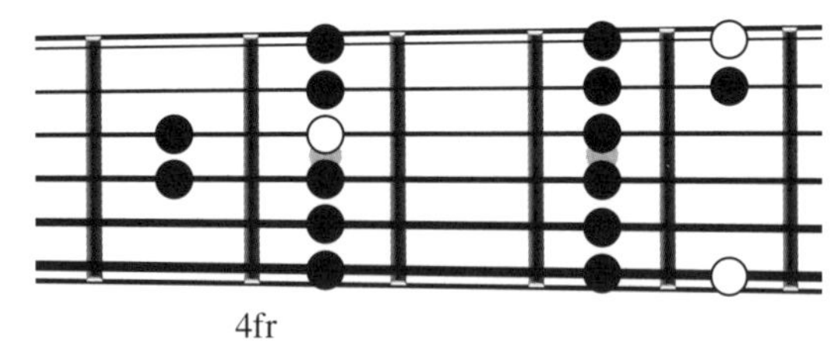

Shape 2 (E-form)

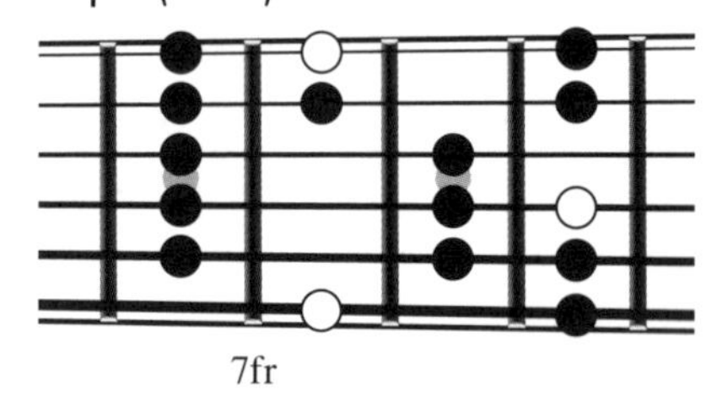

Shape 3 (D-form)

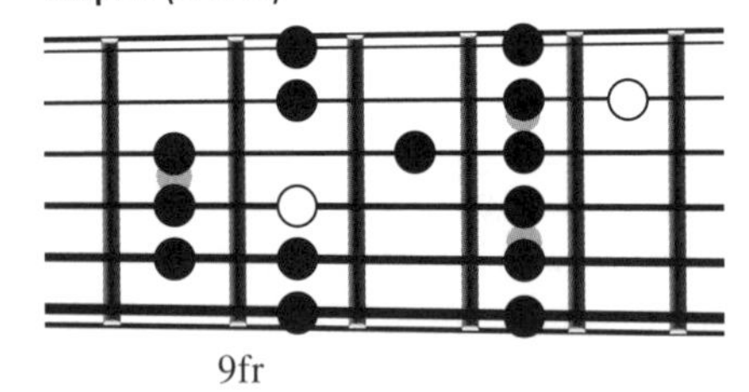

Shape 4 (C-form)

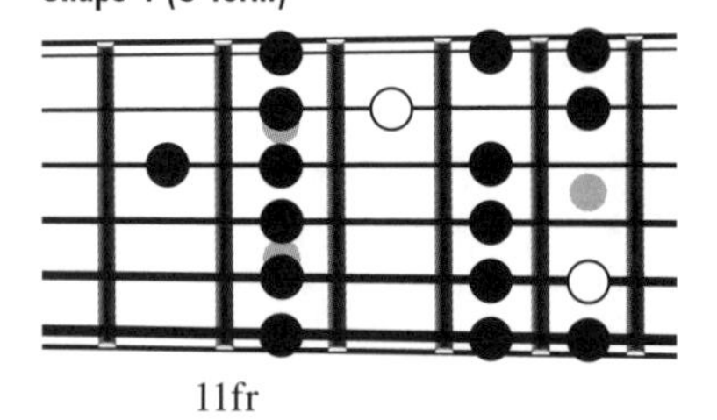

Shape 5 (A-form)

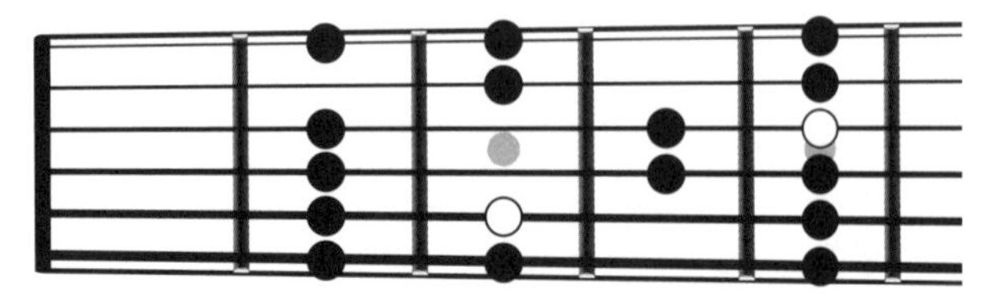

C MIXOLYDIAN

Shape 1 (G-form)

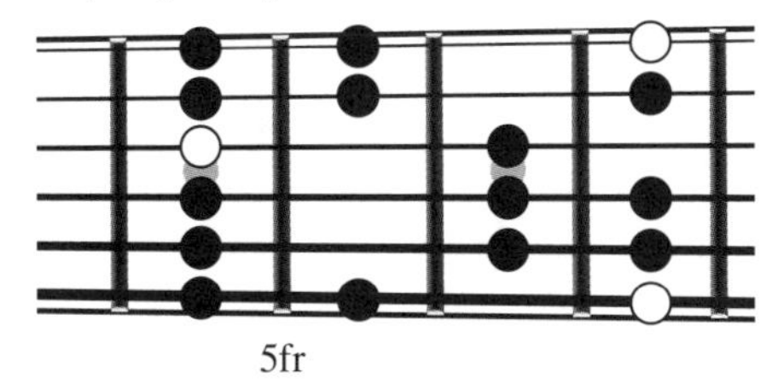

Shape 2 (E-form)

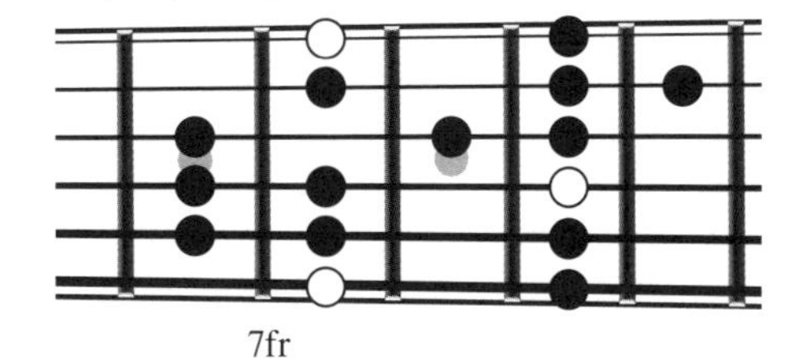

Shape 3 (D-form)

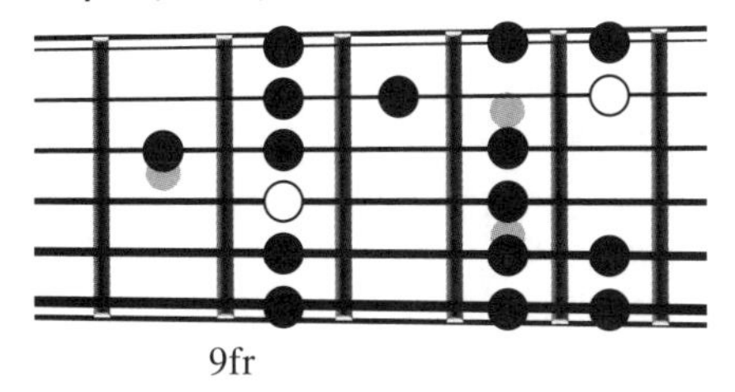

Shape 4 (C-form)

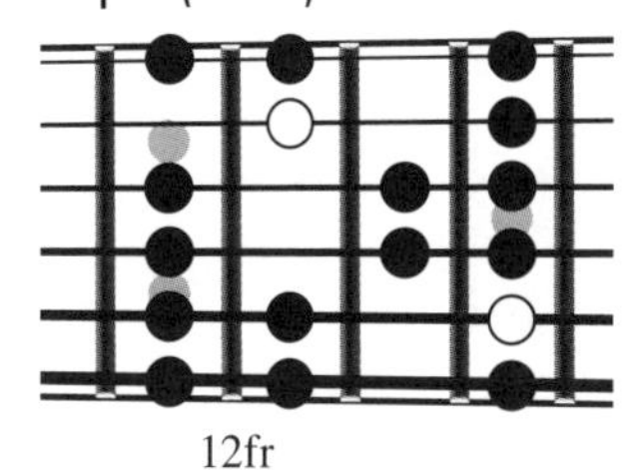

Shape 5 (A-form)

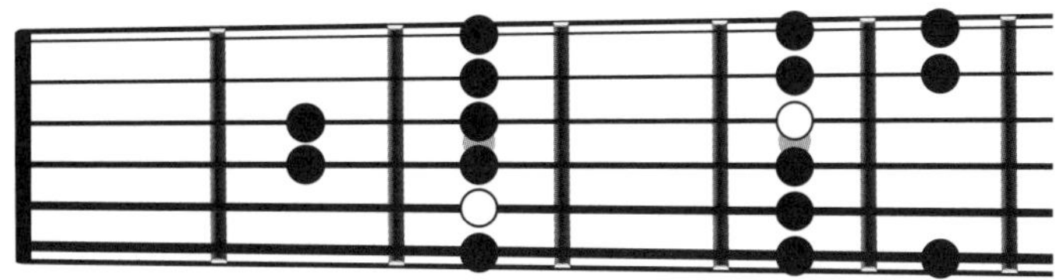

C LOCRIAN

Shape 1 (G-form)

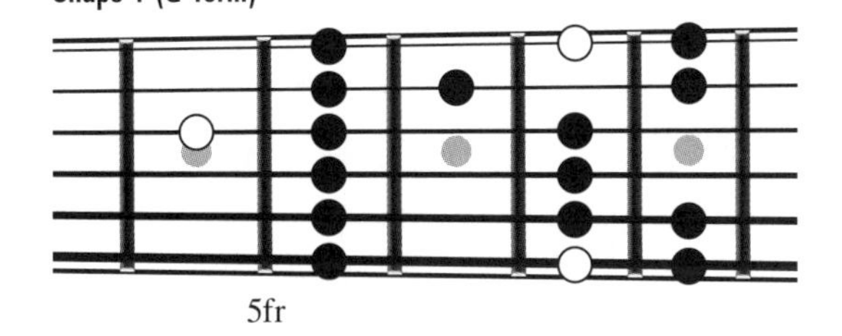

Shape 2 (E-form)

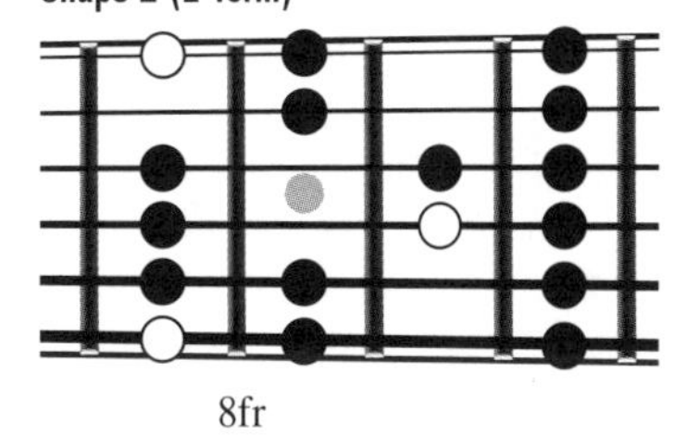

Shape 3 (D-form)

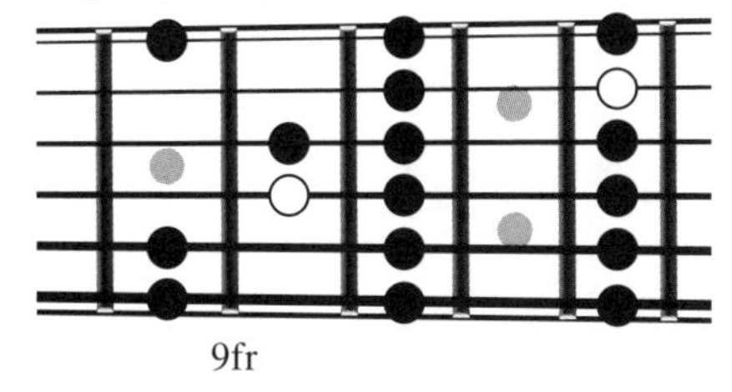

Shape 4 (C-form)

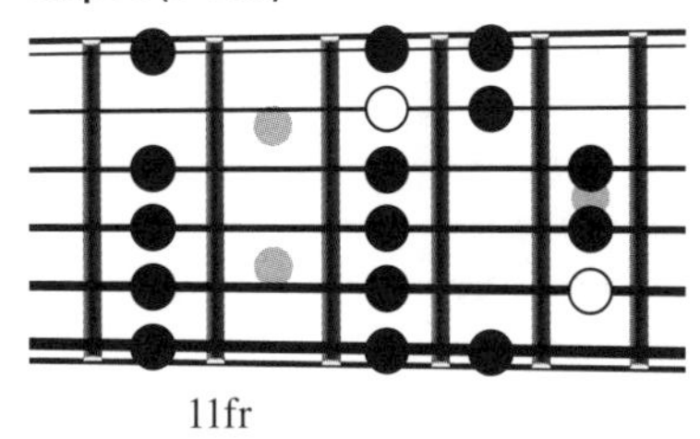

Shape 5 (A-form)

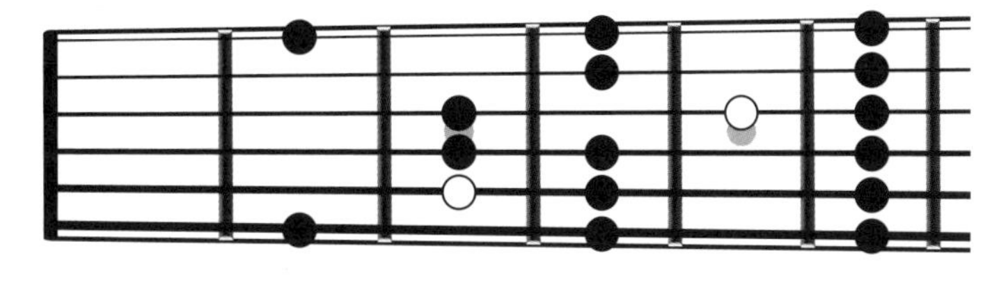

C HARMONIC MINOR

Shape 1 (G-form)

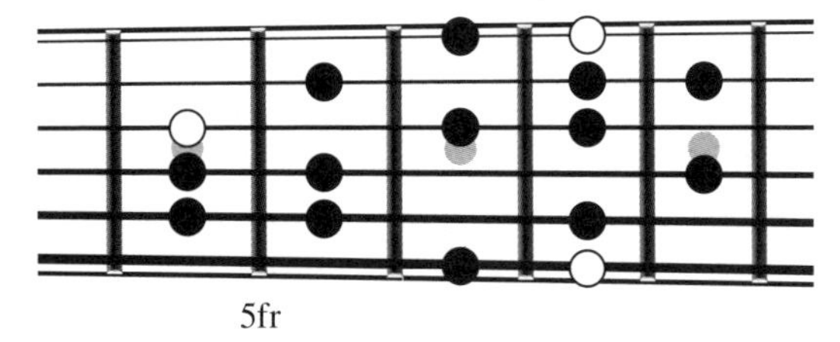

Shape 2 (E-form)

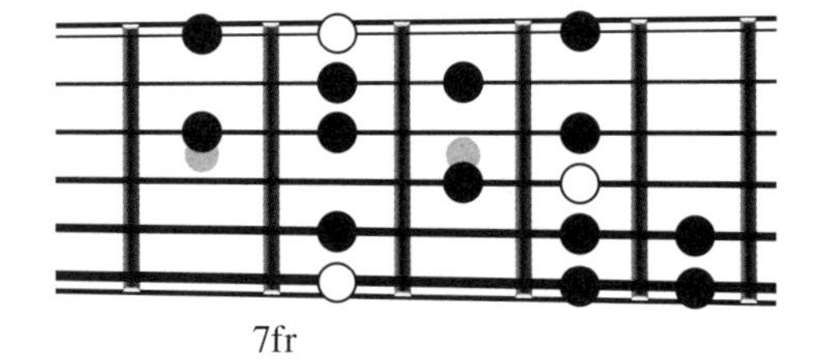

Shape 3 (D-form)

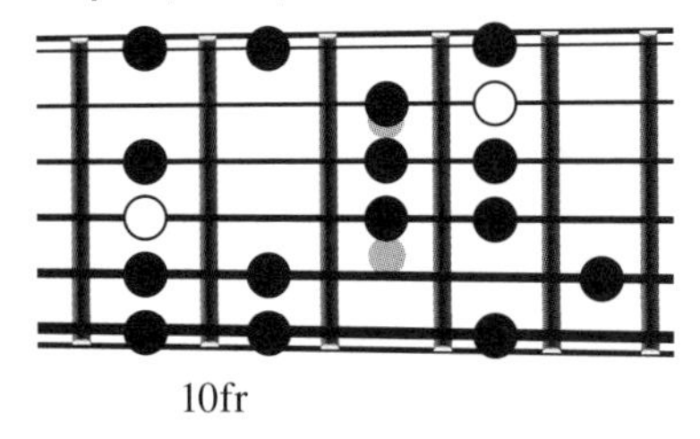

Shape 4 (C-form)

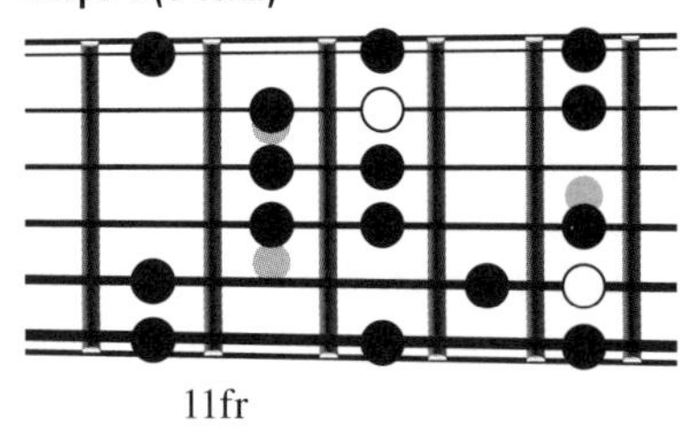

Shape 5 (A-form)

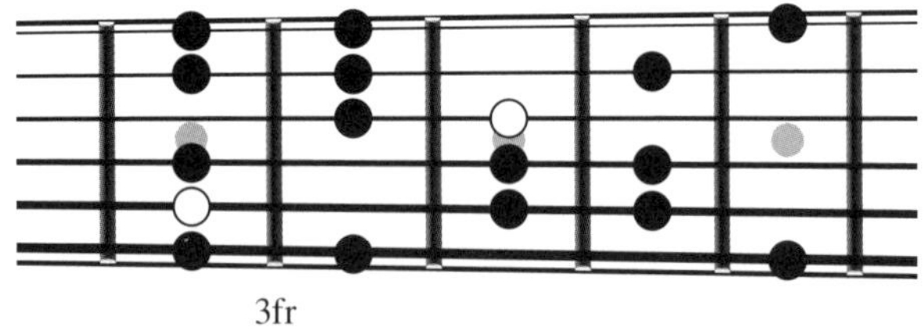

C MELODIC MINOR

Shape 1 (G-form)

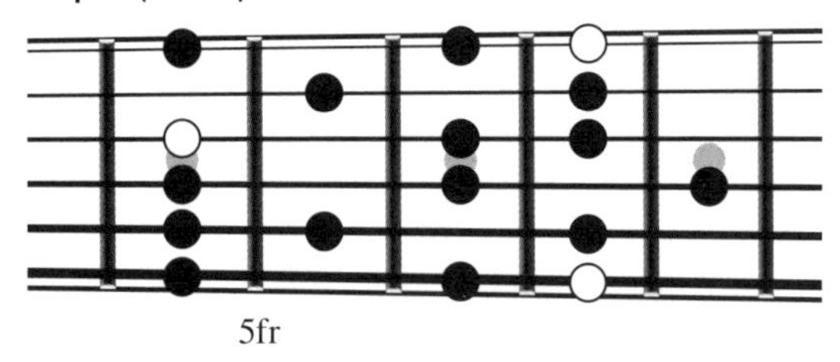

Shape 2 (E-form)

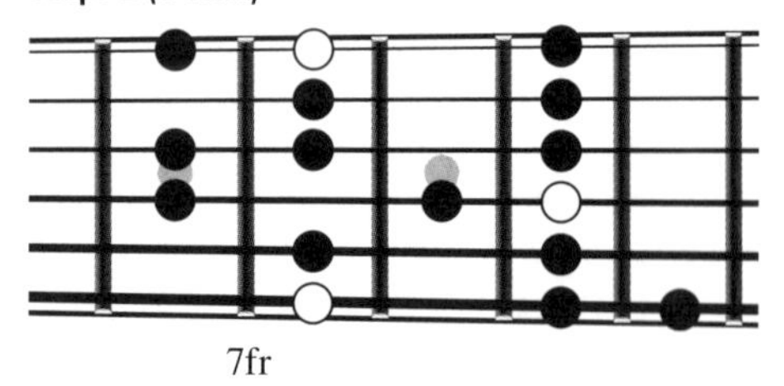

Shape 3 (D-form)

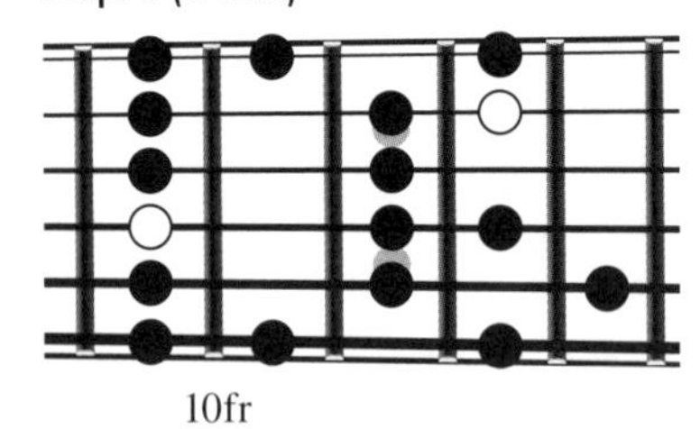

Shape 4 (C-form)

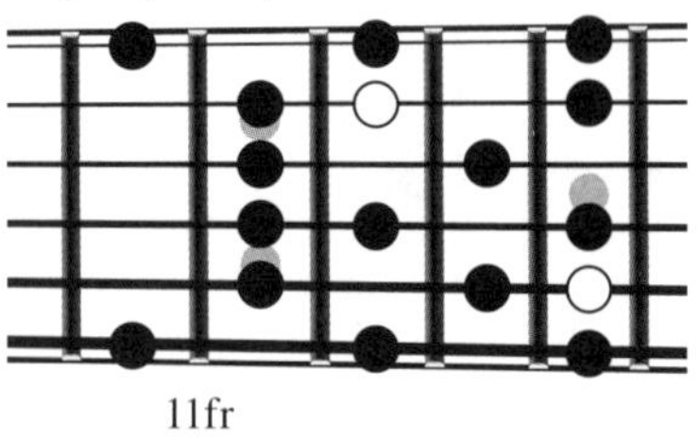

Shape 5 (A-form)

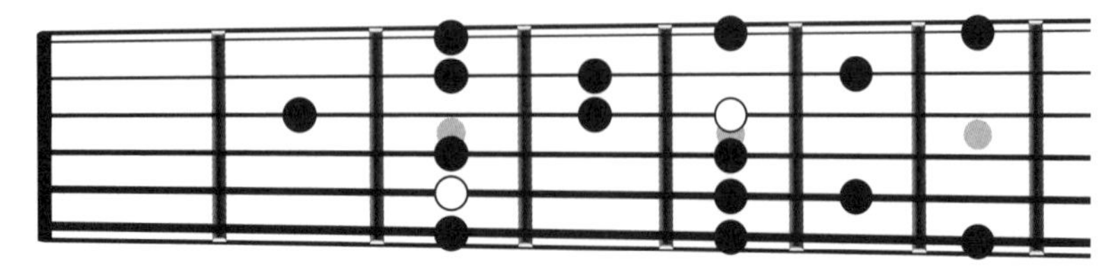

C LYDIAN DOMINANT

Shape 1 (G-form)

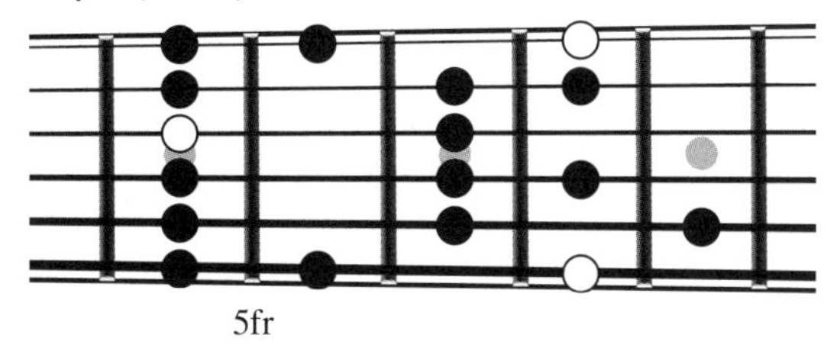

Shape 2 (E-form)

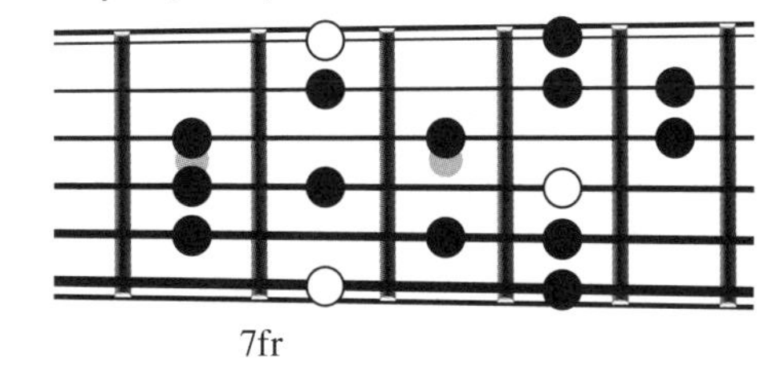

Shape 3 (D-form)

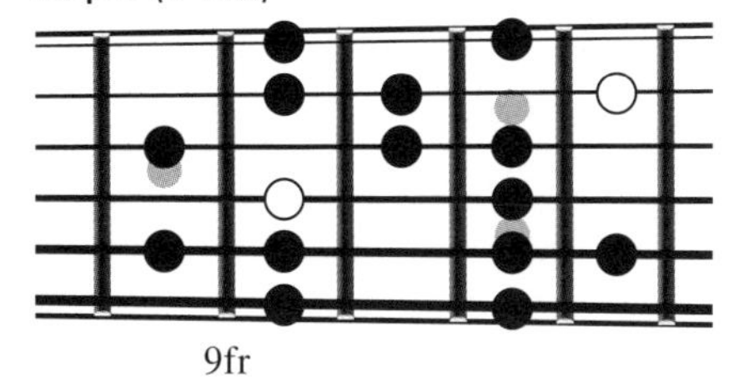

Shape 4 (C-form)

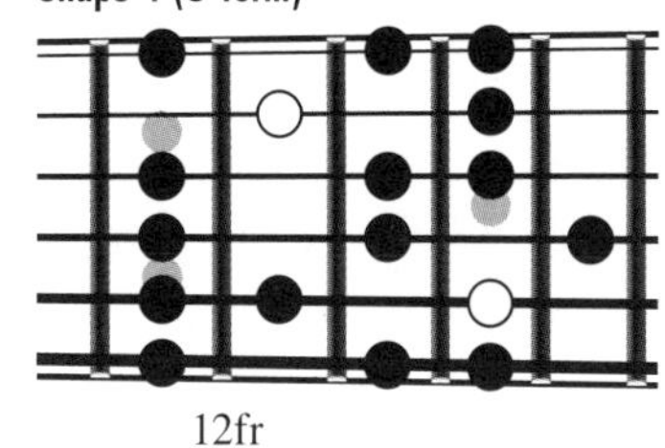

Shape 5 (A-form)

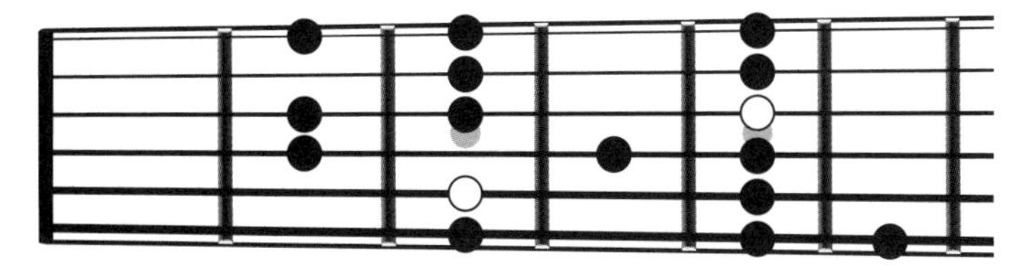

C SUPER LOCRIAN

Shape 1 (G-form)

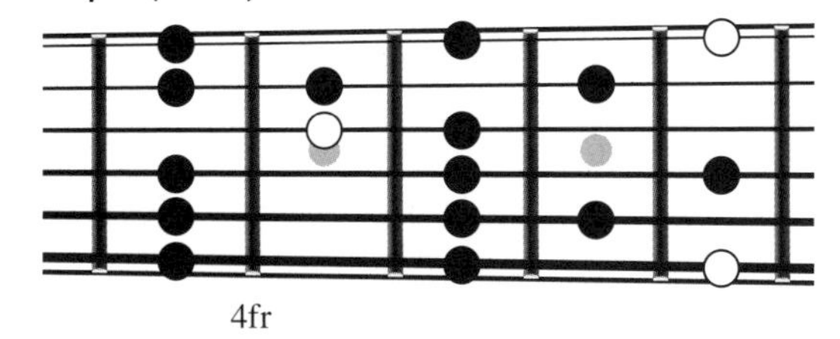

Shape 2 (E-form)

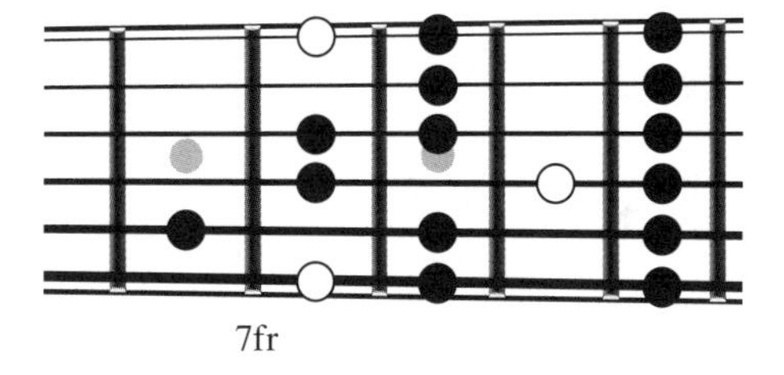

Shape 3 (D-form)

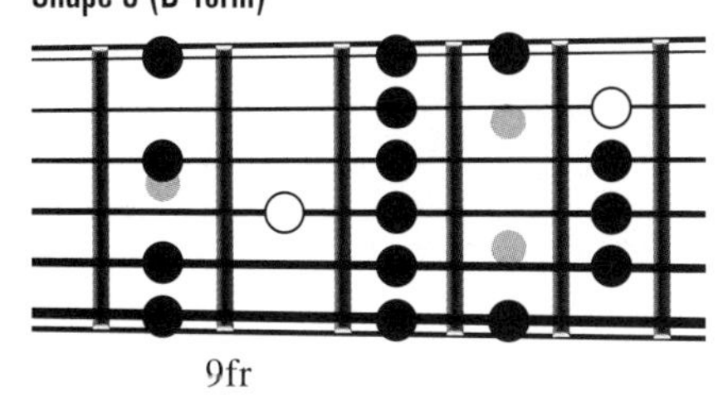

Shape 4 (C-form)

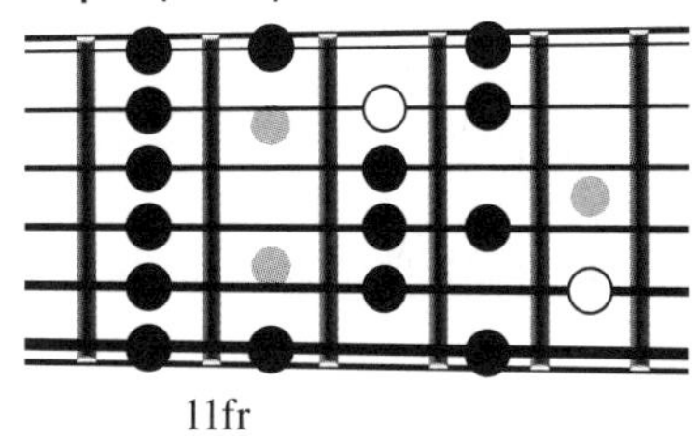

Shape 5 (A-form)

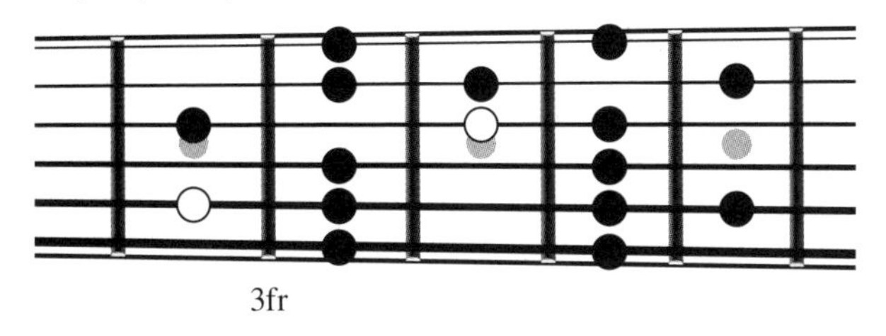

APPENDIX B: CHORD PROGRESSIONS AND PLAY-ALONG TRACKS

Here are several common progressions for you to practice over. I've included suggested scales for most of them, but remember that you have many other options, as presented in Chapter 10.

MAJOR AND MINOR DIATONIC PROGRESSIONS

Progression #1: I–IV in C major (C major scale)

TRACK 96

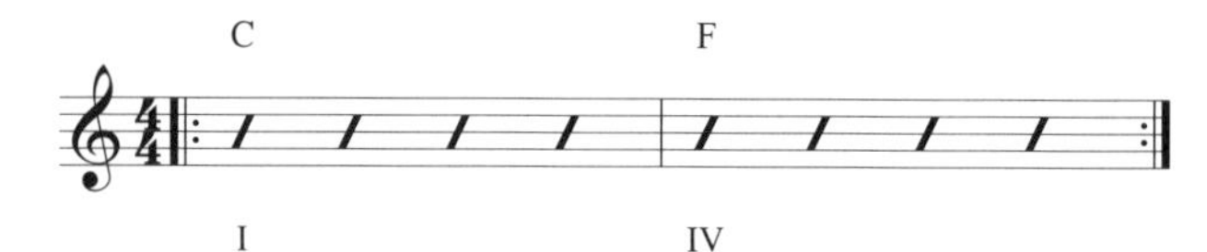

Progression #2: I–IV–V–I in E major (E major scale)

TRACK 96
(1:06)

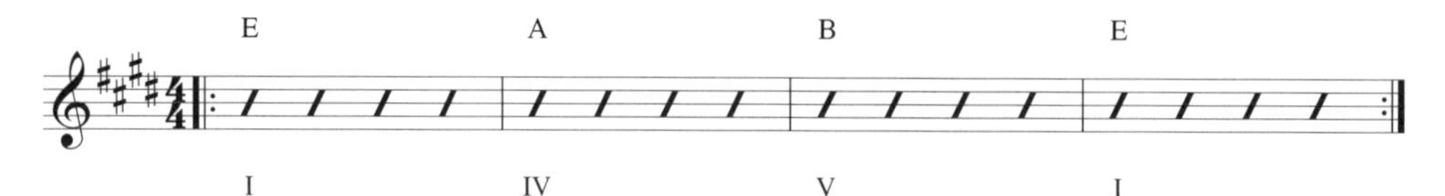

Progression #3: I–V–vi–IV in D major (D major scale)

TRACK 96
(2:05)

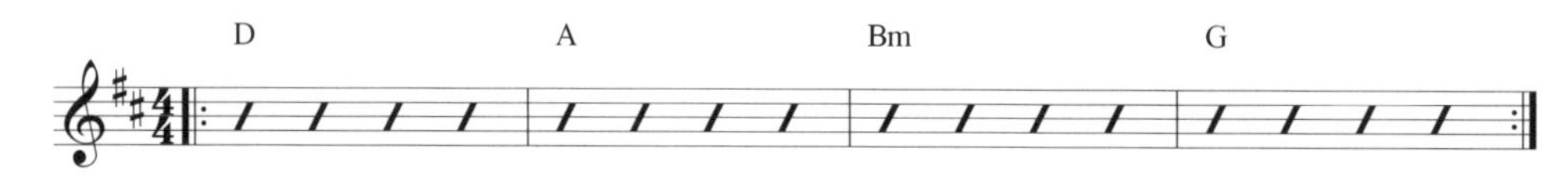

Progression #4: i–♭VI–♭VII–i in C minor (C minor scale)

TRACK 96
(3:03)

MAJOR AND MINOR PROGRESSIONS WITH NON-DIATONIC CHORDS

Progression #5: I–I7–IV–iv in G major (I, IV: G major scale; I7: G Mixolydian; iv: G minor scale)

TRACK 97
(0:00)

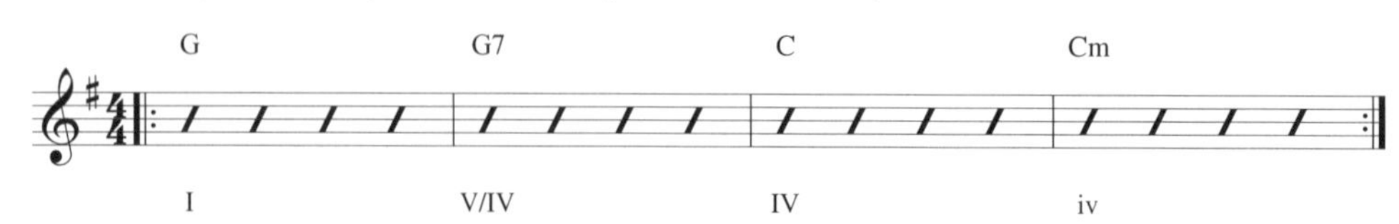

Progression #6: I–♭VI–♭VII–IV in B major (I, IV: B major scale; ♭VI, ♭VII: B minor scale)

TRACK 97
(1:00)

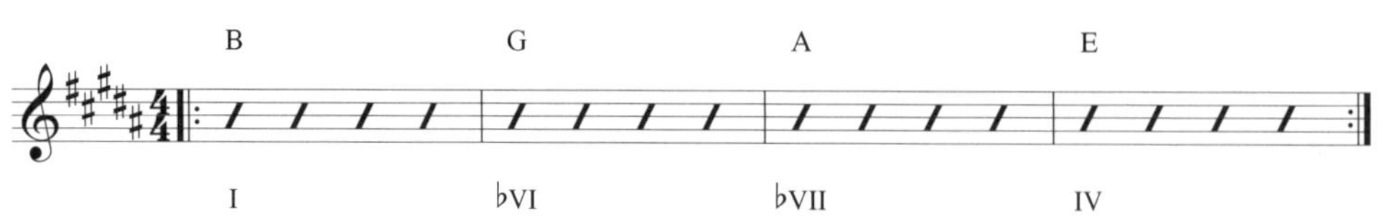

Progression #7: i–♭VII–IV–V in A minor (i, ♭VII: A minor scale; IV: A Dorian; V: A harmonic minor)

TRACK 97 (2:00)

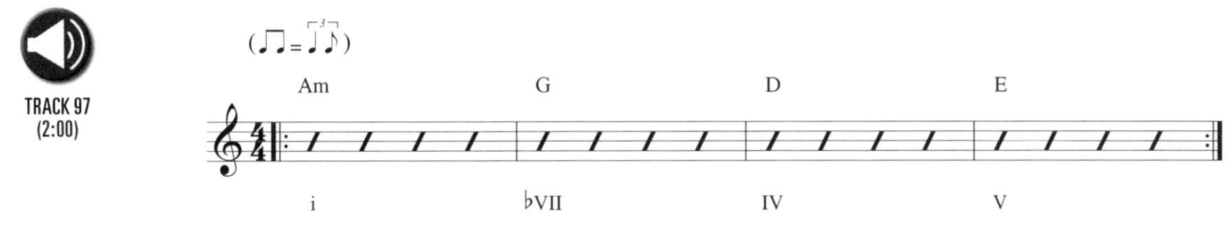

Progression #8: i–♭III–IV–♭VI in E minor (i, ♭III, ♭VI: E minor scale; IV: E Dorian)

TRACK 97 (2:59)

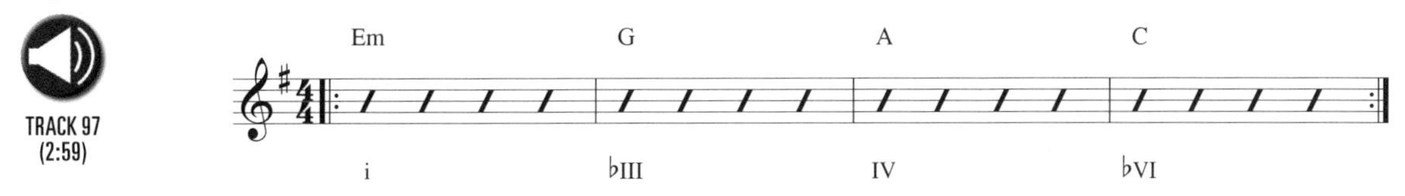

MODAL PROGRESSIONS

Progression #9: I–♭VII–IV in E major (E Mixolydian)

TRACK 98

Progression #10: i–♭VII–IV–i in B minor (B Dorian)

TRACK 98 (1:00)

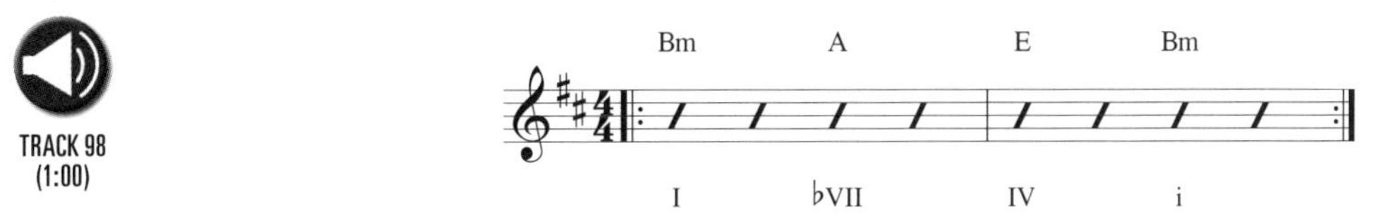

Progression #11: i–IV in D minor (D Dorian)

TRACK 98 (2:05)

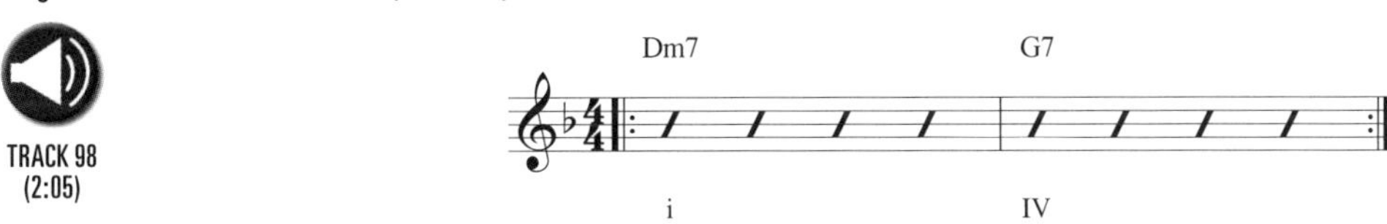

BLUES PROGRESSIONS

Progression #12: 12-bar blues shuffle in A major

TRACK 99

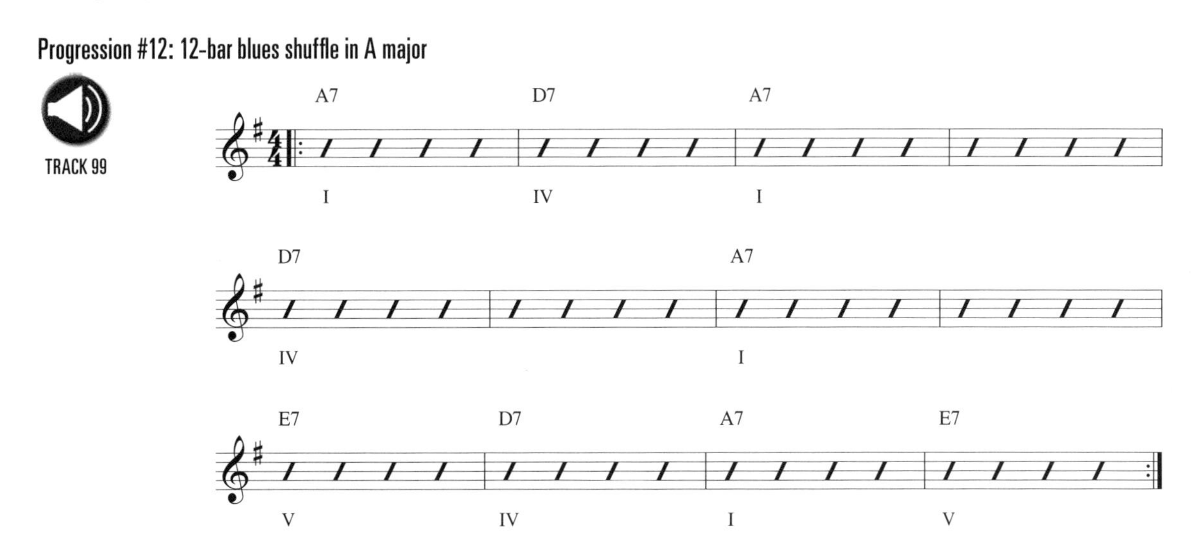

Progression #13: funky 12-bar blues in C major

TRACK 99 (1:35)

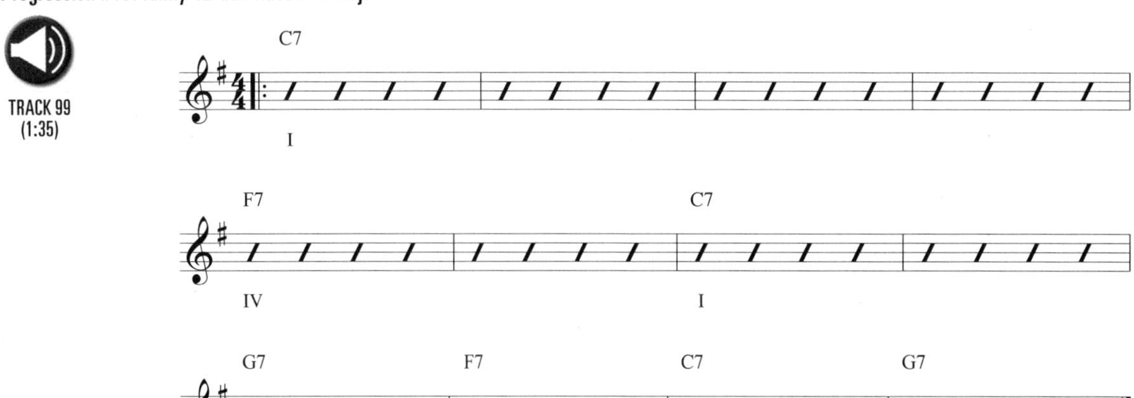

Progression #14: rock-style 12-bar blues in B minor

TRACK 99 (3:18)

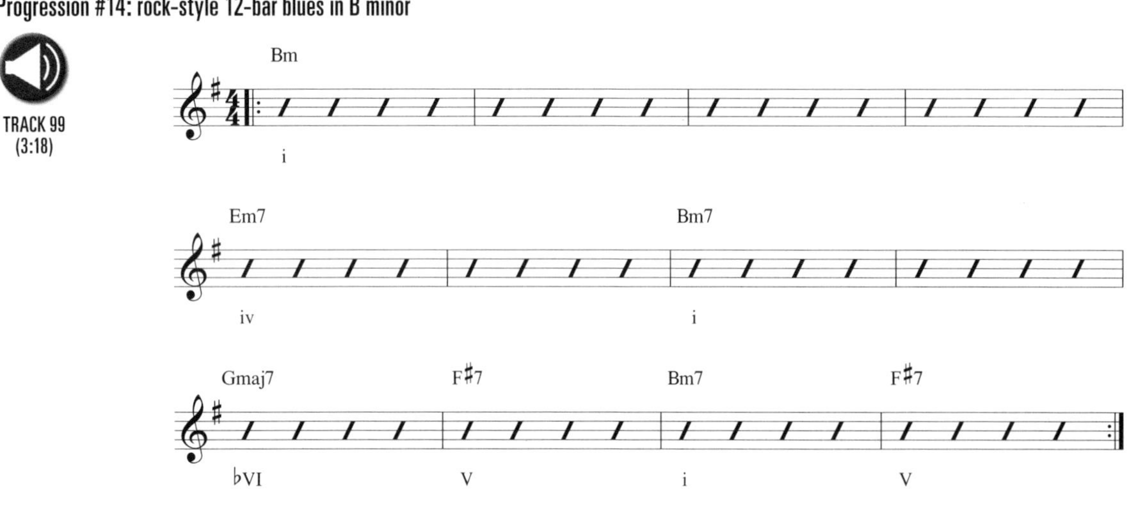

Progression #15: slow 12-bar blues shuffle in E minor

TRACK 99 (5:02)

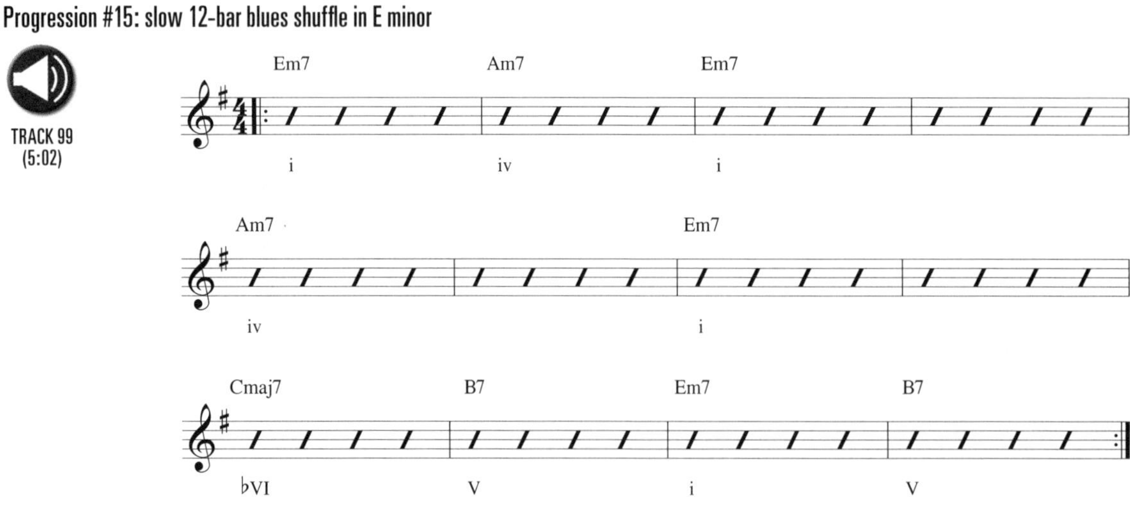